Celtic Radicals Series

David Lloyd George

Celtic Radicals Series

David Lloyd George

Emyr Price

UNIVERSITY OF WALES PRESS
CARDIFF
2006

British Library Cataloguing-in-Publication Data
A catalogue record for this book is available from the British Library.

ISBN 0-7083-1947-5 (paperback)
      0-7083-2004-X (hardback)

Printed in Malta by Gutenberg Press, Tarxien

To my grandson,
Osian Prys McGuinness

CONTENTS

PREFACE

'He saw it [The Young Wales League] primarily as a political instrument for uniting Welsh constituency parties and thereby putting pressure on the Liberal Party leadership and the London based party machine.'

K. O. Morgan 1995

'He had never intended to be the Parnell of Wales in any sense but one – that he wanted to control the Welsh MPs and to make use of their corporate power'.

John Grigg 1973

These two quotes from two eminent biographers of Lloyd George reflect their somewhat withering view of Lloyd George's leadership of Young Wales and his championing of the first modern movement for federal self-government for Wales, particularly in the period of the Young Wales League from 1894 to 1896. Grigg, especially in his *The Young Lloyd George* (1973, reprinted 2002), has interpreted his nationalist stance as posturing as the playacting rebel who used the movement as a stepping-stone for power and fame as a future Westminster politician of renown. K. O. Morgan also interprets his leadership of Young Wales as first and foremost an exercise in pressure group politics and also criticizes the movement as having but 'vaguely conceived labour policies', although he is less critical of Lloyd George's role as 'the Welsh Parnell' than Grigg.

Other historians who have written about his early career, like B. B. Gilbert, J. Graham Jones and even his nephew W. R. P. George, have also tended to see his career up to 1896 and the promotion of his nationalist crusade as either a temporary vessel for his ambitions, climbing the greasy pole of British politics with a Welsh base at his command or else have seen it as a naïve and self-deluding exercise by a young and egotistical exhibitionist and nothing more than a prelude to his later glittering career as a Westminster star.

The Welsh Parnell, the founder and leader of Wales's first modern and overtly political nationalist movement has been dismissed as both being the young parliamentary raver and conversely a pragmatist, while also being depicted as either a monkey portrait or a young nationalist hothead guilty of self delusion as the leader of Young Wales. Perhaps it is time to re-assess his early career and the long-term influence of Young Wales on Welsh politics and to show that this episode in his career was far from being mere posturing and that the movement was much more than a temporary pressure group for a politician on the make. As John Grigg has noted in his volume *The Young Lloyd George* (1973): 'the last word will never be written on Lloyd George or on any part of his career. With the passage of time, new facts will emerge, new explanations and interpretations provided.'

This book seeks to present a quite different interpretation of the Young Lloyd George than that portrayed in Grigg's and other historians' work. It is based partially on my original MA thesis on the young Lloyd George, on subsequent research over a lengthy period in his own and his friends and family's personal papers, and on extensive delving in many Welsh-language newspapers of the 1880s and 1890s (a source not comprehensively used, indeed disregarded, by many of his biographers). Unlike Grigg and others, I have sought to interpret his career before 1896, not as a pragmatist and posturer and not just as a prelude to Westminster success but as a period when David Lloyd George had a committed and visionary view of a self-governing Wales which could create a vibrant, more progressive and a more equal society than a country governed centrally from Westminster.

Between the early 1880s and 1896 and the fall of Young Wales, Lloyd George had a powerful, strong commitment to Home Rule, to a labourist and even feminist agenda for the movement and especially to a groundbreaking aspiration for the Welsh Language to be deployed fully in Wales at a time of much opposition to its resurgence. He was to press for full official status for the language in government, in the law courts and in the workplace – a cause which has almost entirely been disregarded by his biographers. Indeed, he campaigned fearlessly for a visionary New Wales in the teeth of fierce opposition (especially from the Liberals in Wales) which could well have ended his political career there and then. I also argue in this book that he did not renege on Young Wales in 1896 but that the movement was brought down primarily by anti-nationalist Welsh Liberals and Tory opposition; subsequently he had no option but to concentrate on a Westminster career to satiate his ambition to be a social reformer and to continue to press for Welsh devolution and establish and finance Welsh institutions such as the National Library of Wales and the National Museum of Wales.

During his period in power at Westminster from 1908 to 1922 much of his drive, especially as a social reformer up to 1912, was empowered by his Welsh background and values, and it is my contention that too much of a distinction has been drawn between his alleged Old Liberalism and the New Liberalism of 1908 onwards. His links with Wales continued as war Prime Minister although he became increasingly divorced from Welsh life and Welsh aspirations. Indeed, during the last phase of his prime ministerial career and as the 'Wizard in the Wings' in the 1920s and 1930s his Welshness and his reputation in Wales certainly waned, but on occasions he still continued to champion Welsh issues. Finally, despite the failure of the Young Wales movement to achieve its immediate aims its long-term influence upon Wales should not be under-estimated. After Lloyd George's death politicians in the Liberal, Labour and Plaid Cymru parties in their respective ways were deeply influenced by the Cymru Fydd cause which eventually led to the creation of the National Assembly for Wales in 1997.

Lloyd George was the first architect of Welsh devolution and its most famous advocate, but though he would have been glad to see the Assembly established, he would have surely denigrated its lack of powers to create a dynamic, bilingual and more equal new Wales.

Despite its shortcomings, his Young Wales movement was much more than a temporary stage for 'a playacting rebel'. It was a significant milestone in Welsh history and a movement he led with great courage and passion.

ACKNOWLEDGEMENTS

I wish to express my gratitude to the following while I compiled this book for publication. Firstly, my thanks to the director of the University of Wales Press, Ashley Drake, for inviting me to write this book in the Celtic Radicals Series. I owe a considerable debt, too, to the staff at the Press for their courtesy and efficiency in preparing this work meticulously from the manuscript stage to final publication, particularly Sarah Lewis, Dafydd Jones and Nicola Roper, and to Janet Davies for her patient indexing.

I should also like to place on record the many kindnesses I received over many years from the staffs of various libraries and archives, throughout Wales, including Gwynedd Archives Services, the National Library of Wales, Cardiff Central Library, Gwynedd County Council Library and the archivists at the University College of Wales, Bangor.

I owe a particular debt, as well, to the historians, Emeritus Professor, J.Gwynn Williams, D. Litt., of the Welsh History Department at the University College of Wales, Bangor and the late and much lamented head of the History department there, Professor C. L. Mowat, himself a biographer of Lloyd George. Both were responsible for supporting my application for an University of Wales Research studentship which enabled me to begin my work on Lloyd George's early career and many other kindnesses. They truly baptised me into the eddies and currents of that tumultuous period in Welsh history and the emergence to prominence of the 'Little Baptist'.

Moreover, over the years, one has to be indebted to those scholars in the same period, in particular the ground-breaking work of Dr K. O. Morgan (now Lord Morgan of Aberdovey) and the writings especially of John Grigg, B. B. Gilbert, Dr W. P. George and Dr J. Graham Jones. Their foundation work has enabled me to suggest a somewhat different and perhaps controversial emphasis on Lloyd George's leadership of Young Wales and other facets of his early career, although nobody can claim a defintive analysis of this period.

I would also like to thank my close friend, Dr H. G. Williams, a former senior lecturer at University College, Bangor and an expert on the social history of Victorian Wales, for his constant help, advice and support while I wrote this work. I am also indebted to Mrs Philippa Williams for her diligence in typing part of this work and deciphering my handwriting. My greatest debt, as ever, is to my wife for her constant support and forebearance, often at difficult times.

Any shortcomings in this work are my own. Despite a lifelong interest in Lloyd George and the politics of his period, I would like to echo Lord Morgan of Aberdovey's trenchant remark in his work, *Lloyd George, Family, Letters, 1885-1936*:

> Lloyd George remains an enigma, with a political style unique in recent history. An ultimate understanding of him will probably always baffle the historian. (10)

My hope, however, in this book, is that I have shed some new light on that career, particularly with regard to Lloyd George's stance as a pioneering, progressive, left of centre Welsh radical nationalist, during his early period as a politician.

*

I would like to express a final sentiment to Lord Dafydd Elis Thomas and to Rhodri Morgan, who, in their respective ways, are seeking to bring Wales nearer Lloyd George's goal of Federal Home Rule.

Emyr Price

Caernarfon, 2005.

I

THE RADICAL AND NATIONALIST
APPRENTICE, 1863–1884

Significantly, Lloyd George's political baptism preceded his religious immersion into the minority Campbellite Baptist denomination, known somewhat disparagingly in the Welsh vernacular as *y Batus Bach* (The Little Baptists) because of their small membership. As was the Baptist custom, he had to wait until his teens before being baptised in the river near the Penymaes chapel at Cricieth. There his uncle, the shoemaker, Richard Lloyd, was the unordained and unpaid 'minister' and assiduous leader of his flock of 'the disciples of Christ'. Long before this event, however, at the precocious age of five years the young David had experienced his political baptism in his boyhood village of Llanystumdwy.

There he had led the victory procession and carried the Liberal banner of the Madryn squire, Love Jones-Parry, who had taken on and defeated the entire might of one of Carnarfonshire's largest landowners, the Tory, Anglican and Anglicized, George Sholto Douglas Pennant, the heir to the vast Penrhyn estate and to the huge Penrhyn slate undertakings.[1] This formative experience in a momentous and bitter election in Welsh history in 1868 had symbolic significance in the nurturing of the radical and nationalist politician, as it had on the development and growth of Welsh Liberalism. It was an election which was to pave the way a decade and more later in promoting the political career of Lloyd George himself, but with a far more radical and nationalist brand of Liberalism than the squire of Madryn's tepid, Whiggish politics, devoid of any nationalist content. The child is father of the man and the carrying of the Liberal banner through 'the blackest Tory parish in the land' at an impressionable age was a portent for the future.

Liberal anti-Tory anti-landowning politics was an integral part of his upbringing and politics for him was always a higher priority than religion. He was a modern secularist, critical of sectarianism and religious fundamentalism – one who believed throughout his career in the need to establish a more just and fairer society here on earth rather than the fundamentalist view that this life was a preparation for the next world.

From his early teens he was to devote himself not only to securing Welsh Nonconformist political gains but, of greater importance, to building a new just society with a strong Welsh dimension to that process. Although many of his values were shaped by the Welsh Nonconformist conscience, he had no desire to associate himself with the negative aspects of Puritanism nor its overtly spiritual side. But he was determined to use the positive elements of dissent to build a better world for his people, for the needy and disadvantaged.

It is important to stress too that, though his sometimes traumatic experiences during his boyhood at Llanystumdwy played a substantial role in shaping his career, it is something of a myth held by many of his biographers that his experiences there, dominated by the Tory Anglican squire Ellis Nanney and the Gwynfryn estate, were the most important influences to shape the radical and nationalist politician. Indeed, it was only after leaving Llanystumdwy at the tender age of fourteen to become an articled solicitor in the teeming radical town of Porthmadog that his political values flourished and his Welsh nationalist radical ideas crystallized. Nevertheless, it cannot be denied that his boyhood at Llanystumdwy was of singular influence upon him.

There, at five years of age, he had started his political journey in the election of 1868. Then, some years later, in the village's Anglican school in the presence of the headmaster, David Evans, the local rector David Edwards and in front of Ellis Nanney, he had staged and led a rebellion of remarkable bravery against the reading of the catechism in front of the holy Anglican trinity. This was despite the fact that the schoolmaster helped him and his brother William with extra Latin lessons, an essential requirement if they were to become solicitors.

At Llanystumdwy, too, from an early age he had read avidly the books in his late father's extensive library. William George, the well-read left-wing-leaning intellectual schoolmaster from Pembrokeshire, had left a treasure trove, which his son loved to devour. Amongst a plethora of books he read the works of Dickens, constitutional history volumes and classics such as Victor Hugo's *Les Miserables*. This was another crucial factor moulding his social and political values. These literary works deepened and reinforced the social injustices he witnessed during his upbringing in a society he regarded as being exploited by an Anglicized Tory landowning elite.

When David was eight years old the enumerator's census of 1871 was to reveal the social divisions in Llanystumdwy, especially within the central part of the parish defined as 'all that part of the parish lying to the east of the Dwyfor and all the village both sides of the Dwyfor'. It was a village and parish which bred in him a compelling urgency to carve out a career as a champion of the underprivileged.

There were seventy-six households in this particular area of the parish – forty-six within the village itself. Amongst the heads of the households were the following occupations – one schoolmaster, one sea captain, one corn merchant, one farm bailiff, one butler, one artist, four innkeepers, two blacksmiths, one stonemason, two tailors, one grocer and postmaster, one employed shoemaker, Richard Lloyd, employing two men, one butcher, one farmer-miller and three other farmers. There were also two railway workers, one washerwoman, one quarryman, one widow and one gardener. The remaining heads of households were farm labourers.

In the thirty-five households beyond the village were several farm labourers, a cobbler, many widows of farm labourers, granite quarrymen and railway workers. But the majority were farmers – many being smallholders and tenants of the Gwynfryn estate. The biggest farmer was George Jones of Aberkin farm, with 170 acres, employing four men. Significantly, however, the most prominent landowner in the area was Samuel Owen Priestley of Trefan, an Englishman. He was a Tory and a JP. He employed eight hands and housemaids. Another leading Tory was the rector, David Edwards, a proud and domineering man, living in some splendour at Bron Eifion with his English-born wife, two unmarried daughters and two servants. David Evans, the schoolmaster, was also a Tory, employing one servant.

In the two other districts of the parish, beyond the village, the majority were tenant farmers of the Gwynfryn estate. At the Plas Gwynfryn mansion Ellis Nanney lived in luxury. His influence over the village and beyond was profound with so many parishioners dependent directly or indirectly upon his wealth. In 1871 he was a bachelor with a retinue of eight servants, including a parlour maid and a butler.[2] He became the Tory candidate in the Caernarfonshire by-election of 1880 and thereafter Lloyd George's first opponent in the Caernarfon Boroughs by-election of 1890 in the epic struggle between the Llanystumdwy squire and the nephew of the local shoemaker.

Inevitably, Lloyd George's social background was to drive him into the Liberal fold. Although many of the parishioners were Anglicans and Tories, such as Robert Williams Felin Bach, the local miller and Church sexton, the majority were chapel members like Richard Lloyd. Although he paid rent for his home and business premises he was economically independent from the Gwynfryn estate.

Many of Lloyd George's biographers have perpetuated the myth that Lloyd George was the cottage-bred boy; yet the family's social and economic position, despite the onerous pressures upon them, was somewhat better than the workers and numerous farm labourers living in the parish. His mother had an annuity of £46 and a building society savings scheme, which enabled David and his younger brother William to pursue a legal career with its high costs of paying for their articles. Richard Lloyd also employed two men in addition to a part-time gardener at Highgate and he was regarded by the villagers as a local leader. He would preside over social and political issues in the local smithy, the village parliament. There were also close family links to some of the better-off tenant farmers in the locality, like William Griffiths, Betws Fawr.

However, although Lloyd George's social background was relatively comfortable and quite different to the traditional interpretation of his material status as being poor, many leading biographers of Lloyd George, most notably John Grigg in *The Young Lloyd George*,[3] have surely exaggerated his social status. Grigg claims 'the family was probably the best off in Llanystumdwy'.[4] This is surely nonsense, as is Grigg's description of Uncle Lloyd as Hans Sachs, the master craftsman of Wagner's creation.[5]

The family may have been better off than several local workers and farm labourers but it was not as well off as many in the parish who had their own businesses or those who were major employees on the Gwynfryn estate. Richard Lloyd did not own Highgate, while the shoemaking trade during his nephew's youth was an increasingly fragile occupation with new, more mechanized processes of shoe production emerging. Richard Lloyd had to support his adopted family on often irregular and meagre earnings.

Grigg further claims that Lloyd George 'had been born into the Welsh political elite'[6] – another misguided statement. Richard Lloyd could well be regarded as being a member of the labour aristocracy or a member of the petite bourgeoisie but he was far from being within the privileged circle of the established middle-class mandarins who were in the late 1870s and early 1880s the leaders of Caernarfonshire politics. An analysis of the social structure of the leaders of Liberalism in Caernarfonshire before the Third Reform Act of 1884–5 shows the wide divide between them and Richard Lloyd and his family.[7]

The chairman of the Caernarfonshire Liberal Association in 1884 was W. A. Darbishire, an English-born owner of the Penyrorsedd slate quarry, in the Nantlle Valley. The secretary was the moderate sober and ponderous Caernarfon solicitor, R. D. Williams of Porth yr Aur, whilst other members of the association were well-off members of the established middle class, for example, the brothers, R. Pugh Jones and J. T. Jones, of Parciau Mawr, Cricieth – landowners and barristers at law. Hugh Pugh, of Llys Meirion, Caernarfon, was a banker and wealthy businessman while O. M. Roberts of Porthmadog was a professional architect. The Revd D. Evan Davies of Pwllheli was both a Calvinistic Methodist minister and a property developer and J. Bryn Roberts of Bryn Adda, Bangor was a wealthy barrister and prospective parliamentary candidate in 1885 for the newly formed constituency of Eifion, Caernarfonshire.[8] He was a right-wing Gladstonian, as was the businessman from Llanberis, D. P. Williams JP, who later became a fierce critic of Lloyd George's militant radicalism and nationalism. T. C. Lewis of Caederwen, Bangor was also a wealthy businessman, reflecting the fact that it was a combination of Whigs and laissez-faire Gladstonians who controlled Liberal politics in Caernarfonshire in the period when Lloyd George first emerged on the political scene. Within the executive only John Davies (Gwyneddon), himself a banker, and Morgan Richards (Morgrugyn Machno), a bard and local quarry agent, were anti-laissez-faire radicals. There was no one of Richard Lloyd's background on the executive and certainly no one from a working-class background. Neither Richard Lloyd nor his nephew were remotely part of the Welsh Liberal elite of the time.

Richard Lloyd and his nephew were undoubtedly political outsiders in north-west Wales as Lloyd George prepared in 1877 to leave Llanystumdwy and embark upon his legal training. He and his uncle were also religious outsiders in a period when sectarianism and interdenominational rivalry were rife with much disdain expressed, especially by the Methodists towards the radical minority sect of the 'Little Baptists', a denomination which employed no paid pastor while devoting their collections for the relief of their fellow members when they fell on hard times. They were often disparaged because of their radical theological views and inferior socio-economic status.

The Campbellite Baptists had no chapel at Llanystumdwy and village members walked to their meeting place at Penymaes chapel at Cricieth. According to the Religious Census of 1851 they had only 15 per cent of the seating of all religious denominations in the town whilst the Calvinistic Methodists had 38 per cent, with other denominations having more seats than the 'Little Baptists'. Lloyd George's future wife, Margaret Owen of Mynydd Ednyfed farm, had had a private education at the Dr Williams School for girls at Dolgellau and was the daughter of a prosperous Calvinistic Methodist tenant farmer of 180 acres.[9] While courting her in the 1880s he found out for himself the prejudice held against his religious and social background. Margaret's parents were reluctant at first to see a relationship developing between Margaret and Lloyd George.

K. O. Morgan, in his lecture 'Lloyd George and Welsh Liberalism',[10] has stressed that Lloyd George was an outsider as he prepared to leave Llanystumdwy in the mid-1870s and suggests that his main aspiration was to join the middle class and adopt its values – 'the aspirations and ambitions of the small town bourgeoisie'.[11] But this is partly misguided because, although he was certainly an outsider, his aim was not to share the values of the middle-class-dominated Liberal establishment, as Morgan suggests, nor to adopt their political standpoint. While he rose slowly into the middle class as an aspiring solicitor his aim was to eradicate the moderate, respectable laissez-faire Liberalism of that class, which he regarded as being overtly Anglicized and anti-radical. His aim, indeed, was to change fundamentally that British centric radicalism in his local area and throughout Wales, to turn his party into a radical nationalist movement in the 1880s and early 1890s and to imbue that radicalism with labourist ideas and policies. Lloyd George had been influenced by his boyhood experience at Llanystumdwy of witnessing the poverty of workers and farm labourers and, though his family did not share completely such hardship (since their social status was somewhat higher), the difference between them was not great. He felt a closer bond with them than with the local Liberal mandarins and his fight for better conditions for the underprivileged would be a priority.

His Uncle Lloyd had also suffered punishment at school for talking in Welsh, punishment which had rendered him deaf in one ear. This incident, together with Lloyd George's own experience of a highly Anglicized Church school and the social snobbery associated with Plas Gwynfryn and Bron Eifion, had bred in him feelings of nationalist antagonism and formed within him Welsh national aspirations which had not yet crystallized into a coherent form in the 1870s. In time, however, he would aspire to merge social reform with the call for Federal Home Rule for Wales. On his way to Porthmadog in 1877, therefore, he was ready not to become part of the political Liberal elite but rather to transform the party's politics and create a new radical, nationalist base for himself and like-minded contemporaries. These aims and aspirations were to take shape in the Porthmadog of the 1880s, which undermines the myth that Llanystumdwy was the greatest influence shaping his early career, despite its indelible influence upon him.

Indeed, Lloyd George, as his brother William noted in *My Brother and I*,[12] was delighted to leave the narrow-minded confines of Llanystumdwy, recording in his diary, 'Left Llanystumdwy without a feeling of regret, remorse or longing!!' A new world was opening out before him free from the Tory influences of the parish and from the Puritanism of his uncle – an opportunity for a red-blooded youth to roam free. There was also the opportunity in the burgeoning maritime town of Porthmadog to extend his political horizons and to learn the arts and crafts of politicking in addition to sharpening his radical and nationalist views.

He was registered as an articled solicitor with Breese, Jones and Casson for the princely premium of £180, a significant sum for the family to raise (as well as financing his brother, William's articles). C. E. Breese was a prominent Liberal in Merioneth, the party's agent there, although he was an Anglicized Whiggish politician. One of the founding members of the firm was David Williams, of Castell Deudraeth, who had been returned as the Liberal member for Merioneth in the 1868 election, although he was no great radical nor a particularly prominent politician.

Lloyd George lost no time in helping Breese publicly canvass and register voters in Merioneth in preparation for the general election of 1880, invaluable experience for an aspiring politician. He was also to take advantage of Breese's comprehensive library at his home, Morfa Lodge, to educate himself further in political and social matters. But he also had some free time to court several young ladies and continued to be fascinated by the fair sex throughout his life. He was also not averse to occasional public house visits, in contravention of Welsh Nonconformist opposition to strong drink, and he also participated in military manoeuvres with the Porthmadog Volunteers, again rebelling against Nonconformity's pacifist sympathies and certainly those of Richard Lloyd. But politics was his great passion and it was at Porthmadog between 1877 and 1885 that he served his political apprenticeship. There he was to learn the tricks of the trade as an exciting, pioneering new-style politician who would become by the end of the 1880s and early 1890s the champion of Cymru Fydd (Young Wales), a groundbreaking nationalist and radical political movement.

At the beginning of 1880, with C. E. Breese the Liberal agent for Merioneth and with the Liberal leader, W. E. Gladstone, intent on toppling the Tories and forming another Liberal government, Lloyd George further sharpened his political skills by canvassing in the county. He carried out similar work in the Porthmadog area, in Caernarfonshire, enjoying his first taste of real electioneering.

In the constituency of Caernarfonshire the Liberal candidate, the barrister Watkin Williams, faced the entire might of the Penrhyn estate and their influence over the Ogwen Valley. The heir to the estate was the Tory candidate, George Sholto Douglas Pennant, with a vast income coming to the family from the Penrhyn slate quarry and other undertakings. Being only seventeen, Lloyd George did not appear on the public platform but he canvassed zealously for Williams. He also listened intently to the speech-making, for example, Watkin Williams's speech at the Town Hall, Porthmadog, on 16 March. He noted with some disdain in his diary how ineffective were Williams's rhetorical abilities: 'Speech at Town Hall ... very good ... but nothing brilliant.'[13] However, after Williams's victory, on the day of the count, 7 April, he greeted Williams's victory over the county's richest and most formidable landowner and industrialist with great joy, penning in his diary the remarks: 'The victory beyond the most sanguine expectations ... Figures 3,303 Williams ... 2206 Pennant ... a great blow to landlord terrorism.'[14]

Soon afterwards, in October 1880, there was a by-election in Caernarfonshire after Williams's appointment as a judge. His replacement as the Liberal candidate was the wealthy Liverpool businessman and ship owner, William Rathbone, who this time was opposed by none other than the Llanystumdwy squire, Ellis Nanney, for the Tories. This time, and still only seventeen, Lloyd George played a far more prominent role in the election campaign. He not only helped with the canvassing and registration but also, for the first time in what was to be a long association with the press, he wrote several election pieces in a local newspaper the *North Wales Express* under the pseudonym 'Brutus'.

In his first article he castigated the Tory leader, Lord Salisbury.[15] In his second article, 'A contest in Caernarfonshire', the venom of his writing was directed at his *bête noire*, the local Tory candidate, Ellis Nanney.[16] Then, in his third article, 'Irish grievances', he compared the similarities between Irish and Welsh grievances and aspirations for greater social justice, by calling for a similar programme of fundamental land reform in Wales to that being fought for on the other side of the Irish Sea.[17] Although there was ambivalence in Lloyd George's approach to Catholic Ireland throughout his career, he was to resort to the Irish example to fight for land reform and political freedom for Wales in his early career.

Although his journalistic baptism in the by-election brought him no direct personal publicity as his efforts were written under a pseudonym, the experience was to prove invaluable. It enabled him to begin to cultivate the essential attributes of penning trenchant political articles in his first foray into journalism, and paved the way towards his extensive use of the press in the future for political purposes. Securing expertise in this prominent medium in the Victorian era was essential for an ambitious politician, and it was a baptism which gave him much pleasure and confidence to see his work in print for the first time. He had also established valuable contacts with the influential Liberal press barons of the *North Wales Express* with this exercise in political propaganda, another portent for the future.

In this period at Porthmadog he also had the opportunity to develop his political views in a far more radical direction than the orthodox aspirations of Welsh Liberal Nonconformists, centred upon the disestablishment of the Anglican Church in Wales and temperance and tithe reform. In the town, he came into contact with labourist and republican views in the heady surroundings of the workshop of one local republican candle maker, John Roberts, who belonged to the same sect as Richard Lloyd. Indeed, Roberts was a close friend of Uncle Lloyd, both sharing the Campbellite Baptists' belief in democracy and the formation of a more egalitarian society. While frequenting discussions at the workshop Lloyd George was influenced by the radical ideas of a clutch of progressive reformers such as Michael Davitt, the Irish land socialist and nationalist; Michael D. Jones, from Bala, the pioneering Welsh nationalist; John Ruskin, the socialist; and the historian Thomas Carlyle. Although Lloyd George was never a dogmatic republican, the influence of these meetings in the candle maker's workshop was considerable at an especially receptive period.[18]

In 1881, however, Lloyd George moved from his lodgings at Porthmadog to stay at his uncle's new family home at Cricieth where he had retired from his shoemaking business at Llanystumdwy. His family was now living in a terraced dwelling, Morvin House, and the family depended on meagre savings and the keeping of visitors. Lloyd George then travelled daily to his office at Porthmadog by train sometimes staying there late to talk with John Roberts but especially to add another string to his bow. After passing the solicitors' intermediate examination in 1881, he began to attend and participate in his first 'parliament' as a member of the Porthmadog Debating Society. It was run on parliamentary lines and was conducted through the medium of English.

He joined the society in November 1881 and made his speaking debut there in January 1882 on the highly contentious subject of the Irish Land Act, calling for similar legislation for Wales. The local papers gave him much personal publicity; the *North Wales Express* noted: 'His argumentative and nervous speech shook the very foundations of the landlords' claim to compensation.'[19] He continued to attend the Debating Society's meetings for another year, securing much attention in the local press in both the Caernarfon-based *Herald* papers, in the Aberystwyth-based *Cambrian News*, which had a high circulation in the Porthmadog area, and in the *North Wales Express*.

He spoke mainly on Welsh Nonconformist aspirations, although he also participated in debates on wider matters such as the proposals at the time to extend the franchise, securing publicity in the local press every time he spoke. In his speeches at the Debating Society he made constant references to the need for Liberals to adopt the radical course of reform promoted by the party's most radical advocate, Joseph Chamberlain.[20] His final appearances at the Debating Society came in the session 1882–3 and on the last occasion he attended the society, in November 1882, he ventured into the field of foreign affairs. In this debate he praised Arabi Pasha, the champion of anti-British nationalism in Egypt, praising him to the skies and bringing in comparisons with the need to press for a national awakening in Wales. His speech was much lauded in the *Carnarvon and Denbigh Herald* of 18 November 1882 where his oratory was highlighted: 'The speech would undoubtedly have gained praise had it been delivered in the House of Commons.'[21] Certainly his speech had its Welsh affinity for Lloyd George and its own personal significance, as he declared in his peroration: 'Arabi Pasha is a man who has arisen from amongst the peasants of his country – a man who knew all about their wants, because he has felt those wants himself.'[22] The combination of the national leader desirous of improving his people's social condition together with a call for national freedom, as represented by Arabi Pasha, was particularly attractive to the young Lloyd George.

Although Lloyd George remained on the fringes of politics in 1882, in his first electioneering exploits and in his first newspaper articles and debating society speeches he had served a fruitful apprenticeship. He had begun to develop two crucial requirements for a budding politician – the refinement of his oratorical skills and the art of propagandizing in the press. He had also begun to shape his political viewpoints and objectives, although they were not yet clarified. In the general election of 1880 W. E. Gladstone had formed another administration, the Liberals in Wales winning 29 of the 33 Welsh seats. During this administration the Welsh Liberal members had been able to exert pressure to secure specific Welsh legislation in the form of the Welsh Sunday Closing Act of 1881 and had pressed at Westminster unsuccessfully for measures dealing with Welsh Church disestablishment and moderate land reform. The Welsh Liberal representatives in Parliament, almost invariably moderate Gladstonians, were not nearly radical enough for Lloyd George, who was more attracted by the radical Chamberlainite wing of the party and was anxious to see a clearer Welsh identity and profile given to his party in Wales. These aspirations were to become an increasing feature of his thinking in the subsequent few years both before and after the Third Reform Act of 1884 as he expressed the view that young radical-nationalists needed to be adopted as Welsh parliamentary candidates. In the aftermath of the Gladstonian victory in 1880 he had made a revealing note in his diary, noting who were his favourite idols in the political sphere: 'Statesmen – Gladstone, Chamberlain and Parnell.'[23]

Though he had some admiration for Gladstone, Lloyd George's real hero was Chamberlain, then a radical within the party and the upholder of municipal socialism, whom he had repeatedly extolled in his speeches in the Porthmadog Debating Society. By the eve of the Third Reform Act of 1884 and Chamberlain's subsequent promotion of his radical new 'Unauthorized Programme'[24] which included neo-collectivist reforms, antagonistic to Gladstone's views, Lloyd George would align himself with Chamberlain and his call, too, for Home Rule All Round for the various nations of the United Kingdom. In 1882 Lloyd George was proceeding towards such radical views and his nationalistic sentiments were also to be reflected in 1885 when he established at Cricieth a Welsh-speaking debating society whose minutes of meetings show how events there were dominated by basically Welsh and radical issues.[25]

Before qualifying as a solicitor in 1884, politics was not his only interest and passion, however. There is no doubt that Lloyd George was a thoroughly red-blooded young man. Indeed, this author found a significant reference in Myrddin Fardd's diary in the National Library of Wales showing that Richard Lloyd had confessed to his friend, Myrddin, a notable Welsh bard and antiquarian, that Lloyd George had been flirting with various girls on his way home from school when he was twelve years old. This knowledge had been relayed to Richard Lloyd by the schoolmaster. But at Porthmadog, free from his uncle's shackles, he had several dalliances with local girls, causing concern to his family, although they knew of only some of his adventures. Undoubtedly, he had much appeal to the fair sex and he was aware of the pitfalls of such pursuits and the criticism that would come from various quarters. In a note in his diary on 17 January 1880, he criticized his own behaviour, although he did not refrain entirely from such ventures. He wrote: 'This I know the realisation of my prospects, my dreams, my longings for success are very scant indeed, unless I am, prepared to give up what without mistake, are indeed the germs of a fast life.'[26]

He also wavered from the narrow path of Welsh Nonconformity, with its emphasis on temperance, through occasional visits to local taverns. For instance, in August 1882, although he had signed the anti-drinking pledge of the Blue Ribbon Society (a temperance movement) some months earlier, he noted in his diary on 12 August how he had enjoyed a somewhat intoxicating experience on a legal trip from Porthmadog to Beddgelert:

> To Beddgelert with 11 o'clock coach . . . walking, fearfully hot, had my feet and face blistered . . . bathed them in Llyn Dinas, serving writs. Had a glass of port with police officer, had a glass of beer before starting for Port with J.B., another at Prince Llywelyn Beddgelert and a glass of port with some bread and chop at Thomas's house, so that's keeping the Blue Ribbon pledge grandly![27]

He also kicked over the traces in this period by attending military exercises, even as far as Llandudno, with the Porthmadog Volunteers in the company of their leader, Randall Casson, one of his employers. This activity was not to the liking of his Uncle Lloyd, the pacifist. Here, too, he imbibed strong drink. Lloyd George was never a substantial drinker and in his teens he could not afford to be. Indeed, such activity could be detrimental to someone harbouring political ambitions, with temperance one of the major beliefs of many Liberal Nonconformists. Temperance platforms were also potential avenues of advancement for an aspiring politician to exploit. Indeed, neither strong drink nor the fairer sex were Lloyd George's prime passions. It was politics, and soon after he curtailed his tavern visits and began declaiming strongly on temperance platforms where he called for more control of the liquor trade through local option, seeking further legislation to strengthen the Welsh Sunday Closing Act of 1881.

In 1883 and 1884, however, he had to give up politics temporarily while concentrating on his solicitors' final examinations. Because of the financial pressures on his family he had to pass these exams at the first hurdle so that he could proceed at once to earn a living, as his family had also to finance his brother William's articles. Richard Lloyd had retired and the family at Cricieth were living on his mother's savings and were also dependent on keeping visitors and tourists during the season.

In May 1884, much to his family's and his own relief, he qualified as a solicitor, but with only third class honours in comparison to his brother's achievement later in securing first class honours in his finals. Shortly before sitting his finals, Lloyd George noted in his diary that he was considering going to London to work, intimating some disgruntlement at the way of life in Eifionydd:

> I am inclined for a London career – a fellow may make a successful career down there and amass a tidy sum, though not a large fortune, but as for any higher object-fame – London is the place for that. If I were to pursue my great ambition, to be eminent as a public speaker in Wales that would almost be an impossibility. For one thing, there are so many good, excellent public speakers already. Another thing, I would have to speak in Welsh so that after all my reputation would after all be confined to this stinted Principality – *a la Londres*.[28]

Lloyd George made these remarks when he was under considerable strain while facing his final examinations and when his relationship with a local singer, Lisa Jones, had finished (she then married a prominent local musician, J. Lloyd Williams). Lloyd George's nephew, W. R. P. George, in his work *The Making of Lloyd George* has interpreted these remarks as confirmation from the outset that his uncle was bent on a London career.[29] John Grigg, too, is of the same view and writes that Lloyd George's early championing of Welsh affairs was a pragmatic, tactical pose:

> He started with a broad outlook . . . he always cared about Wales but only in the context of United Kingdom and Imperial politics. His apparent preoccupation with Welsh affairs during the first phase of his career reflected a shrewd eye for tactics rather than a parochial mentality.[30]

This is an erroneous interpretation of Lloyd George's early career. True, he had called Wales 'a stinted Principality' at a time of depression and, of course, from an early age he desired a seat in the House of Commons. But Grigg is mistaken in his view that tactics were his main preoccupation in standing up for Welsh interests during his early career. Indeed, what Grigg calls his parochial mentality was from the mid-1880s onwards to incorporate a desire based on conviction for a considerable degree of Welsh autonomy. Naturally, he desired a Westminster seat as this was the only platform available from which he could fight realistically for a Welsh parliament within a British imperial context – a controversial stance regarded with hostility by many from his own ranks. In no way was this parochialism, but by the early 1890s his formation and leadership of the Cymru Fydd (Young Wales) movement was to involve calling for an independent nationalist-based Welsh Liberal party with a European slant to it. Then he was to be called 'The Welsh Parnell'.

This militant position as a radical nationalist with labourist views was yet to manifest itself clearly in the early 1880s when he was a trainee solicitor but in 1884, after qualifying as a solicitor and the advent of a more radical era with the Third Reform Act of 1884, he began the process of refining his political ideas which would place Home Rule at the forefront of his activities allied to Chamberlainite social reforms. Indeed, in the six months during which he stayed reluctantly with his employers as an solicitor before opening his own business, he was to devote all his spare time to radical politics, carving out a reputation for himself locally as an embryonic radical nationalist and the 'people's attorney'.

The onset of the Third Reform Act would provide Lloyd George with a golden opportunity to appeal to the new electors on the register by supporting a programme of neo-collectivist policies associated with Chamberlainite radicalism allied to a new approach to Wales as a political entity. This reform programme went far beyond the Gladstonian orthodox line and the traditional Welsh Nonconformist programme of disestablishment, tithe reform and temperance measures.

In Caernarfonshire, with the extension to the franchise and the redistribution of seats, there was a marked if not revolutionary change in the political process. Three new constituencies were formed out of the previous two electorates of the Caernarfon Boroughs and the county of Caernarfonshire. Socially and economically, too, the whole county was ripe for a new radical to cultivate.

The census of 1881 showed the county had a small select elite of rich landowners, who in some cases, like the owners of the Faenol and Penrhyn, were also major capitalist industrialists.[31] These were at the apex of the social hierarchy and a prime target for Lloyd George. There was also a small solid, established middle class of businessmen, some of them Tories and beholden to the gentry; others were orthodox and traditional laissez-faire Liberals for whom Lloyd George had much antipathy. The census showed that 1,400 men were employed in professional work and 600 in prominent commercial occupations. There was a lower middle class comprising hundreds of shopkeepers, 219 tavern keepers, 528 blacksmiths and five pawnbrokers. Amongst this category Lloyd George could hope for some support, although he was highly unlikely to secure the backing of the licensees.

The working class, particularly the slate and granite quarrymen, were by far the most numerous urban sector. There were 8,408 slate quarrymen and 1,184 granite quarrymen; 2,868 were classed as labourers and 217 were lead miners; 500 worked on the upkeep of the county's roads. There were 354 railway employees, especially numerous at the regional centre, Bangor, while 3,109 were employed in the building trade. The remainder of the working class were employed in other miscellaneous trades. Although many of these workers were without the vote, amongst them were the newly enfranchised whose support Lloyd George sought.

In the rural sector there were 2,925 farmers, many of them tenants of the large estates of the county. By far the most numerous group at the base of the rural pyramid were the 4,602 farm labourers. This group Lloyd George sought to champion, though many did not qualify to vote after 1884. He was also anxious to continue to win the tenants' support. At extreme poles of the social structure in the county there were 14,868 people returned under 'property, rank and not by any special occupation'. The majority were the old, infirm and the unemployed and Lloyd George cultivated the support of those who had the vote. The minority were the wealthy landowners who were the dominant force in the county and the backbone of the Tory Party in the main with their retinues and those directly employed by them.

Lloyd George had joined the lower middle class as a lawyer but his sympathies were with the working class and he also hoped to win over those segments of the middle class who had radical views, although he was no friend of the established middle class who held old-fashioned Liberal values. Attracted by municipal 'socialism' and by the teachings of the American radical Henry George and his work *Progress and Poverty*, he was intent on winning the newly enfranchised to his cause and to promote policies which would undermine the hegemony of the landed and industrial elite in the county. The two Caernarfonshire constituencies had small electorates before the Third Reform Act – in Caernarfonshire 6.2 per cent of the population could vote with 14.2 per cent able to vote in the Boroughs constituency. After the reform of the franchise there was a substantial increase in voters in the Boroughs and in the new constituencies of Eifion and Arfon. Although many of the working class and all women were voteless, the newly enfranchised were a challenge for the people's attorney and it was imperative that he would win their support, if he were to make a political breakthrough in the area.[32]

Not only would he have to declaim on traditional Nonconformist and rural matters but he would also have to champion measures such as trade union reform, leasehold enfranchisement, bringing land into community and municipal control and reforms to secure health and housing changes. He needed to be a social reformer and to associate himself with the national awakening emerging fitfully in the Wales of the 1880s, including measures to give status to the Welsh language. He needed to coalesce radicalism and nationalism and to project himself as a left-wing nationalist of a new pioneering kind in Wales.

He did not rest on his oars in May 1884 after qualifying as a solicitor but immediately began to carve a reputation for himself locally as a reformer. Only a fortnight after becoming a solicitor, he appeared alongside his Uncle Lloyd before the Criccieth Vestry, to protest against the local Burial Board, which was under the dominant influence of the local Tories. He alleged that they favoured Anglican burials in the town's cemetery, even for Nonconformists. Some months later the original Burial Board was disbanded and a new predominantly Nonconformist board was put in its place. Lloyd George was appointed the new board's first official solicitor and experience gleaned in this post proved invaluable to him subsequently, especially in the Llanfrothen burial scandal of 1888.

However, in July 1884 he had other challenges to face, including his first appearance as an advocate in court. This appearance was before Justice Gwilym Williams at Porthmadog where he won the case.[33] This success was repeated in the local courts, especially in defending poachers, which brought to him much capital at the expense of local Tory landlords. At the same time he appeared in the local Registration Courts, alongside the Liberal secretary for the county and boroughs of Caernarfon, R. D. Williams, fighting for those who wanted to vote for the first time since the 1884 Reform Act. The people's attorney was blending successfully the law courts and politics.

The young solicitor also used the temperance platform to his advantage. Although he had partaken of strong drink as an articled solicitor he now mended his ways and became a leading temperance advocate locally. He addressed several meetings organized by the well-known local leader of the UK Temperance Alliance, H. J. Williams (Plenydd),[34] and also became friendly with another temperance reformer, D. R. Daniel, who later became a notable trade union official.[35] Daniel was also a personal friend of Tom Ellis, shortly to be elected as the Liberal-Nationalist MP for Merioneth. Daniel was to forge the link between Ellis and Lloyd George in 1886, which brought the two most enthusiastic young nationalists in Wales together to fight for a new agenda in Welsh politics.

In 1884, however, the temperance platform was not the only vehicle of publicity that Lloyd George used. He also resorted once more to the local press to shape public opinion. This time he used the pseudonym 'J. Pen' in the Liberal weekly, the *North Wales Observer and Express*. The editorial board knew exactly who the young columnist was, enabling him to forge further valuable contacts in local Liberal circles. He wrote three articles in 1884 for the paper, each a paean of praise to Chamberlainism and the need to marry that radicalism and Welsh national aspirations. The newspaper was part of the newspaper combine, the Welsh National Newspaper Company, known locally after its Welsh language weekly, *Y Genedl Gymreig* (The Welsh Nation). One of the company's leading lights was W. J. Parry, the leader of the Slate Quarrymen's Union, who was also a strong supporter of Welsh Home Rule.[36] Later Lloyd George would use these papers to win the Caernarfon Boroughs and in the mid-1890s he would effect a takeover of the papers in order to underpin the Cymru Fydd (Young Wales) movement. Now in 1884 the articles he wrote, starting on 5 September, castigated the local undemocratic nature of the Liberal hierarchy and parliamentary representation, demanding new style, more radical Welsh parliamentary candidates for the future and the need to adopt Chamberlainite policies. This was the drift of his second article a week later, which appeared coincidentally in the week that Chamberlain, at Newtown, expressed publicly for the first time his support for Welsh Church disestablishment – the first prominent Liberal to do so, much to Gladstone's displeasure.[37] In his third and final article on 7 November he was again critical of the county's Liberal caucus, calling for more democracy, as the general election of 1885 approached. All these articles urged the radicalization of his party and the need for it to cultivate a powerful Welsh identity, underlining his own personal and political priorities.

By January 1885, in order to seek to fulfil those aspirations, Lloyd George was intent on leaving his employment at Breese, Jones and Casson to set up in business on his own so as to become more independent financially and politically and free from the Whiggish influences of the company. He was to leave the company in acrimonious circumstances, causing much embarrassment and concern to his younger brother, William, who had to remain there while completing his articles.

Indeed, he was determined that nothing would stand in his way in order to carve out a political career for himself. He confided this ambition to Margaret Owen during their courtship. After a quarrel between them over his frequent absences to pursue his political activities, he told her bluntly that not even his love for her would stand in his way, as he sought to build a reputation for himself as a social reformer and politician. In a letter to her, undated, but probably written in 1885 he had said: 'My supreme idea is to get on. To this idea I shall sacrifice everything except

I trust honesty . . . I am prepared to thrust even love itself under the wheels of my juggernaut.'[38]

The juggernaut was about to move into a higher gear as he faced a new era in his life at the beginning of 1885. Although several of the biographers of his early career have claimed that his primary objective from the outset was to build a London-based career and to acquire British-wide prominence, in the first decade of his public life from 1885 to 1896 he would give priority to Wales, and in doing so he pioneered often unpopular, controversial policies, especially his support for Welsh Home Rule. He was ready to advocate such a policy even in the teeth of hostile criticism from his own party – a standpoint that could easily have led him into political oblivion.

It is nonsensical to suggest, as so many of his biographers have done, that such a militant stand was only a temporary ruse to bring him publicity and that he would shelve such parochial views once he had gained prominence. Indeed, it was only after a decade of pursuing a long sustained campaign of conviction for radical policies allied to Home Rule that he finally abandoned the project when it was torpedoed by his own party in 1896. Indeed, in 1885, as he really entered the fray in Welsh politics, he was ready to embark on a campaign which entailed a fundamental change in the way Wales was governed within the British Isles which led 'the Parnell of Wales' into dangerous and controversial territory.

II

JUGGERNAUT IN ACTION BUT FAILURE IN MERIONETH, 1885–1886

When Lloyd George opened his solicitor's business at Cricieth and then Porthmadog in 1885, a new phase in his political career was about to begin. After establishing his business in these two towns, he also soon expanded his practice to Harlech and to Blaenau Ffestiniog in Merioneth. At the beginning, his business was far from prosperous until his brother William joined him in 1887 and to a large extent bore the everyday brunt of the practice. Extending the business to Blaenau Ffestiniog, in particular, was a significant step in Lloyd George's political career, because it was there, in the most populous, industrialized area of Merioneth in 1885 and 1886 that he was to launch his first bid to secure a parliamentary nomination.

He was drawn to Merioneth for several reasons. He had already been despatched there to the westernmost parts of the county to register Liberal electors at the behest of C. E. Breese; also during his last six months at Breese, Jones and Casson he had undertaken several legal cases in the county, which had brought him local press publicity. He also knew full well that Blaenau Ffestiniog and its environs with its burgeoning population was fertile ground both for his business to flourish and, especially, for him to gain political renown amongst the slate quarrymen and those workers dependent on the slate industry directly and indirectly. In addition, the railway connection between Porthmadog and Blaenau Ffestiniog enabled him to attend court cases and political meetings. Similarly, he could use the Cambrian Coast line service to expand his activities as far as the southernmost regions of the Merioneth constituency.

Inevitably, therefore, he was drawn to Merioneth for these reasons; but the socio-economic and political set-up in Merioneth was also ripe for the radical and nationalist agitator to exploit. He foresaw that it was possible to usurp the commanding but fragile Liberal hierarchy which ruled the roost in the constituency by challenging this traditional, Anglicized and predominantly middle-class coterie of tepid Liberals. At the dawn of the new democratic era, ushered in by the Third Reform Act and the Redistribution Acts of 1884–5, he was determined to be as critical of the established middle-class caucus in Merioneth, opposed to Welsh national aspirations, as he had been contemptuous of the County Liberal Association of Caernarfonshire before the Third Reform Act.

He was also critically aware that landlordism, which he aimed to attack, continued to dominate life in the county, not only in agriculture but also because the landlords owned quarries, industrial land and leaseholds upon which ordinary slate quarrymen had raised their houses.[1] Twelve of the 'greatest landlords' owned 128,593 of the county's 427,810 acres – 33.2 per cent of Merioneth's landmass. These landlords owned the great estates of the county like Penllyn, Rhiwlas and Tan-y-Bwlch. Below this rural elite there were thirty-seven squires owning between 1,000 and 3,000 acres of land, sharing control with the greatest landowners of over half of the county's landmass. This second rung of landowners, with some exceptions, tended to be Tory in politics, Anglican in religion and Anglicized culturally and linguistically. Lloyd George sought to undermine their hegemony, although some families, like those at Castell Deudraeth and Dolserau, were Liberal in politics – but not the new-style Liberalism with its Welsh national dimension which Lloyd George sought to champion.

Below the top two elements in the landlord pyramid, apart from the 96 yeomen who owned between 300 and 1,000 acres, the majority of the agricultural population was in a very inferior position. There were 1,004 smallholders owning less than an acre: 346 owned between 2 and 100 acres and those above them possessed between 100 and 300 acres. These groups, many of whom had had the vote since the Second Reform Act of 1867, had in the main voted Liberal since the controversial 1868 election in Merioneth which witnessed the ejection of several tenant farmers from their holdings for voting publicly (without a secret ballot) for the Liberal cause. Both the small owners and tenants had been a thorn in the Tory side for two decades. However, the county's largest agricultural group was that of the farm labourers, landless and without the vote after 1867 and many of them still voteless after 1884. However, Lloyd George was intent on bringing them within the political process and championing their rights. In rural Merioneth, therefore, Lloyd George sought both to consolidate Liberal votes after 1884 and to secure the support of the newly enfranchised. This aim he sought to fulfil not only by appealing to old Liberals on the thorny issues of Welsh Church disestablishment, tithe and temperance reform and the call for fair rents, but also by promulgating and championing new issues such as the Chamberlainite demand for municipalization of the land, the provision of allotments, leasehold enfranchisement and trade union reform for farm labourers (and, indeed, for slate quarrymen, who had established their own union in the 1870s).

Indeed, Lloyd George's main preoccupation in 1885 and 1886 was to champion the cause of the Nonconformist slate quarrymen's desire to improve their standard of living and secure radical reforms. They were employed in various parts of the county but the main conglomeration of slate workers was based in the Blaenau Ffestiniog slate quarries. Here was to be Lloyd George's potentially richest vein to quarry. According to the census of 1891, 25.1 per cent of the county's waged population worked in the slate industry. Amongst this numerous group of workers he could support measures such as trade union reform and leasehold enfranchisement, which would enable quarrymen to acquire the freehold on the land upon which their houses were built. In addition, he could press the Chamberlainite emphasis on providing municipal homes and other civic facilities. Joseph Chamberlain in his 'Unauthorised Programme' also promised cheap allotments for workers in urban areas and improvements in public health reform.

The county of Merioneth had also witnessed the emergence of a small but influential middle class of professionals and the self-employed in towns such as Barmouth, Blaenau Ffestiniog, Bala and Dolgellau. Although many of these were far too moderate Gladstonians in Lloyd George's opinion, amongst them were a small minority of radicals and nationalists aware of the need for social reforms to aid the underprivileged. This group Lloyd George hoped to court.

Before the Reform Act of 1884, it was the established moderate section of the middle class and the enfranchised small property/agricultural owners and tenants who formed the backbone of Liberal support in the county. The electorate was small, with only 6.7 per cent of the population enfranchised whilst in the 1880 general election only 3,169 voted out of a population of 52,038. Yet, though some quarrymen had had the vote since 1867, not one of them was a member of the Liberal Association's caucus. Indeed, in its entirety, the Liberal Association hierarchy were middle-class businessmen and professionals opposed to radical changes; in the 1880 general election the elected Liberal MP's manifesto, that of Samuel Holland, the local quarrying magnate, was devoid of any reference to social welfare legislation and measures to improve the lot of the working class. It was a rural-based, Nonconformist programme aimed at Church disestablishment, tithe reform and temperance measures; the manifesto made no claim for Welsh devolution nor social welfare measures. It was the traditional Gladstonian party-line approach.

In 1884, before the onset of the Reform Act, the Merioneth Liberal Association was chaired by the Dolgellau doctor, E. O. Jones; the secretary was John Cadwaladr Jones, a Blaenau Ffestiniog accountant, while a typical member of the business class, represented on the caucus, was Thomas Jones, Brynmelyn, a corn merchant. The Liberal MPs of the county since 1868 had been drawn from the prosperous upper middle class. David Williams, solicitor and landowner of Castell Deudraeth, was the first Liberal MP for the county, a ponderous and moderate Liberal and an Anglican. Samuel Holland, his successor,was both a squire and quarry owner, while the prospective Liberal candidate for the 1885 general election was Henry Robertson of Pale Hall, Llandderfel, a Scottish-born entrepreneur who had made his fortune in railway building and as an investor in the coal-mining industry. He was no radical.

Lloyd George was to label the Merioneth bigwigs 'a set of respectable dummies' and desired to see them replaced by more democratic figures, especially from amongst workers and quarrymen imbued with radical and nationalist aspirations. To him, the emerging nationalist, they were unrepresentative and outmoded figures who were not fit to take radicalism in Wales in a more egalitarian direction. They mirrored similar Liberal associations not only in Lloyd George's boyhood Caernarfonshire, but throughout Wales on the verge of a new area in Welsh politics in the mid-1880s, with the electorate in Merioneth, for example, having expanded threefold from 3,469 in 1880 to 9,333 by 1885. Lloyd George wanted the new voters to be drawn to a more advanced radicalism, with the Liberals selecting candidates from his social, linguistic and nationalistically inclined background. Here was an opportunity to galvanize radicalism in north-west Wales and head it in a new direction, on the basis of the Chamberlainite creed, while contemporaneously merging it with a nationalistic slant. It was no surprise that he concentrated most of his energies in the 1885 general election on Merioneth rather than on the county of his upbringing, especially as the three Caernarfonshire constituencies, Eifion, Arfon and the Caernarfon Boroughs, had already chosen parliamentary candidates, all of whom were moderate Gladstonians. He was especially anxious to make a mark for himself at Blaenau Ffestiniog with its large working-class electorate. There were 1,789 on the register there in 1885, triple the number in 1880, many of them quarrymen. This was potential fertile territory for him to cultivate and set up a marker for the future and, in time, secure a parliamentary foothold.

In 1885, Lloyd George lost no time in engaging in political controversy. Indeed, some months before the 1885 general election, which was to take place in November, he made much political capital out of a contentious legal case in the north-west of the constituency at Penrhyndeudraeth, where many quarrymen employed in the Ffestiniog quarries lived. The case was heard before the Penrhyndeudraeth Magistrates Court in July 1885. He appeared before them on behalf of over 400 petitioners in what had been a protracted controversy concerning the drink trade. One year before the hearing, the ratepayers had presented a petition to the Tory-dominated bench to seek a limit to the large number of taverns in the area. The bench had to yield reluctantly to this demand by closing several public houses, but later allowed one of these taverns, the Victoria Inn, to reopen with a new licence. In the court case in July, Lloyd George claimed that the Victoria's new licence was illegal, but after three hours of bitter legal wrangling the inn was given a new licence. Lloyd George then proceeded to accuse the bench of blatant prejudice and further alleged that it was one member of the bench of magistrates who was really the applicant for the licence, which had been applied for in another's name. There was uproar in the court and in the columns of local papers. For example, *Y Dydd*, a leading Merioneth weekly, devoted its front page to the case and the rumpus which had ensued.[2] However, Lloyd George was more than delighted with the publicity he had gained, noting in his diary, 'Got on I think remarkably well. Never felt more fluent.'[3]

At the same time, at Blaenau Ffestiniog, he also joined 'Senedd Bethania', the 'Bethania Parliament', another parliamentary debating society. Its deliberations were comprehensively reported in the local press, especially in *Yr Herald Cymraeg*, where William Jones (Ffestinfab) had a weekly column. William Jones was a part-time journalist and a quarry clerk and one of the few working-class radicals on the county's Liberal Association. Ffestinfab gave considerable space in his column to Lloyd George's exploits in the debating society. But this was not the only public platform Lloyd George exploited in 1885 at Blaenau Ffestiniog. In January, in the spacious Assembly Rooms in the town, he sounded forth on temperance reform, noting with much self-satisfaction and immodesty in his diary: 'Spoke with much fire and impetuosity and heard general praise of me amongst the workmen.'[4]

In a similar vein, in February at the same venue, he shared the platform with the editor of the *North Wales Observer and Express*, Abel Jones Parry, noting again in his diary that his contribution was 'the highlight of the night'.[5] He also participated in other political meetings in the area before the onset of the general election of 1885 and in his boyhood county of Caernarfonshire, where he addressed several meetings, urging the adoption of Chamberlain's 'Unauthorised Programme'. These activities brought him press publicity, which percolated through to Merioneth. When the general election of 1885 was eventually held, Lloyd George was ready to adopt a radical-nationalist stance, in particular in the Merioneth constituency, espousing the Chamberlainite creed that the new county councils should embark on municipal socialism and land and housing reform, especially taxation on the increase in land values and the enfranchisement of leaseholds. He was determined too to imbue his campaign with the call for devolution for Wales. In Merioneth, as well, he was ready to take a rebellious stand against his own party; he was determined to create a radical-nationalist reputation for himself, which would become ever more strident and clear cut in the Cymru Fydd era after 1886 and especially in the first half of the 1890s.

In the Merioneth election of 1885, he was prepared to be an anti-estab-
lishment rebel.

Indeed, long before polling day, he entered into a particularly
controversial development, which caused much dissention in Merioneth
Liberal politics. Morgan Lloyd, the Trawsfynydd-born barrister and former
MP for the Anglesey Boroughs, decided to challenge the choice of Henry
Robertson, the wealthy Scots-born railway entrepreneur, as the official
Liberal candidate for Merioneth. Robertson had been chosen by the
Liberal caucus in the county three years earlier to succeed Samuel Holland,
another wealthy, Anglicized moderate Whig, as the parliamentary
candidate. In a public meeting extensively reported in the press, Morgan
Lloyd accused the Liberal clique of selecting Robertson secretly and
undemocratically, without offering the opportunity for others to contend
for the candidature. With the electorate having tripled, Lloyd also insisted
that there was now a need to revoke Robertson's original choice and
reconvene a new selection meeting. He claimed he would oppose
Robertson and set himself up as 'the people's choice' for the Liberal
cause[6]. Following Lloyd's missive came the call from Ffestiniog quarrymen
for Lloyd to be nominated as the Liberal candidate instead of Robertson,
a demand repeated by Liberal branches in Harlech and at Barmouth.
Then on 20 August, at a packed meeting of Blaenau Ffestiniog quarrymen
organized by then vice-president of the North Wales Quarrymen's Union
D. G. Williams (Tanymarian), Lloyd George was asked to support the
challenger's candidature,[7] although it must be stated that Morgan Lloyd
was far from being a democratic, radical, nationalist candidate in Lloyd
George's view. Indeed, during the controversy, Lloyd George wrote in
his diary: 'I back him not as a supporter of his candidature, but against
the mode of selecting a candidate; his views are not half radical enough.'[8]

In his speech at Blaenau Ffestiniog, however, Lloyd George pounced
upon the opportunity to boast that they were cultivating new ground,
namely, electing candidates who were the choice of the people, rather
than being selected by a clique of an unrepresentative elite who did not
have the right to speak on behalf of true Liberalism. He ended his speech
by asserting emotionally that Robertson's selection to represent the
people of Merioneth was 'a deceitful travesty'.[9] Lloyd George, apart from
this speech, played no other role in Morgan Lloyd's campaign, perhaps
realizing that he had ventured enough by supporting him publicly at the
outset of the campaign. Indeed, he feared that Morgan Lloyd's campaign
could split the Liberal vote in the constituency and allow the Tories to
win the seat, as he noted in his diary after the count: 'Glad that Robertson
won, rather than lose the election to the Conservatives.'[10]

Lloyd polled badly, securing only 1,907 votes, the Tory, W. R. M. Wynne,
winning 2,209 votes, whilst Robertson came out on top of the poll with a

total of 3,784 votes. Lloyd George, however, had sided with the quarrymen's choice, thus bringing him into the public eye within the county's slate-quarrying community. Although he was undoubtedly a radical and a nationalist, he had also been cunning enough to support a very moderate Liberal, if not an old-style Whig, in the Caernarfon Boroughs constituency in the election, namely, Sir Love Jones-Parry, the prodigal squire from Madryn, Llŷn. In the Eifion constituency, he had also supported the sober Gladstonian, J. Bryn Roberts, with whom he was to come to severe blows at the most controversial stage of the Cymru Fydd League in 1895 and 1896, with Roberts opposing, with great hostility, Lloyd George's call for Welsh Home Rule and an independent Welsh radical political party. Indeed, while supporting Roberts in Eifion in 1885, he also ensured that he used his public appearances there to champion the left-wing Chamberlainite 'Unauthorized Programme'. He noted in his diary during the campaign: 'Replying to attacks on Chamberlain, pointing out that every Tory mushroom thought he ought to attack Chamberlain . . . I was tremendously cheered . . . I felt I had made another stroke at Criccieth.'[11]

During the election of 1885, Lloyd George had expressed clearly that what Merioneth expected (like other Welsh constituencies) was for young, militant, parliamentary candidates, with a resolute policy of promoting Welsh national aspirations, to be chosen to fight elections, rather than privileged English-born wealthy nominees. Immediately after the hustings, he began to seek to strengthen his position in Merioneth radical circles, especially in the slate-quarrying communities. This aspiration was soon evinced in 1885, when he came into contact with his boyhood hero, Michael Davitt, a politician and rebel, a land socialist and Irish nationalist – a hero he had called in his diary at the beginning of the 1880s 'my most admired character in real life'.

In February 1886, he was presented with the opportunity of sharing a platform with his hero at Blaenau Ffestiniog. The Welsh land socialist and nationalist, E. Pan Jones, the editor of Y Celt, had arranged for Davitt to address several meetings in north Wales where Davitt, the former political prisoner, would lead the call to establish a Welsh Land and Labour League. The Welsh Liberal establishment did not wish to be associated with Davitt and his 'criminal' background and even Thomas Gee and his Baner ac Amserau Cymru were lukewarm about his visit to north Wales.[12] But Lloyd George was more than pleased to accept an invitation from the nationalist and socialist pioneer, Michael D. Jones of Bala, to share a platform with the Irishman. The invitation for him to speak at Davitt's meeting at Blaenau Ffestiniog was forthcoming because the controversial nature of the tour meant that there was a dearth of Welsh speakers to share a platform with Davitt. Lloyd George, however, had no hesitation in accepting the invitation to speak at Blaenau Ffestiniog where a crowd estimated to be 1,800 strong had gathered to listen to the Irish reformer. In his speech, Davitt called for land nationalization and no compromise with landlordism; he insisted, too, that rural and industrial workers should be an integral part of the campaign and that legislation to defend their rights and welfare should be forthcoming. He also called for fair rents and municipal housing.

Lloyd George had been asked to thank Davitt and, according to his diary entry, he was agitated and nervous before rising to speak – 'biting my nails to the quick'. But, after he began to speak, his nervousness receded and he spoke eloquently, attacking the 'lukewarm Liberals' who had opposed Davitt's visit, those tepid Liberals who were misrepresenting Wales in Parliament. He also called for young, radical and nationalist candidates to represent constituencies such as Merioneth. He was, without doubt, pressing his own case, while at the same time calling for the overthrow of landlordism, many Merioneth landlords being also quarry owners. He said: 'While workers starved, the "byddigion" (landlords) were feeding their pheasants with food which should have gone to the people.'[13] He received tremendous applause at the end of his speech, according to *Y Genedl Gymreig*[14] (and numerous other papers, too), while Michael D. Jones told him after the meeting that he should seek a parliamentary candidature in order to promote the cause of Welsh Home Rule and Welsh radicalism. Lloyd George noted ecstatically in his diary (with his customary immodesty): 'My speech gone like wildfire through Ffestiniog – they're going to make me an M.P. Michael D. Jones for it. Long talk with him. Pan Jones and Mr Davitt at the L. and N.W. Railway Hotel – scheming future of agitation – I feel I am in it now.'[15]

Undeniably, the meeting at Blaenau Ffestiniog was a real incentive for Lloyd George and a boost to his confident, perhaps overconfident, belief that he could soon secure a parliamentary candidature on a radical-nationalistic ticket. Indeed, he attempted to sound out leading Liberals in the Caernarfon Boroughs constituency as to whether he might replace Love Jones-Parry as a candidate, unsuccessfully because he was often drunk or in trouble with various women. However, it was to Merioneth that Lloyd George turned to satisfy his ambition, and to Blaenau Ffestiniog, in particular, where there was continuous criticism of Henry Robertson, even after his election as MP in 1885.

At Blaenau Ffestiniog, the centre of radicalism in the county, Lloyd George proceeded after the election and the Davitt meeting further to carve out a name for himself in the district as a labourist radical championing the workers' cause. This aim was evident when he addressed the Blaenau workers' branch of the Leasehold Enfranchisement Society in April 1886.[16] This was an issue of considerable concern to many slate workers who did not own the leases of land on which their houses had been built. This meant that when the lease expired, the land and house would revert to the landowner. Lloyd George could exploit this issue to the utmost because it sought to undermine not only landlordism, but also the fact that many quarry owners were the possessors of leases in the area; indeed, many of them were leading, tepid Liberals who dominated politics in the county. He pressed for leaseholds to be converted to freeholds at reasonable prices.

During the same month he also made two speeches at Rhiw Chapel and at the Assembly Rooms in the town, on the more traditional, Liberal programme of temperance reform, claiming that the controversial clause in the Welsh Sunday Closing Act of 1881, known colloquially as 'the man on his travels', should be deleted from that legislation – a measure, he claimed, that would decrease Sunday drinking on the sly in Wales.[17] He had alleged, too, that many licensees had abused this clause in the act, which had been meant only to provide alcoholic refreshment for resident visitors at hotels. Then, in June 1886, he spoke on the same subject again at the annual general meeting of the Merioneth Temperance Union, meeting there for the first time a like-minded, young radical-nationalist, Tom Ellis, the son of a tenant farmer from Cefnddwysarn, Merioneth and an Oxford University graduate. Lloyd George had already heard about his advanced views and his radical leanings from their mutual friend, D. R. Daniel, the Llanuwchllyn-born trade unionist and temperance reformer, who was to play a crucial role later in the late 1880s in securing for Lloyd George his first parliamentary nomination.

Tom Ellis, within a short space of time after meeting David Lloyd George, would, however, prove a thorn in the flesh of Lloyd George's parliamentary aspirations in Merioneth. Nevertheless, both would prove to be close colleagues in promoting the Welsh national awakening in the late 1880s and early 1890s, though by the mid-1890s their paths would diverge as Lloyd George championed the Cymru Fydd League movement for Home Rule and an independent Liberal Party for Wales.

Another obstacle for Lloyd George to overcome appeared in 1886, as a result of the seismic split in the Liberal Party over the contentious issue of Home Rule for Ireland, favoured by Gladstone and advocated by him publicly for the first time in March 1886. Joseph Chamberlain immediately criticized the policy, advocating instead 'Home Rule All Round' for all the nations in the British Isles, not Federal Home Rule, but less extensive devolutionary powers. Lloyd George, already a Chamberlainite in socio-economic terms, believed Chamberlain's Home Rule programme was of far greater immediate benefit to Wales, than the priority accorded to Ireland by Gladstone.

Chamberlain resigned from the government in order to oppose Gladstone and in the great controversy that ensued, especially in the run-up to the election of 1886, Lloyd George played a curious dual role, despite his Chamberlainite sympathies. In April 1886, at Cricieth, he rejected Gladstone's policy,[18] but later that month he spoke up for Gladstone at a Blaenau Ffestiniog meeting.[19] Then in June he wrote to Tom Ellis, a Gladstonian, that he was 'at Llanbedr a few weeks ago addressing a meeting to support Home Rule'. More controversially, again it was revealed in his diary that he intended, later that month, to attend at Birmingham, Chamberlain's power base, a great meeting to establish Chamberlain's Radical Union. However, he seems to have missed his train connection to Birmingham and, in so doing, saved his political career, for if he had joined Chamberlain's ranks, he would have inevitably become in the course of time a Liberal Unionist, a member of the breakaway party which found little favour in Wales. Such action would have ensured for him political oblivion.

This great dilemma for Lloyd George in the summer of 1886, between Gladstonianism and Chamberlainism, was mirrored by another personal/political dilemma for him in the 1886 general election, caused by the Home Rule crisis. The election brought a Liberal vacancy in Merioneth when Henry Robertson decided not to stand again and Lloyd George, despite his earlier seemingly anti-Gladstonian stance, decided to seek the county Liberal nomination. He made several inquiries amongst Liberal members and branches in the county as to possible support, and he secured the nomination of the Harlech branch, so that his name could go forward to the selection stage. He undertook this action despite the fact that his friend Tom Ellis had already been nominated as a prospective candidate by many branches throughout Merioneth. Morgan Lloyd was also in the race for the nomination. In comparison with Lloyd and Tom Ellis, Lloyd George, much to his disappointment, was a rank outsider in the race, having won only one nomination. Consequently, before the final selection meeting at Dolgellau, he pulled out of the race for the candidature after realizing he had no hope of winning and because Tom Ellis's brand of radical-nationalism was in many respects on the same wavelength as his own, despite their differing views during the Chamberlain–Gladstonian split. Indeed, Lloyd George went to great lengths to support Ellis's candidature, stressing in a personal letter to him on the eve of the selection meeting that Ellis represented the new forces of radicalism and nationalism, coursing through Wales. He stated with much gusto: 'I am strongly convinced . . . that you are destined to rescue Wales from respectable dummyism.'[20]

Of course, Lloyd George had no real hope of winning the nomination, with Ellis far ahead in the race and his nomination by fourteen branches, in contrast to Lloyd George's one branch, Harlech. His flirtation with the Chamberlainite policy had not been of advantage to him either. The choice for the nomination finally lay between Ellis and Morgan Lloyd, and Lloyd George, despite his disappointment at failing to secure the nomination, decided to write a letter to the *Cambrian News* on the eve of the selection meeting commending Ellis's cause, whilst at the same time not neglecting to praise his own involvement in Merioneth politics. In his letter to the press he said, without modesty:

> I observe that my name was submitted to the Liberal Association as one of the proposed candidates for the representation of the county. Since Mr. Robertson's resignation, I have received numerous communications from different parts of the county, favourable to my candidature. Having, however, at the outset, pledged myself to support the candidature of Mr. Tom Ellis, Cynlas, I decided not to enter the lists . . . It would appear to me that Ellis possessed beyond any other candidate named, the qualifications essential to constitute an effective Welsh member. Born and brought up amongst the people, he knows their wants. Of their own race and religion, he thoroughly sympathises with their sentiments. Living as they do in democratic times, Members of Parliament must now represent their constituents, not only on professed opinions, but also in real sympathies. This Mr. Ellis does. He has, moreover, shown that he possesses the ability to express with vigour and effect, any opinions he may entertain.[21]

Tom Ellis won the nomination after a lengthy, acrimonious campaign, following a public allegation from Morgan Lloyd that misdemeanours had taken place during the counting at the selection process. However, Ellis was duly elected and Lloyd George had failed in his first ever attempt, at twenty-three years of age, to secure a parliamentary nomination. He had also seen his hero, Chamberlain, splitting the party and his rejection by the majority of Liberals in Wales and their preference for the Grand Old Man. The Liberals in Wales had not followed Chamberlain into the Liberal Unionist ranks (and eventually to the Tory Party) and did not support him in the 1886 general election. In that election, Lloyd George, in a state of some melancholia, was to play an uncharacteristically subdued role, as no doubt he still retained some sympathy for aspects of Chamberlain's policy, despite his action in splitting the Liberal Party. He had, of course, realized that he could well have entered the political wilderness if he had not supported the official Liberal Party. That is why he had supported Tom Ellis, but he did not take any part in Ellis's election campaign in Merioneth in 1886, judging from the complete absence of any press references to any speeches there, and despite the fact that one of Lloyd George's biographers, J. Hugh Edwards, claimed erroneously that: 'In various parts of the constituency he delivered fervid speeches, which kindled the enthusiasm of the audiences and materially contributed to Ellis's victory.'[22]

Lloyd George adopted a similar, low-key stance in the election campaigns in the Caernarfonshire elections, in the Eifion constituency and in the Caernarfon Boroughs, underlining his disappointment at his ambitious attempt to secure the Merioneth nomination. His juggernaut had come to a clear halt in 1886, albeit temporarily. He had suffered a severe blow to his ambitions (and to his ego), which led him to note in his diary on 20 June 1886, that he might well have been over-ambitious at twenty-three years of age, with few financial resources, in seeking a parliamentary nomination and that, in future, he would have to be better prepared before seeking another candidature. He noted realistically in his diary: 'I would not be in nearly a good position, as regards pecuniary, oratorical or intellectual quality to get to parliament now as say five years hence.'[23]

However, his efforts in Merioneth during 1885 and 1886 had not all been in vain, despite the rebuffs he had suffered. He had established important political contacts there and beyond the county in the period. He had acquired more expertise in public speaking, political campaigning and in his use of the press – essential attributes for the future. In addition, he had to come to terms with failure, which, nevertheless, made him more resilient and decidedly more determined to create a name for himself in politics.

He had also established a crucial contact point with Tom Ellis, which paved the way for him to play a continuing and even more prominent role in the future in fostering Welsh national consciousness, associated with the Cymru Fydd movement. This development was a further incentive for him to seek to transform the Liberal Party in Wales into a more socially progressive and more nationalistic party, and, by the early 1890s, to bring into the Welsh Liberal political domain a more labourist approach to reforms, which he believed could be facilitated by a Welsh parliament.

He had also learnt, however, that at times a politician had to adopt a more pragmatic role (especially with regard to the Chamberlain controversy) in order to secure his objectives. Lloyd George, nevertheless, during the remainder of his pre-parliamentary career (and, indeed, during his championing of the Cymru Fydd, Young Wales League, 1894–6), with the exception of his first election in the Caernarfon Boroughs in 1890, was not prepared to take a moderate stance in his social and political objectives, nor in his nationalistic views.

After the rebuffs of 1886 in Merioneth, he had to turn to political activity in Caernarfonshire, the county of his upbringing, in order to re-build his political ambitions. He was determined to rise from the ashes like a phoenix and, as he cast his eyes over the Caernarfonshire political landscape, he hoped not only to resurrect his career there, but also to transform his country's political future in a more radical and nationalistic direction. He was determined to show that his juggernaut had only been stopped temporarily in its tracks.

III

THE ANTI-TITHE AGITATOR AND RADICAL NATIONALIST, 1886–1888

Lloyd George was a resilient political animal, even at the tender age of twenty-three. After failing to secure a parliamentary nomination in Merioneth, and although he had to end his political affair with Chamberlainism, he was not prepared to turn his back on future political ambitions and concentrate only on a legal career. Neither was he ready to give up his ambitions to be a social reformer. He was intent on pursuing radical and social economic objectives to meet the welfare needs of the newly enfranchised and, indeed, those without the vote.

Having established contacts with Michael D. Jones and Tom Ellis in 1886, he was also ready to adopt a more emphatic commitment to secure Welsh national aspirations and champion federal Welsh Home Rule, which was already implicit in his support for the more diluted self-government proposals in Chamberlain's policy of 'Home Rule All Round'.

There were obviously considerable difficulties obstructing him as a Welsh radical-nationalist, as he sought to reactivate his career in 1886. It was by no means an easy task for him to fulfil his ambition of securing a parliamentary nomination and follow in the footsteps of Tom Ellis, and to aim to prioritize Welsh aspirations within a party to which labourist and nationalist objectives were inimical. Lloyd George was, after all, a relatively poor, young attorney without the necessary financial clout to fight for a parliamentary nomination, and especially to maintain a parliamentary career at Westminster since MPs were unpaid at this time. Another major obstacle was the fact that he was without doubt beyond the pale of the Anglicized, middle-class-dominated, Liberal elite in north-west Wales and in the county of his upbringing. Moreover, he belonged to a minority religious sect, the smallest denomination in his constituency and in Caernarfonshire. This was at a time when interdenominational rivalry was at its most fervent, while the largest denomination in the area was the Calvinistic Methodists. They were antagonistic towards not only 'Y Batus Bach' (the Little Baptists), but also, in the main, towards any nationalist or labourist issues. Above all, therefore, he would have to make his radical and nationalistic aspirations acceptable to Liberals (who were naturally inclined towards Gladstonian and Nonconformist policies) or seek to effect a change in the personnel of local Liberal associations with their dominant middle-class, moderate members. His main hope was to show that Welsh Liberals needed young, radical candidates of his own ilk and to appeal to the more progressive sectors, emancipated by the Third Reform Act.

In the summer of 1886, his prospects of securing a parliamentary foothold appeared to be clouded by uncertainty, but there emerged, albeit unclear, a silver lining, which raised his spirits and opened a new window of opportunity for him to acquire more prominence locally, and enhance his hopes of a potential parliamentary candidature. Within a month of his failure in Merioneth in the general election of 1886, he was able to begin the process of raising himself, phoenix-like, from rejection, with the advent of the anti-tithe war in Wales. In August 1886, tenant farmers in the Llandyrnog area in the Vale of Clwyd began to agitate against the payment of tithes to the Anglican Church in Wales. This was the first battle to be fought in the long, drawn-out and increasingly tempestuous war against landlordism and Anglicization in the 1880s, with tenant farmers demonstrating against the imposition of the tithe, which they resented paying to what they, as Nonconformists, regarded as an alien church. Lloyd George pounced upon the opportunity to participate to the utmost in this campaign in his own locality, which enabled him to resuscitate his political prospects while also contributing further to the 'national awakening' in Wales.

The tithe issue (*pwnc y degwm*) had long been a contentious matter in Wales, indeed, since the 1830s. Since 1859, Thomas Gee, the influential Denbigh press baron, through the columns of his newspaper, *Baner ac Amserau Cymru* (the Banner and Times of Wales), had sustained a long and vigorous campaign of opposition to tithe payments by Nonconformists. By the 1880s, with an undercurrent of a depression in farming, tenant farmers driven by Gee began to agitate, through non-payment, for the abolition of the tithe system; this led to the beginning of a long and bitter campaign against the Church and the authorities. Gee impelled the farmers to organize, on a widespread basis, and to set up an efficient organization to highlight their grievances, although Gee hesitated to advocate the breaking of the law. The organization was called, to begin with, the Anti-Tithe League, with its first branch established at Ruthin in September 1886. This was the first step, which culminated in the winter of 1886 in the organization called Y Gymdeithas Er Cynorthwyo Gorthrymedigion y Degwm (The Society for Promoting the Tithe Oppressed People). The society would sustain and support those throughout rural Wales who were prepared not to pay the tithe.[1]

The movement had three objectives. Firstly, it proposed using all constitutional and legal means available to decrease the amount of tithe paid to the Church. Secondly, it proposed financially helping all farmers who had their stock taken from them in lieu of the tithe they had failed to pay. Lastly, it proposed providing the best legal advice to farmers facing the consequences of not paying the tithe. Although the movement claimed it was not in favour of lawbreaking and violence, it was certainly seeking to use methods of civil disobedience (and, inevitably, violence ensued).

By the winter of 1886, the movement had spread like wildfire throughout rural Wales and in its wake Lloyd George's own political prospects were revivified. The anti-tithe agitation fell like manna from heaven into Lloyd George's lap. He realized that he could use the issue to raise radical and national consciousness in Wales. The campaign could be manipulated, not only to attack landlordism and the Church, but also to heighten the national consciousness in Wales by attacking the Church as an alien, foreign establishment, *Yr Estrones* (The Foreigner), the English Church in Wales. The campaign, he foresaw, could be exploited, too, to highlight farming grievances; but unlike Gee, he wanted it to branch out in another direction, namely to urge in his locality and throughout Wales the formation of a militant union for farm labourers, many of whom were employed at very low wages in Caernarfonshire. Indeed, he could foresee the league expanding into the labourite sphere, championing also the grievances of slate and granite quarrymen in his locality, who were exploited by an alien elite who were their employers.

There is no doubt that allying himself with the Anti-Tithe League would secure much publicity for Lloyd George in Caernarfonshire, while in the county there were two political doors ajar for him, which could lead, potentially, towards the goal of a parliamentary candidature. J. Bryn Roberts, the barrister from Bryn Adda, Bangor and Liberal MP for Eifion after the Third Reform Act, was by 1886 rumoured to be in line for a county court judgeship and, therefore, would have to resign his seat. At the same time, another avenue of opportunity opened for Lloyd George, with the resignation of Love Jones-Parry, as a future candidate for the Caernarfon Boroughs seat. He had lost the election in the constituency in 1886 to the Tory barrister and land agent, Edmund Swetenham, from Wrexham. Under pressure from the local Liberal Association and bedevilled by ill health (gout) from loose living, he decided to announce in December 1886 that he would no longer stand for the Liberal cause in the constituency. After his resignation, in the most radical papers in the constituency, such as *Y Genedl Gymreig* (The Welsh Nation) on 8 December 1886 and *Y Werin* (The People) on 9 December, came the call for the new candidate to be young, local, Welsh speaking and drawn from the ranks of the people – a similar candidate to Tom Ellis in Merioneth. Although no mention of Lloyd George as a possible successor was made in December 1886 in any of these press reports, he could utilize the tithe controversy, alongside other political initiatives, to cultivate the ground in order to create a further reputation for himself locally and put in a bid for the nomination when the time was ripe. A chink of light was emerging, for the political prospects of the young attorney of the people, both in the Caernarfon Boroughs and in the Eifion constituency.

It was, consequently, no coincidence that the first outbreak of anti-tithe agitation in Caernarfonshire should happen within Lloyd George's own local area in Eifionydd.[2] He appeared not to be present during the first outbreak of protest against the tithe in the area, but he was the secret instigator impelling local farmers to protest. This first protest in Eifionydd took place in parishes adjacent to Llanystumdwy, namely Llangybi and Llanarmon, where some of the farmers were tenants of the Gwynfryn estate. On 26 October, in a meeting held at the Board School, Llangybi, the tenant farmers demanded a 15 per cent decrease in the payment of tithe. This initiative was followed three days later by a similar meeting in his boyhood parish, when a 20 per cent reduction in tithe payment was demanded.[3] In this case, however, David Edwards, the rector, said he could not consent to the demand. Then, after a petition was launched, the rector refused to yield a second time. Consequently, a branch of the Anti-Tithe League was established in the parish, which had as its motto, 'Rhyfel hyd y carn' (War to the hilt).[4] It was significant that it was in Lloyd George's boyhood village, that the first anti-tithe league branch was formed in the whole of the Llŷn and Eifion area.

Lloyd George's name did not appear in any newspaper extracts or reports of these two apparently spontaneous developments in Eifionydd in the autumn of 1886. However, it is possible, indeed probable, that he was the hidden instigator behind these events from the very start. Indeed, one of his earliest biographers, Hubert du Parcq, has remarked (without specifying the date) that he delivered his first salvo in the tithe war at Llangybi Board School.[5] Also, Lloyd George was the first guest of honour at the first event organized by the anti-tithe movement, on New Year's Day 1887. This appearance seems to confirm his earlier involvement there and at Llangybi and that he was the hidden puppeteer, pulling all the strings from the outset. He had bided his time, tested the water, before becoming immersed in the campaign.

In his New Year's address in his boyhood village, to the expectant audience of tenant farmers, and in the wake of a virulent attack upon him locally for leading the agitation, he vigorously denied that he had no right to intervene in a matter involving the farming community and the Church. Indeed, he countered that he had every right to get involved, as the controversy was an issue which affected the entire well-being of society.[6] These remarks underline how determined he was to justify his intervention from the outset and that he had, undoubtedly, launched the agitation in the area, from the very beginning. He had shown great cunning in conveying the impression that the agitation arose spontaneously and naturally from the farmers themselves, rather than being his own work.

Nevertheless, once the movement in the area was up and running (and once he had identified himself publicly as its leader), Lloyd George then proceeded, during 1887, to expand the agitation throughout the whole area. Naturally, this would elevate him to public prominence, in two electoral seats where there was a possibility of a vacancy. Publicity would be gained, not only in rural areas, but also in the three southern towns of the Caernarfon Boroughs, namely Nefyn, Pwllheli and Cricieth, where Love Jones-Parry had vacated the Liberal candidature, and where Lloyd George hoped to emulate Tom Ellis. Indeed, in this period, he was in constant communication with Ellis throughout the campaign. Both of them saw the agitation not only as a means of championing the farmers' cause, but as an opportunity to propagandize for social and trade union reforms in urban areas, be it quarrying areas or towns where many farm labourers lived. They hoped to achieve this by transforming the Anti-Tithe League, by 1888, into a wider movement called the Welsh Land, Commercial and Labour League.

After his initial appearance at Llanystumdwy on New Year's Day 1887, Lloyd George reappeared in public at the same venue on 6 January, which was the customary date for the payment of the annual tithe.[7] At Lloyd George's prompting, all the farmers of the parish refused to pay, even though the local squire and Lloyd George's future election opponent, Ellis Nanney, had offered to help them with their payments. Not unexpectedly, Lloyd George's promptings incurred the wrath and barbed hostility of the local Anglican and Tory press, with the county's Welsh-language Tory weekly, *Y Gwalia* (Wales), and the English-language Tory organ, the *North Wales Chronicle*, berating his appearance at Llanystumdwy. The *Chronicle* alleged that external influences had motivated the usually obedient farmers of the area to embark upon illegal actions, while *Y Gwalia*, in a vituperative editorial, 'Eifion yn Ymwyddeleiddio' (Eifion becoming Irishized), poured scorn on Lloyd George:

> It appears that it was one Mr 'Oliver' George, solicitor from Criccieth, who was the hero of that meeting under consideration. It is not known if he is related somehow to the arch revolutionary, Henry George, or not, but we know one thing, that we have never heard of him before as an authority on the subject of the tithe.[8]

This article ended on a particularly vindictive note:

> It saddens us that some of the most respectable, hard working
> and thrifty farmers of Eifionydd have allowed themselves to be
> part of the torrent of errors preached by the Radical press. They
> will realise, one day, that solicitors are not their best friends.[9]

Gwalia knew full well the hatred of many farmers towards solicitors,
but the paper's poisonous condemnation did not disturb Lloyd George.
Any publicity was good publicity as far as he was concerned, especially
gratifying being the comparison drawn between himself and the American
land reformer, Henry George, who had been his hero since the early
1880s. Indeed, the criticism levied against him by the Conservative press
impelled him to redouble his efforts in the tithe war and to expand his
activity into the Llŷn area in January. In an anti-tithe meeting at Llithfaen,
near Pwllheli, he shared a platform with the movement's most powerful
spokesman, apart from Thomas Gee, namely John Parry, Llanarmon-yn-
Iâl, from the Vale of Clwyd. This meeting was a prelude to a further, larger
gathering some days later, at Pwllheli, to establish a regional branch of
the league, encompassing the whole of south Caernarfonshire. At this
meeting, which secured much publicity in the Liberal and Tory press,
Lloyd George delivered an inflammatory oration, declaring:

> The country thinks it's about time the gentry should finance
> their own religion at their own cost; that they should spend less
> on their hunting dogs and spend more on the parsons – to get
> rid of one set of hounds in order to keep another set![10]

Lloyd George was not prepared to temper his rhetoric in this address,
even availing himself of the opportunity to attack the monarchy. At this
meeting, he was chosen as secretary of the newly formed south
Caernarfonshire branch, by the hundreds of farmers from all parts of Llŷn
and Eifionydd, who had crowded into the Town Hall at Pwllheli. Tudwal
Davies, a farmer and crowned bard of Brynllaeth, Aber-erch and a close
friend of Lloyd George, was elected joint secretary.

As an elected leader of the campaign in south Caernarfonshire, in
February 1887, he once again addressed a meeting at Llanystumdwy,
when he implored the members to continue to refuse payment of the
tithe, while pouring scorn on those who had already yielded by paying it.
At this meeting, he chided the Anglican Church for being a foreign
establishment, claiming that Nonconformists should not pay for the
upkeep of an alien Church and its head, Queen Victoria. In the course of
his speech, he said: 'Although I have no objection to God Saving the

Queen, I believe this country pays more than enough for her upkeep.'[11] He was, therefore, ready to use inflammatory, anti-English and anti-monarchical language to arouse passions in the campaign. Not unexpectedly, the *Gwalia* newspaper responded fiercely to his accusations, claiming, 'the leaders of the movement were those who did not have to pay the tithe', and adding, 'the innocent farmers were being led by those who cared nothing about their success'.[12]

Despite these attacks upon him by the Tory press, Lloyd George continued to escalate the tithe issue in April 1887, when he resorted to the courts of law to promote the cause – revealing how adept the 'people's attorney' was in exploiting the law to bring about political change. In the wake of the Llanystumdwy farmers' refusal to pay the tithe to the local rector, David Edwards, the clergyman responded by refusing to pay to the parish vestry the annual poor rate. He had informed the parish overseer, Henry Jones, that he could not afford the £15 payment because the farmers had not paid the tithe to him. Lloyd George then put pressure on Henry Jones to issue a summons against the rector to appear before the local magistrates' court at Pwllheli for non-payment. Not surprisingly, Lloyd George agreed to take up the case on behalf of the parishioners, knowing full well that it would attract considerable publicity locally, and more widely via the press.[13]

On the magistrates' bench sat four of the area's most notable Anglicans and Conservatives, who despised the anti-tithe agitation. The chairman was R. Carreg, owner of the Carreg estate, near Aberdaron; B. T. Ellis of the Rhyllech estate was another rabid Tory, as was Owen Evans of the Broom Hall estate in Eifionydd, and the remaining magistrate was the rector of Llanengan, the Revd Thomas Jones. When the hearing took place, with the court crowded and hundreds milling outside, Lloyd George pounced on the opportunity to make the case an explosive issue between himself and the bench. At the beginning of the hearing, the chairman pronounced they were not ready to accept the summons and to listen to the case against the rector, arguing that the Overseer, Henry Jones, had summoned only David Edwards, while disregarding the others in the parish who had not paid the poor rate. Lloyd George retorted that the rector was the only one who had not paid the poor rate, while the others were in the process of paying. After the chairman alleged that the case was politically motivated and that the granting of the summons would need longer deliberation, Lloyd George resorted to a tactic he was to deploy frequently as the 'people's attorney'. He claimed that his client would never receive justice at the hands of such a prejudiced Tory bench and that he would take the case to a higher court. After further exchanges, however, the summons was accepted, although the chairman warned Lloyd George that the overseer, Henry Jones, should always act in a neutral manner while conducting his job. The case was then adjourned for a further hearing a fortnight later where, again, a huge crowd had assembled. However, much to their disappointment, it was announced that David Edwards, the rector, had paid his debt to the parish.[14] Nevertheless, the case had been a feather in Lloyd George's cap and a victory over the forces of the Church and landlordism.

In rural Wales, in May and June, the anti-tithe agitation reached a crescendo of discontent with riotous behaviour at Mochdre and Llangwm in Denbighshire. At Llangwm, the rioting had led to the notorious and notable prosecution of the 'Llangwm Martyrs' at the High Court in London, on a charge of rioting. Amidst accusations of rural terrorism, Lloyd George welcomed the escalation of protest, while insisting that he was not an advocate of violence and alleging that the rioting was the result of overreaction by the police and the authorities.[15] In a letter he also informed Tom Ellis, in May, that: 'This tithe business is proving to be an excellent lever wherewith to rouse the spirit of the people.'[16] In the same letter he added 'The people are looking to you for the development of a national policy which they are tired of waiting for from their own representatives.'[17] Once more, Lloyd George was aware that he could identify himself with the anti-tithe movement in order to effect for himself a political breakthrough as a new-style Ellis-type nationalist candidate.

Lloyd George proceeded in June and July to raise the political temperature and to escalate the agitation in the Llŷn area, especially by attending the hiring fairs there, to stir excitable crowds to a frenzy. In hiring fairs at Sarn Meillteyrn and Aberdaron he was intent on stirring the cauldron of discontent further. At the Sarn fair, near the village of Bryncroes, where local farmers had refused to pay the tithe, he addressed the crowd spontaneously, although he had arranged carefully for pressmen from the radical papers, especially *Y Genedl Gymreig*, to be present. Indeed, *Y Genedl* and its sister labourite paper, *Y Werin*, gave much publicity to his speech there.[18] In the course of his declaration he alleged:

> The Church is a foreign body foisted on the Welsh by the state: its endowments were the fruits of larceny; its clerics did not do their work properly and they were worse than Robin Hood, who stole from the rich to give to the poor, but that they [the clerics] were stealing from the poor.[19]

While speaking at Sarn, he was attacked by the local Anglican duo, the vicar and curate of the parish. There followed a series of highly emotional statements from both sides, which, according to *Y Genedl*, lasted for close on two hours. The proceedings came to a dramatic climax when the crowd, at Lloyd George's Moses-like urging, divided into two sections – one section in favour of disestablishment and the other against the proposal. Reports in *Y Faner* on 6 July and *Yr Herald Gymraeg* on 5 July both claimed that the vast majority of the crowd sided with Lloyd George. A few days later, he aroused much fervour and dissent at the Aberdaron fair. The Tory newspaper, *Y Gwalia*, published a vitriolic report on both fairs on 6 July, pouring cold water on Lloyd George's alleged histrionics, noting sarcastically: 'Only 13 had congregated to listen to him in the fair at Aberdaron on Jubilee Day.' Lloyd George was, nevertheless, on top of the world after his whirlwind tour, noting in his diary without any hint of humility after his visit to Sarn: 'I spoke on the street there with much "hwyl" [inspiration] . . . crowd appeared to be much impressed . . . I spoke on top of a beer barrel . . . hwyl fawr iawn [great inspiration].'[20]

In similar vein, on the day of the Nefyn fair (one of the six Caernarfon Boroughs) he was again on the anti-tithe rampage. In his speech, he took a deliberate swipe at the Caernarfon Boroughs Tory MP, Edmund Swetenham, and called him and his fellow churchmen 'highwaymen robbers'. With Caernarfon Boroughs still with a parliamentary vacancy for the Liberal nomination, his direct attack upon Swetenham was significant, as he branded the Tories the defenders of 'an English establishment with its many hangers on'.[21]

He was again heckled here by opponents and was forced to continue his address outside the hall he had hired for the meeting. But, in the open air, he concluded his speech when he urged the farmers to demand a 10 per cent reduction in the tithe payment from the local squire, Wynne Finch of Cefn Amwlch. He further warned that the farmers would oppose to the hilt any attempt by the bailiffs to seize their goods in payment for the tithe. Following this meeting, he also arranged a further demonstration at Pwllheli a few days later to open a fund to support the 'Llangwm Martyrs'.[22]

These activities brought to a climax his inflammatory campaign in 1887, apart from a notable meeting at Cricieth in December, which drew many supporters as the main speaker was the legal spokesman for the 'Llangwm Martyrs', John Parry of Llanarmon-yn-Iâl.[23] This meeting was called to organize the non-payment of tithes in the area, which would be again due in January 1888. Once more, Lloyd George aroused the ire of *Y Gwalia*, which noted sourly that only a few came to listen to Lloyd George and Parry – 'proof that the Criccieth people were reluctant to swallow their doctrines'.[24]

The Tory press's hostile reaction to his campaigning in 1887 reflected their fear that Lloyd George had had a considerable effect throughout Caernarfonshire and via the press on a wider scale. Indeed, there is little doubt he had come to considerable prominence in Caernarfonshire and had resurrected his hope of securing a parliamentary candidature in the Boroughs of Caernarfon. Indeed, by the end of 1887, he began to think that he had a realistic chance of capturing the nomination, because there had been continuous friction and delay over securing a successor to Love Jones-Parry within the Boroughs' Liberal hierarchy.

In 1887, several suggestions as to a possible candidate had been put forward, and, as expected, in what was a very conservative and Conservative-held seat, most of the names being bandied about were either rich, moderate Whigs, or sober Gladstonian party-line nominees. For example, two of the names most consistently featured were A. C. Humphreys-Owen, the Glansevern estate owner in Montgomeryshire and close confidant of Stuart Rendel, the Gladstonian MP for Montgomeryshire, and Clement Higgins QC, a Whig-inclined English Liberal. These were candidates Lloyd George would have placed in the category of 'respectable dummies'. However, in the changed climate of the new, democratic era, post-1885, the mandarins who controlled Liberal politics in the Caernarfon Boroughs could not blithely avoid the possibility of selecting a candidate from the same background as Tom Ellis and by association, therefore, a politician like Lloyd George. Also, the more radical of the Welsh Liberal press, such as the *Genedl* company in Caernarfon (with their three papers, two in the Welsh language), were calling continually for an Ellis-type candidate.

Significantly, by October 1887, Lloyd George (like several others of his background and political views) had been elected, for the first time, as a member of the Caernarfon Boroughs Liberal Association.[25] Therefore, despite the fact that several of the old-guard Liberals remained members and were inimical to his views, there were changes taking place gradually in the composition of the Boroughs' politics. Thus, there was the possibility that, sooner or later, opinion could crystallize in favour of a new, radical, nationalist candidate. Though many obstacles, financial, religious and political, still stood in his way, he noted in his diary of 4 September 1887: 'I want to cultivate the Boroughs and if the Unionist government holds together another 3 years, I may stand a good chance to be nominated as Liberal candidate.'[26] However, he was going to delay any premature public move for the candidature, remembering that he had felt he had acted too impetuously in Merioneth in 1886. But when the Caernarfon Boroughs on 26 November 1887 once more postponed the choice of a candidate, he knew that, sooner or later in the new year, he would have to take steps, without declaring himself publicly at first, to seek the nomination. In December 1887, in a letter to his friend, D. R. Daniel from Four Crosses, near Pwllheli, who was also Tom Ellis's close friend, he asked Daniel to sound out whether Ellis would support him.[27] Undoubtedly, his links with Ellis had been strengthened during the tithe controversy. It was his exploits in this 'war' which led Lloyd George to believe that he could emulate Ellis and carve out a parliamentary niche for himself.

He would eventually, by January 1889, secure his objective of a parliamentary foothold, as a new-style, radical-nationalist, but a fundamental part of his plan, at the start of 1888, was not to come out publicly as one who desired the nomination until the time was ripe. He was careful to tread warily in the first six months of 1888, until he was sure that three of the six boroughs (Nefyn, Pwllheli and Cricieth) would choose him before embarking upon the capture of the more difficult and populous boroughs of Caernarfon, Bangor and Conwy. Only then would he be prepared to launch a public bid for the northern towns.

One essential factor, which secured for him the favour of these three southern boroughs by mid-1888, was his continuing activity on the anti-tithe front in south Caernarfonshire. In particular, at the beginning of 1888, the movement was renamed The Welsh Land, Labour and Commercial League and, as its new title implied, it had a strong, labourist element to it. This was of particular importance to Lloyd George as he aimed to secure the support of agricultural labourers and granite quarrymen in the southernmost boroughs. Lloyd George was acutely aware of the need to press labour issues. He remonstrated with Thomas Gee's son, Howel Gee, when he received from him details of the new league's constitution, that it lacked a strong commitment to labour issues. In particular, there were few references to matters such as leasehold enfranchisement and the need to provide housing and allotments for farm labourers. He told Gee in a letter: 'Inexplicable omission. Here is a class more numerous and more fearless than our cautious Welsh farmers. The Government's allotment scheme is a sham and a delusion; falls far short of Chamberlain's scheme, which was really a great idea.'[28]

Many farm workers lived not only within the southern boroughs, but also in the northern boroughs. But more numerous and politically more crucial for him were the urban workmen, who had the vote. As he had done in Merioneth in 1885/6 he was anxious that workers should be allowed to buy, at reasonable rates, the leases on which their houses had been built, instead of their houses reverting to the Tory landowners and slate owners. He was also anxious for the new league to agitate for municipal housing for the working class in the boroughs, with fair rents, while calling for the redistribution of wealth by taxing ground rents and also taxing capital appreciation and profits on changing mineral and land values. He made this explicit in his letter to Thomas Gee: 'Another glaring omission. We ought to add the fixing of fair ground rents and the enfranchisement of leaseholds upon that basis and I shall tell you why – the Conservatives seem to have a stronger hold upon the towns than the counties.'[29] He also appealed to Gee to ensure that the league's constitution catered for the needs of slate miners, quarrymen and granite workers, with their voting presence in the Caernarfon Boroughs. He wanted the league to support reforms to improve their working conditions and their trade union rights, showing how he was moving gradually in a collectivist direction, as early as 1887–8. He informed Gee: 'Land question as it affects mining interests is completely ignored. This will lose support of miners and quarrymen – their grievance is quite as acute as any of the farmers.'[30]

When the new league's constitution was finalized, some of Lloyd George's recommendations were incorporated within it, although the league did not prove to be as aggressive as he had hoped. Nevertheless, in 1888, he was more than ready to use the movement, as far as possible in the first six months of that year, to secure personal and political publicity and to air his progressive views with their strong, labourist elements. Lloyd George was also anxious to see new branches of the revamped league established in the area and in March 1888 he arranged several meetings for that purpose, addressed by himself and by John Parry the anti-tithe leader. At a crowded meeting at Pwllheli to establish a branch there, he used the occasion to call upon Welsh Liberals 'to choose parliamentary candidates who would demand at Westminster the rights of Welsh workers'.[31] His appeal was derided by the Welsh Anglican weekly journal, *Y Llan a'r Dywysogaeth* (The Parish and the Principality), which held that he was preaching revolutionary doctrines, while also seeking to undermine the Church and its clerics by 'throwing mud in the faces of people who were not only honourable but a blessing to society'.[32]

This further blast from the Tory press did not deflect him from rhetorical flourishes against the landowners and the Church. A month later, another golden opportunity presented itself to court more publicity, at Cricieth and Pwllheli. He had persuaded the chief baron of the Welsh-language press, Thomas Gee, to accompany him around Caernarfonshire to address meetings of the league, which would ensure considerable publicity not only in Gee's papers, particularly *Y Faner*, but also in a host of other papers circulating in north Wales.

During the visit, which brought Lloyd George much attention, he and Gee spoke together at large, open-air meetings coinciding with fairs held in various locations. At Cricieth, his Uncle Lloyd had been perceptive enough to hire the local town crier to tour the whole area to announce that the meeting was being addressed by the 'Pope of Welsh Nonconformity' himself. There was a flurry of excitement long before the meeting took place, as Gee had already condemned the local landowner and Tory, Ellis Nanney of the Gwynfryn estate, in *Y Faner* for evicting a local farmer from his tenancy because he had refused to pay the tithe and because he had joined the Land, Labour and Commercial League.[33]

At the meeting, Lloyd George pulled out all the stops and, indeed, dramatically took out of his pocket the tenant's eviction order and with a theatrical flourish revealed its contents before the audience. He did this, knowing that Nanney's land agent, W. B. C. Jones, was present in the crowd. There was a highly charged response to Lloyd George's ruse which led *Y Gwalia* the following week, to remark with great hostility that Lloyd George was 'that ambitious one from amongst the legal fraternity, who was drawing honest tenants into a trap' – a remark which sounded much more hostile in Welsh – 'yn un o wŷr uchelgeisiol y gyfraith, sy'n hudo tenantiad gonest i'r fagl'.[34]

However, Gee's visit to Cricieth (and also to Pwllheli) proved to be a considerable coup for Lloyd George during this vital stage in his career. Gee and his powerful newspaper henceforth played a crucial role in his career up to and including the establishment of the Cymru Fydd League (Young Wales) in the mid-1890s and was also instrumental in his securing his first parliamentary nomination by the end of 1888 and preparing the way for him to come out publicly for that prize he so coveted in the summer of 1888.

On the threshold of the public declaration of his intent to secure the Boroughs nomination in July 1888, Lloyd George once again visited the hiring fair at Sarn in Llŷn, to secure more publicity in the press. His visit there again, not unnaturally, aroused the ire of the Conservative and Anglican press – a development which delighted him as it added to his reputation amongst his supporters. The Tory press continued to attack him as one who deployed Irish terrorist tactics to influence people to break the law and face imprisonment. *Y Gwalia*, in its editorial on 3 May 1888, painted him as a terrorist agent, adding: 'The fair was visited by a swarm of Irish type Welshmen, led by a beardless boy from Criccieth.'

The *Llan a'r Dywysogaeth* was equally vitriolic, publishing a vindictive collection of verses on 6 July, under the heading 'Y Dyn Ymyrgar' (The Interfering Man), alleging that his activities would prove counter-productive by incurring the hostility of those whom he was seeking to seduce. Nevertheless, these Conservative slights were a boon to Lloyd George, as they brought him increasing prominence in south Caernarfonshire and beyond, via the press reports. Soon after the Sarn hiring fair on 6 July, there came the public announcement (which almost appeared to be spontaneous) that he had been provisionally selected by the Liberal Associations of Pwllheli, Cricieth and Nefyn as the next Liberal candidate for the Caernarfon Boroughs.[35] However, there was a lengthy, difficult struggle ahead, to secure the support of the more conservative (and, indeed, Tory-biased northern boroughs of Bangor, Conwy and Caernarfon). But securing by July the provisional support of the southern boroughs gave him a vital platform to succeed.

Undoubtedly, one of the major factors which had resurrected his political hopes since 1886 had been the anti-tithe and labourist activities in Llŷn and Eifionydd, during a tempestuous two-year period. It had also helped him to fan the flames of nationalism and identify himself as a radical-nationalist. In 1888, however, it was not only the tithe and land issues which were to secure for him a vital base in the southern boroughs, but also another crucial development – the launching of a weekly newspaper which was largely his own in the area – *Yr Udgorn Rhyddid* (The Trumpet of Freedom), which he was to describe as 'thoroughly nationalist and socialist'. In the first six months of its existence, it was to play a fundamental role in securing his first parliamentary candidature, by consolidating his base in the three southernmost boroughs of Caernarfon.

IV

HIS NATIONALIST AND SOCIALIST 'TRUMPET OF FREEDOM', 1888

From the early 1880s, Lloyd George had realized how influential the press was as a medium of political propaganda, and had written trenchant articles for local newspapers in Caernarfonshire. In early 1888, as his political star rose in the wake of the anti-tithe campaign, he embarked on a further, more intense exercise in press propaganda by founding his own newspaper.

In January 1888, with the acquisition of the Caernarfon Boroughs nomination firmly fixed in his mind, he was not content to depend on other newspapers alone to sustain his campaign and secure the goal of a parliamentary candidature. He was determined to possess his own newspaper, a development which became even more marked during his later career. His first step in the process of newspaper proprietorship was the establishment of a Welsh-language weekly, circulating in the Caernarfon Boroughs, especially in the three southern boroughs of Pwllheli, Nefyn and Cricieth. The town of Pwllheli was its publishing base and *Yr Udgorn Rhyddid* (The Trumpet of Freedom) was launched there on 4 January 1888.

It would enhance his efforts to secure a parliamentary nomination and be the vehicle to propagate his political objectives as a new-style radical and nationalist, who would not flinch from having federal Home Rule for Wales as one of his main aspirations. That would be a fully fledged, domestic parliament for Wales, which would not only effect Nonconformist legislation, such as Church disestablishment and temperance and tithe reform, but would also seek a more labourist role, with the type of reforms he had outlined to Howel Gee, as they formed the constitution of the Land and Labour League in 1887.

Not surprisingly, therefore, while preparing to launch his newspaper at the end of 1887, he informed one close colleague that he should be involved in the venture and that the paper should have a radical and nationalist message. In a letter to the temperance organizer, trade union reformer and Cymru Fyddite, D. R. Daniel of Four Crosses, near Pwllheli, his closest confidant at the time, he told him that the paper would 'revolutionise the country'.[1] In a further letter to Daniel he outlined his militant objectives in more detail:

The project is in a fair way to realisation. In conjunction with
D. Evan Davies, William Anthony and one or two others, I decided to embark on the enterprise. Will you join? We propose
raising a capital of say £100, and limiting our liabilities to that
amount, so as to escape the injurious consequences of libel suits.
It is to be thorough, nationalist and socialist – a regenerator in
every respect.[2]

Lloyd George foresaw a venture which would be so controversial as to
verge on libel, as it sought to attack landlordism and the deficiencies of
capitalists, who owned the major slate and granite quarries in
Caernarfonshire. He was determined to propagate progressive views,
which he termed as 'socialist' – in the sense that he would reflect the
views of reformers, such as Michael Davitt, E. Pan Jones, Henry George
and the municipal socialism associated with Chamberlainism.

Lloyd George was responsible for formulating the new weekly's title,
Yr Udgorn Rhyddid (The Trumpet of Freedom). His use of the word
'trumpet' reflected how that instrument was deployed by anti-tithe
agitators to summon protestors to farms, to prevent bailiffs from seizing
the goods and animals of those who had refused to pay the tithe. In a
letter to D. R. Daniel on the eve of *Yr Udgorn*'s launch, when he urged
Daniel to help edit the paper, he showed he was proud of the title: 'Why
not Udgorn Rhyddid? Something stirring! Never mind the bombast if the
stuff that's in it is good, as it will be if you undertake the editorial duties.'[3]
Lloyd George used all of his persuasive powers to bring Daniel on board
the new venture. Their aim was to activate opinion in the area and to
undertake a radical and nationalist crusade. Tom Ellis MP had encouraged
its publication and had informed D. R. Daniel on 21 December 1887,
before its launch: 'I think a great deal of The *Udgorn* and feel that I can
already hear it sounding forth.'[4] Tom Ellis was, therefore, an enthusiastic
supporter of the venture, whose main shareholders, apart from Lloyd
George, included two leading figures in Liberal circles in the town. D. Evan
Davies was a Calvinistic Methodist minister and property developer,
while William Anthony was a wealthy draper; both of them, significantly,
were leading lights of the Liberal Association of the Caernarfon Boroughs,
but they were not on the same radical wavelength as Lloyd George.

Other backers of the venture were the town's mayor, Edward Jones
JP, a local merchant, again a moderate Liberal, and H. Tudwal Davies, the
farmer and eisteddfod crown winner from the village of Aber-erch. He was,
conversely, a supporter of Lloyd George's advanced views and had
already played a prominent role in the anti-tithe agitation in 1887.

The presence of both radicals and moderates on the paper's board of
directors was soon to become a constant irritant to Lloyd George; this

was reflected in a letter he wrote to D. R. Daniel at the beginning of February 1888, when he claimed that those directors on the board who were of a moderate, orthodox persuasion were interfering with editorial policy:

> It is a wretched paper as now conducted. Articles of considerable interest, which I managed to secure have been totally suppressed, whilst some stuffy nonsense written by D. Evan Davies and O.N.'s smooth varities are published in prominent type . . . I shall resign or get a better understanding.[5]

This letter had been written at a time when Lloyd George had not been able to devote as much attention to the paper as he had hoped. Indeed, he had been married to Margaret Owen, of Mynydd Ednyfed, during the first week in January. The marriage and the honeymoon had meant that he was not able to supervise the whole editorial launching of *Yr Udgorn* to the extent that he might have wished, although he did contribute to the paper throughout January and had prepared his first contribution to the first ever edition before embarking on his honeymoon.

Despite the tensions which soon emerged over editorial policy between Lloyd George and his co-directors, he was determined that the venture would be a success. Indeed, he was to make much use of the paper to give prominence to his views and to advance his career. Only a handful of copies of the paper in early 1888 have survived in archives across Wales, but their content reflects how vital a part the weekly played in fostering Lloyd George's ambitions. Moreover, it is evident from diary entries in D. R. Daniel's papers (deposited at the National Library of Wales, Aberystwyth) that Lloyd George, from the outset, was centrally involved in the whole venture and ready to enhance his career (without declaring publicly that he was a candidate for the Caernarfon Boroughs nomination until July 1888). Some of *Yr Udgorn*'s contents were also printed in other Liberal newspapers, which circulated in the Caernarfon boroughs, especially *Y Genedl Gymreig*, *Y Werin* and the *North Wales Observer and Express* – giving his views further publicity.

Lloyd George, according to the Daniel papers, had certainly written the paper's second editorial on 11 January and it may be surmised that he, too, had penned the first article on 4 January.[6] This article was entitled 'Y Dadganiad' (The Declaration) and certainly reflected his views and was couched in his unique rhetoric. The article outlined the paper's objectives and reflected Lloyd George's radical-nationalist priorities.

The paper's first aim was, according to the editorial: 'To promote the welfare of farm labourers, slate quarrymen and coal miners, diligent farmers and honest traders and to protect them from the oppression of landlords and the "crachach" of Wales.' The second aim was to heighten Welsh national consciousness in Wales: 'Wales and the Welsh, the land and the people will be one of its central features.' Thirdly, and finally, Lloyd George's paper claimed that: 'We will fight for the oppressed aggressively but peacefully.'

The paper, therefore, reflected a pronounced nationalist stance and a neo-collectivist line, socially and economically (a stance which would emerge ever more prominently in Lloyd George's views by the early 1890s when he would champion issues such as the eight-hour day, pensions for the aged and death duties on the rich). In *Yr Udgorn*, too, he knew that he would have to keep plugging the issues of Nonconformist reforms, temperance, disestablishment and fair rents. Indeed, in the first edition, the clergy, the brewers and the landowners and quarry owners came under a searing attack.[7] It called on the government to legislate over local control of the liquor industry and strengthen the Welsh Sunday Closing Act of 1881, to stop Sunday drinking in clubs and in hotels on the sabbath. The paper further demanded Welsh disestablishment and the deployment of the Church's endowments to improve the lives of ordinary Welsh people. It also stressed the need for fairer farm rents, in addition to cheap allotments for farm labourers, while claiming that a Welsh parliament would give priority to such reforms.

In *Yr Udgorn*'s second editorial, 'Dechreu yn y Dechreu' (Beginning at the Beginning), on 11 January, Lloyd George welcomed the new national awakening coursing throughout Wales. He called for 'organisation and commitment to demand the people's rights'. Then, in almost Messianic terms, but being careful not to name himself personally, he appealed for the emergence of a leader in the area 'to unite the workers, the farm labourers and small farmers to transform the country'. He also added: 'Let someone appear to gather together the water so that it flows into one river and then we shall soon feel its strength.'

The Baptist imagery was evident in such a comment, with the editorial emphasizing the need for the Caernarfon Boroughs to choose a new candidate from a similar background to his own and with the same aspirations. In the same edition, the paper's objectives were also reflected in an article written by his soulmate, D. R. Daniel, under the pseudonym 'Democrat', and entitled 'The Welsh awakening'. In this article, he asserted that: 'The youth of our colleges and the University had pushed to one side "God Save the Queen" and had embraced "The Land of My Fathers".'[8] In another article by his former mentor on the public stage, H. J. Williams (Plennydd), the temperance reformer had called for 'the spirit of Cymru Fydd (Young Wales) to shake the people of Lleyn'. Also, in the same edition, Tudwal Davies, the poet, had published a string of satirical verses entitled 'The Songs of The Udgorn', which poured scorn on the landlords and their oppression of tenants, farm labourers and quarrymen through their ownership of so many quarries.

In subsequent editions of *Yr Udgorn*, this tabloid formula of using simple satirical verses and articles was used repeatedly, in addition to the inclusion of a weekly 'Irish Letter' (Llythyr y Gwyddyl). These particular articles were written in colloquial Welsh to ensure that they reached the maximum possible audience. Once more, comparisons were drawn with Ireland in order to press home a nationalist message. For example, a column which appeared on 15 February called upon the Caernarfon Boroughs electors to demand a parliamentary candidate who would pursue the same nationalist line as Tom Ellis. The piece ended with the colloquial statement, which included English-language clauses: 'Fi isho pobol Caernarfon a Bangor dewis another Tom Ellis, if they can find one.' (I want the people of Caernarfon and Bangor to select another Tom Ellis, if they can find one.)[9] In this article, as in others in the paper, Welsh and English phrases were intertwined.

A series of articles using an Irish analogy were also published at the very time Lloyd George was delivering a series of public lectures in the constituency entitled 'Welsh grievances and Irish remedies'. *Yr Udgorn* covered these activities, such as the lectures on Ireland, delivered at the Liberal clubs at Pwllheli and Bangor in March 1888, when Lloyd George was using all the means at his disposal to prepare the way stealthily and secretly before launching a public strike for the nomination of the Caernarfon Boroughs, but was being very careful not to display publicly his intent until he was sure of support from the southern boroughs.

He had also ensured, in February 1888 in *Yr Udgorn*, that publicity was given to two dramatic meetings in which he was involved with the Anglican disestablishment campaign in the area. He shared, firstly, the platform at Cricieth with two leading Caernarfon Boroughs mandarins, the eminent preacher Dr John Thomas and the Revd J. Eiddon Jones of Llanrug.[10] Then, a week later, the Church Defence League organized a counter-protest at Cricieth, where the main speaker was the rector of Barmouth, the Revd E. Hughes. Deploying his tactics at hiring fairs (see chapter III), he heckled and argued with the rector publicly to such effect that the meeting had to be postponed.[11] Lloyd George joyfully told his friend D. R. Daniel in a letter that he had made another stroke at Criccieth but also asked him rather cynically whether he could lend him a book on the history of the Welsh Church for future speechmaking.[12] Then, to crown his anti-Church tirade, a week later, despite having to rouse himself from his sickbed, he intervened again at a Church Defence meeting at Porthmadog, destroying once more the rector of Barmouth's speech there. *Yr Udgorn* reported that he was carried triumphantly after the meeting on his supporters shoulders down the High Street.[13] *Y Gwalia* also reported vindictively: 'He was showing off his talent for disruption, to secure personal glory and cause havoc.'[14]

From week to week, his newspaper also published articles criticizing in highly personal and harsh terms many of the leading landowners of the area. These articles, which certainly bordered on the libellous, reflected how he was prepared to go to the limit to secure publicity. Ellis Nanney and the Faenol and Penrhyn families came under attack from *Yr Udgorn* for the treatment of their tenants and quarry workers. Many articles also spotlighted the visit of bailiffs to tenanted farms where the farmers had refused to pay the tithe and, with his widespread contacts within the Land and Labour League, Lloyd George was to obtain reports of rioting from as far away as Flintshire and Cardiganshire to be included in the paper. For example, in the third edition of *Yr Udgorn*, a report appeared which praised farmers at Whitford, Flintshire, for resisting the seizure of stock at various farms. *Yr Udgorn* trumpeted: 'An army of agriculturalists is being formed and is growing continually and the Church and the Authorities are incurring the heaviest costs and losses.'[15]

Lloyd George was also to make frequent use of the editorial column. For example, on 8 February, he incited Llŷn and Eifionydd farmers to oppose the tithe, whilst criticizing vehemently some farmers because they were unwilling to stand up and be counted and challenge the law and the authorities. In his editorial, he stated: 'The tithe controversy appears to be escalating everywhere, except in the Lleyn area . . . the inhabitants are so subdued and quiet they have to be compared to the subjects of Cetewayo in Southern Africa.' He also lambasted the farmers who showed 'servility and cowardice and were fond of the Church and the Tories'.

In the first months of *Yr Udgorn*'s existence, he also returned to agitate on the tithe front in his home village of Llanystumdwy, where he had started the anti-tithe agitation in Eifionydd a year previously. In the 18 February edition of his paper, he launched a series of articles condemning the local squire, Ellis Nanney (Lloyd George's first election opponent in 1890), for the way he allegedly dealt with his tenants. In particular, he condemned his eviction of one tenant, William Evans of Cae Einion, who had refused to pay the tithe, and championed his cause in a theatrical manner in front of a large crowd at Cricieth (see previous chapter). The story ran and ran for several weeks in his paper. Stories were published of similar action by other Anglicized, Tory landowners, especially by the Faenol and Penrhyn estates. These families were the backbone of the Tory cause in the Caernarfon Boroughts of Caernarfon and Bangor and a target for Lloyd George's invective.

Yr Udgorn also made frequent appeals for donations to support the Land and Labour League, especially a fund opened to sustain the Llangwm Martyrs (see previous chapter). This was at a time when Lloyd George had established a close relationship with their defending solicitor, Alun Lloyd, who, as indicated in the previous chapter, accompanied Lloyd George on a speaking tour in Caernarfonshire in April 1888.

Lloyd George's identification with the Land and Labour League was much in evidence in these early editions of *Yr Udgorn*; he also brought an emotional Scottish dimension to the whole issue. Following in the footsteps of Tom Ellis MP, he compared the plight of Welsh smallholders and labourers to the grievances of crofters in the Highlands of Scotland. Indeed, it was a subject referred to in the first edition of *Yr Udgorn*, with comparisons also drawn, between the crofters and many quarrymen who rented small parcels of land from the landowner quarry owners. This article reinforced Lloyd George's plea to Howel Gee in 1887 when the Land and Labour League was formed that the conditions of smallholders and agricultural labourers, let alone the slate quarrymen, should be radically improved.

Much space was devoted, as well, in the journal to another radical measure, which affected slate and granite quarrymen, and an issue which Lloyd George had championed in Merioneth in 1885–6, namely the enfranchisement of leaseholds. The problem was particularly acute amongst quarrymen and workers at Pwllheli (the Glynllifon estate), Nefyn (the Cefn Amwlch estate), Caernarfon (the Faenol estate) and at Bangor (the Penrhyn estate). Consequently, Lloyd George had much to gain from trumpeting this issue once again.

The paper was also used to propagandize on the more traditional and orthodox Welsh Nonconformist issues of temperance and further reform of the Welsh Sunday Closing Act, to curtail drinking on the sabbath. However, he was also prepared to discuss much wider issues, such as the need to reform, if not indeed to abolish, the House of Lords. The article he wrote on 18 January poured out his invective against the Lords (reminiscent of the period when he was Chancellor of the Exchequer). He informed his readers:

> This establishment militates against the spirit of the age . . . The basis of true Government is the voice of the people . . . the House of Lords has secured a reputation as the arch-enemy of all reform. The weakest intellects and the most unclean characters can sit in this noble House. It is admitted readily, even by *The Times*, that the House of Lords requires reform, but its total annihilation is the only cause worth fighting for . . . securing the fall of this god of oppression would count as one of the victories of freedom and a cause of celebration for generations yet to be born.[16]

An extraordinary range of articles were published in the earliest editions of *Yr Udgorn* in 1888 – articles, for example, emphasizing the need for local authorities to spend money on road building and housing, to help the slate and quarrying industry and to alleviate unemployment in the area – an almost neo-Keynesian doctrine. Columns were also devoted to criticizing the Toryism of many Nonconformist denominations, particularly the Calvinistic Methodists. Pwllheli was one borough singled out for Lloyd George's barbed criticism, with a leading article on the subject, alleging that many middle-class Methodist wives attended the local branch of the Disraelian Primrose League (*ledis neis y* Primrose League). Lloyd George's article thundered: 'The establishment of this League is an insult to our nation. If we look at the list of members of the branch at Pwllheli, we find, incredibly, in the list of names, several Non-conformists.'[17]

In order to increase its readership, *Yr Udgorn* also published stories, which were populist 'penny dreadfuls', ranging from jokes about servile quarry stewards, Scottish-born gamekeepers of the gentry and oppressive land agents. Also, the paper published stories taken directly from English papers to entertain the readers – breach of promise cases, and topics such as 'Finding a baby in a basket' and 'Floods in China'. Scandalous London divorce cases were also lifted from the London press and crime and murder featured prominently.

Nevertheless, there is no doubt that the paper's prime objective, in its initial stages, when Lloyd George was obsessively involved with the paper, was to establish a new political agenda. This was the promotion of progressive radical and nationalist ideas, allied to a campaign to prepare the way for Lloyd George to confirm publicly that he was a runner in the race for the Caernarfon Boroughs parliamentary candidature. *Yr Udgorn* continually spun the message that Wales and the Caernarfon Boroughs needed young, democratic, Welsh-speaking radical-nationalists, which reflected a new era in Welsh politics. This was allied to the need for greater priority to be given to airing the grievances of workers in the small towns and industrial conurbation villages of Caernarfonshire. At the same time, it promulgated in particular the needs of tenant smallholders and farm labourers at the base of the rural pyramid. Underpinning this agenda was the demand to revolutionize the structure of British politics, through the establishment of a federal system of government, including Welsh Home Rule (and, indeed, abolition of the Lords). The nationalist and labourist seeds were being sown here, which would come to fruition in Lloyd George's Young Wales – Cymru Fydd League in the mid-1890s.

Although in the first six months of 1888 there were no direct references to Lloyd George as the most suitable candidate for the Caernarfon Boroughs, the inferences that he was hoping to secure the nomination were there in the columns of his newspaper. For example, in the 18 January edition, there was a report from the Criceith Debating Society of a mock election. Not surprisingly, the victor by a large majority was Mr Lloyd George for the Liberal cause – certainly, a straw in the wind and a dress rehearsal for what was to follow in the second six months of 1888.[18]

Another interesting aspect of his life at this time, captured in the columns of *Yr Udgorn*, was the fact that he was by now in business, with his brother William as his partner. William had to shoulder much of the work at Lloyd George and George, as the elder brother became engrossed in his political work, and would have to share much of the financial burden of Lloyd's pre-parliamentary and parliamentary career up to 1911, before the introduction of payment of MPs. The brothers had placed something of a paradoxical advertisement in *Yr Udgorn*, publicizing not only that they specialized in house and property conveyancing, but that they were moneylenders, providing 'ample sources of finance to enable borrowings to be made on land on reasonable terms'.

Another interesting personal reference in the first edition of *Yr Udgorn* was a detailed account of Lloyd George's marriage in January 1888 to Margaret Owen. Interestingly, the marriage did not take place in Margaret's own Calvinistic Methodist Chapel at Criceith, nor at David's Penymaes Baptist Chapel. Indeed, the marriage was held in the somewhat remote village of Pencaenewydd, some six or seven miles from Criceith. The reason for this was certainly not disclosed in *Yr Udgorn*, because the marriage agreement had been the cause of some friction between the parties. Without referring to any friction, or to the fact that it did not take place at Criceith *Yr Udgorn* reported:

> Last Tuesday, Mr D. Lloyd George, Criccieth, Solicitor, was married to Miss Maggie Owen, Mynydd Ednyfed. The two then proceeded after the ceremony to London, so as to secure some joint privacy following the great noise in the town and to avoid being blinded by the light and heat [a reference to a bonfire having been lit to celebrate the occasion].[19]

No mention was made of the fact that the marriage was not held at Criceith, but the fact was that Maggie's parents were devout Methodists (while Uncle Lloyd was similarly a devout Campbellite Baptist). No agreement was possible on a chapel at Criceith, so the ceremony was moved to another location. It is also possible to infer that the Owen family, respectable farmers of a sober Gladstonian Liberal mindset, were anxious for Maggie to have a quiet wedding, as they had certainly, at the beginning of the courtship, distrusted Lloyd George as a 'Batus Bach' and because he had something of a reputation as a ladies' man. Indeed, they would have preferred Margaret to have married the officiating minister at the wedding, the Revd John Owen, MA, who had previously sought Maggie's hand in marriage. Maggie Owen never became a Baptist, but remained a Calvinistic Methodist throughout her life.

Nevertheless, despite all the pre-marriage friction, David Lloyd George certainly benefited from the marriage, because it brought him greater social and financial status in the area and secured for him a foothold in the Calvinistic Methodist camp, an important consideration in the Caernarfon Boroughs constituency, where the Methodists were by far the most numerous denomination. Moreover, it brought him financial benefits. Maggie's father, Richard Owen, although a tenant farmer, was sufficiently well off for him to pay for Maggie's education at a private institution, Dr Williams's School for Young Ladies at Dolgellau, Merioneth. Also, after retiring in 1890, he had enough money to built two substantial houses – one for himself and his wife and the other for Maggie, at Cricieth, which was to be a pecuniary advantage for the rather impoverished young MP. *Yr Udgorn* published many poems and messages of congratulations to the marriage of the 'Little Baptist' to one of the most highly esteemed Methodist families in the area. Personally and politically, his own newspaper had played a crucial role in promoting Lloyd George's career at a crucial period in his life. As was shown in the previous chapter, he had been involved prominently in the land and labour campaign since 1886 and now, by the summer of 1888, he had used *Yr Udgorn* to place himself in a position where he could at long last consider publicly standing as a candidate for Parliament.

In addition, the paper had reported his many activities as a politician bent on setting a new radical-nationalist agenda in the country of his upbringing. *Yr Udgorn* had been used unequivocally to trumpet his own political ambitions as the time to strike for the nomination approached.

Founding his own newspaper was a lesson he was not to forget during his later career: indeed, by the early 1890s, he was to secure control over the three *Genedl* papers in Caernarfon to promote the cause of Welsh Home Rule and the aspirations of Young Wales, based in part on the Italian and Irish models. However, Lloyd George had used *Yr Udgorn* in the first few months of 1888, in the 'Golden Age' of the Welsh-language press, to show that he was a radical and nationalist in the making, ready to establish a new cause and set up a new political agenda in Wales.

V

THE BREAKTHROUGH: SECURING THE CAERNARFON BOROUGHS PARLIAMENTARY NOMINATION, 1888

As the two previous chapters have shown, Lloyd George had elevated himself to real public prominence in his locality by mid-1888, through an energetic, often sensational, combination of activities. With his involvement in the anti-tithe agitation and the Land League (see chapter III), he had carved out a reputation for himself in south Caernarfonshire, including the Caernarfon Boroughs. He had cemented this reputation in the first six months of 1888 by using his own newspaper, *Yr Udgorn Rhyddid*, not only to escalate the activities of the Labour and Land League, but also by his using its columns to court publicity in many other directions (see chapter IV). Thus, by June–July 1888, he was ready to come out publicly as a candidate for the still-vacant parliamentary nomination in the Boroughs of Caernarfon.

As already noted in Chapter III, the nomination vacancy in the constituency since Love Jones-Parry's retirement announcement in December 1886 had resulted, in 1887, in a continuing delay in choosing a new candidate, which had led Lloyd George to believe that he still had a chance of securing the nomination, especially as he had become a member of the Liberal Association for the first time during that year.

However, in 1887, the Boroughs' Liberal Association was still dominated, in the main, by orthodox Gladstonians, who did not share his radical and nationalist standpoint. The chairman was the successful Bangor businessman, T. C. Lewis of Caederwen, while the solicitor R. D. Williams of Porth yr Aur, Caernarfon – a sober, unreconstructed Gladstonian – remained as secretary. The two vice-presidents were H. L. Squires from Conwy, an English-born Gladstonian, while the most radical member of the association was John Davies (Gwyneddon). The other members were Albert Wood from Conwy, a hotelier; Lewis Hughes of Conwy, a businessman and store-owner; D. Lloyd Edwards from Pwllheli, a solicitor; W. Jones Owen, a Pwllheli grocer; and D. Evan Davies – the Calvinistic Methodist minister – a property developer from the same town, who had already crossed swords with Lloyd George over his 'nationalist and socialist' use of *Yr Udgorn*. The other members, such as the Revd John Owen, MA, of Cricieth, the rival for Margaret Owen's hand in marriage, were not kindly disposed towards him. It was obvious in 1887–8 that he had a hard task in front of him if he was to win the nomination.[1]

Nevertheless, although several names had been put forward as candidates, particularly Professor Clement Higgins, QC, and A. C. Humphreys-Owen of Glansevern, Montgomeryshire, confidant of Stuart Rendel, Montgomeryshire's MP and the 'MP for Wales', there had been a considerable reluctance to choose a successor to Love Jones-Parry. Indeed, on 2 November 1887, the Tory paper, *Y Gwalia*, had suggested slightingly that 'a certain Mr "Oliver" George of Cricieth would be more than ready to take the candidature' – a strident, sarcastic, but perceptive remark by the Conservative weekly.[2]

By March 1888, Lloyd George had certainly strengthened his position within the Liberal Association of the Boroughs, because at the association's AGM he was chosen as one of its vice-presidents. Moreover, significantly, at that meeting a prospective candidate was not elected, while a month previously, A. C. Humphreys-Owen had written to Stuart Rendel, complaining that there were machinations by the radical press in the country to prevent his being chosen, as they preferred a Welsh-born radical-nationalist candidate. Indeed, as Lloyd George's reputation in the area was growing, at this juncture for the first time ever in the Liberal press he was named directly as a possible candidate in the Boroughs. *Y Genedl Gymreig* in early May included a report from 'our Pwllheli correspondent', suggesting that he was 'the ideal choice for the Boroughs vacancy'.[3]

Lloyd George's prospects were to be enhanced further, with the most important legal case he was to fight during his pre-parliamentary career, the Llanfrothen Burial Scandal, which was to become (over the remainder of 1888 in three specific stages), a cause célèbre throughout Wales.[4] The first hearing of this lengthy and highly publicized case took place in May 1888, as his political ambitions became public knowledge for the first time. The case involved a long, drawn-out conflict involving Nonconformist burials in the parish churchyard at the village of Llanfrothen, near Porthmadog. The Anglican rector had insisted, despite the Burials Act of 1880, which allowed Nonconformist burials in parish churchyards, that this could not happen in Llanfrothen. Indeed, the rector had persuaded the donor of additional land to the churchyard, where burials had been held, to sign a document in 1881, refusing the right to hold Nonconformist burial rites there. This was despite the fact that the land had been given to the parish in the late 1860s and Nonconformist burials had taken place there.

The whole issue came to a head on 28 April 1888, with the death of a local quarryman, Robert Roberts. His family wished him to be buried in the parish churchyard in that area where the rector insisted that Nonconformist burials could not take place. Not surprisingly, the rector refused the Roberts family their request for burial in the local churchyard. They then consulted Lloyd George. His advice was that they had every right to have the burial at Llanfrothen churchyard, especially because he believed the new document of 1881, signed by the donor, was invalid because the land had been parish property since the 1860s and because the Burials Act was now in existence. He advised the Roberts family to proceed with the Nonconformist service by breaking the lock on the churchyard gate, set there by the rector. The burial went ahead.

On 16 May, the rector took the family to court for trespass and other alleged offences. The case was heard at Porthmadog before Judge Bishop, a renowned Tory and Churchman. Lloyd George defended the quarryman's family. After careful preparation, with diagrams of the new plot of land made by a local Liberal architect, O. M. Roberts,[5] Lloyd George argued that the new burial plot in question had been handed to the parish long before the donor had signed a new declaration in 1881, refusing Nonconformist burials there. The jury seemed to agree with Lloyd George, but, amidst confusion, Judge Bishop reserved judgement and postponed the case so that he could consider further points of law. Despite the postponement, Lloyd George's apparent victory in the first stage of the case brought him much publicity. Local newspapers like the *Carnarvon and Denbigh Herald*,[6] the *Cambrian News*[7] and the *Genedl*[8] papers as well as newspapers much further afield devoted much praise to his handling of the case. It also, secured much publicity for him in the southern boroughs of Caernarfonshire, where he was about to aim publicly for the nomination. The case came at a vital time for him.

Indeed, in the wake of this case, the public announcement came within weeks that Lloyd George was to seek the nomination and that he already had the support of the local Liberal associations in the three southern boroughs. Prior to this announcement, too, on 1 June, Lloyd George addressed a huge meeting at the recently opened Liberal Club in Caernarfon,[9] an establishment for which he had zealously campaigned in early 1888, both at public meetings and in *Yr Udgorn*. At this meeting, he called for a local-born, Welsh-speaking candidate to represent the Boroughs at Westminster. This was, indeed, a portent, for a few weeks later, in the *Carnarvon and Denbigh Herald*, it was reported that the three boroughs, Nefyn, Pwllheli and Cricieth, had all chosen him as a nominee for the candidature.[10]

This announcement was seemingly a bolt from the blue, but Lloyd George had planned meticulously for a long period before making his designs public. Throughout the first six months of 1888, he had been orchestrating events and developments in order to secure this objective, skilfully using all avenues of opportunity to secure his goal. Not surprisingly, he was delighted at the outcome, writing an effusive letter to his friend D. R. Daniel after his selection by the three southern boroughs came out into the open during the first fateful week of July. The letter revealed that he considered himself to be the 'nationalist' choice of the three southern boroughs. He also tempered his delight with caution, knowing that the three northernmost boroughs, Bangor, Caernarfon and Conwy, areas which were more Conservative, Anglican and Anglicized, had yet to support him. He informed Daniel, somewhat exaggeratedly:

> You have heard that the South Caernarfon Boroughs have taken up my candidature. There was a meeting at the Pwllheli Liberal Association to consider the selection of a candidate. This meeting unanimously resolved to invite me out. You may or you may not, according to the depth of your insight into character, be surprised to learn that the only one who found a dissentient note was our mutual friend, D. Evan Davies. He thought, forsooth, that I was too extreme, addicted to socialist ideas. What incredible meanness on the part of a professed socialist! Anyhow, his protests availeth not and he fell in with the current. Nefyn has now followed and lastly Criccieth. In both cases, the utmost unanimity prevailed. Humphreys-Owen was rejected with scorn as totally unadapted to the requirements of the age. If either Bangor or Caernarfon follow suit, I shall be the next Nationalist Candidate for the Boroughs.[11]

Therefore, by July, Lloyd George had, secured his initial task of winning official support from the southern boroughs as a nationalist and a 'socialist', showing that he was intent on winning the candidature on a radical-nationalist ticket. Contrary to the belief of many historians who have written about his early career, Lloyd George was undoubtedly a radical nationalist, with a labourist slant to his social and economic policies. He was intent on pushing for Welsh Home Rule. More than any other contemporary politician, he was ready to press this case to the limits and especially in the early 1890s. This was not posturing nor tactics, as historians like John Grigg have held. Indeed, it was a standpoint held with conviction, and a commitment which was very high-risk, especially in a constituency which was Conservative held and where many Liberals might well scoff at such an extreme policy.

Despite this strategy, Lloyd George, ever the optimist, felt he already had a powerful foothold in the constituency. He was confident that in the months ahead he could use his stronghold in the south of the constituency to win over the remaining boroughs. In reaching this goal by January 1889, he was not only to demonstrate a further commitment to the Cymru Fydd strategy, led by Tom Ellis MP, but he was also to display a ruthlessness and a deft, sometimes dubious, if not devious, use of methods to publicize his cause, especially through a highly manipulated and orchestrated press campaign.

He lost no time in promoting his campaign. On 6 July, to coincide with his selection by Nefyn, Pwllheli and Cricieth, an English-language article appeared in the *North Wales Observer and Express*[12] (reproduced in Welsh a week later in *Y Genedl Gymreig*),[13] commending him as the only choice for the boroughs nomination. No name appeared under this article, but the D. R. Daniel papers at the National Library, Aberystwyth, show that Lloyd George (or a close associate) was the hidden author of both articles. The articles expressed the view that old-type, orthodox, Anglicized politicians, like A. C. Humphreys-Owen (and other like-minded politicians), were unsuitable to meet the needs and aspirations of a new age. A local-born, Welsh nationalist candidate was required, ready to give priority to Welsh affairs – 'one who was destined to total independence from any English party'. The candidate needed to be thoroughly bilingual and 'a champion of disestablishment, land reform, leasehold enfranchisement and advocate of a tax on royalties on industrial mining land'. The article also held that a new candidate 'should not be in servitude to the corrupting influences of London Society'.[14] This latter statement, surely, militates against the argument in W. R. P. George's *The Making of Lloyd George* that he was from the outset, in the 1880s, carving out a London-centric career for himself on the British political platform.[15]

Indeed, Lloyd George had secured support in the three southern boroughs on a nationalist ticket and, as the above articles reflect, he was prepared to promote his campaign by taking an extreme line, advocating the establishment of an Irish-style independent party in Wales. These two articles, written anonymously, were to be but the opening salvo in a blitzkrieg campaign in the press, mainly through anonymous letters, in the summer and autumn of 1888. At the same time as the publication of these two letters, he wrote to D. R. Daniel on 5 July, to urge his friend to organize an orchestrated flood of laudatory nom-de-plume articles in the county press. This letter clearly confirmed a meticulously planned exercise to secure public support and win over dilatory Liberal activists in the northern constituencies. He entreated D. R. Daniel:

> Have you any friends or acquaintances at Caernarfon, Bangor or Conwy, whom you might by writing seek to influence? What about the Rev. M.O. Evans? (Minister of Pendref Independent

Chapel, Bangor). Could not Michael D. Jones do something? Can't you get Plenydd to see and write to his friends? There is another great service which you might render, if so inclined.

Would you not write a spirited letter to *Y Genedl* or *Herald*, favouring my candidature? You know my qualifications. You know I am a Welsh nationalist of the Ellis type. Have more or less thoroughly studied the Church, Land and Temperance questions. Perhaps if you would do me the kindness of placing my elocutionary powers under the microscope of your powerful imagination, you might give a tolerably favourable account of my gift of speech?

Since I have come out at all, I feel bound to do my utmost to succeed. But I can only do so by means of confidential friends. I dare not go canvassing openly for support. It would injure me. But my friends may do a lot for me – it is upon these that I must rely – especially those who did their part in getting me out. Could you not write such a letter for next week's *Herald*? (Tudwal has promised to write to the *Genedl*.) He volunteered to do so.

If you were to send it off tomorrow evening, it would be more likely to appear next week than if it only reached them on Monday morning.[16]

This letter not only reflected Lloyd George's desire and commitment to win the nomination on a Welsh nationalist ticket, but also showed his guile and persuasion in securing the support of his friends in a highly devious fashion to achieve his aim, and revealed how important was the press if he was to attain that objective.

D. R. Daniel responded to Lloyd George's request and the articles appeared in the following week, in both the *Herald*'s papers[17] and in those of the *Genedl* company.[18] 'Demos' was the author in the *Herald* papers; the articles emphasized that Lloyd George was a politician in the same mould as Tom Ellis – a democrat, a nationalist, a man of the people and an eloquent speaker. According to 'Demos', he was 'the nationalist choice for the Caernarfon Boroughs'. At the same time, articles appeared in English and Welsh in the *Genedl* company's three weeklies, under the pseudonym 'Etholwr' (Elector), but written by the crowned bard and farmer, Tudwal Davies. They praised Lloyd George as one of the leaders of Young Wales (Cymru Fydd) and the only worthwhile choice for the constituency. There also appeared in other publications articles of a similar kind, for example, in the Welsh radical weekly, *Y Celt*, edited by E. Pan Jones, the land socialist and friend of Michael Davitt.[19] In an editorial extensive it expressed the supportive views of veteran nationalists such as Michael D. Jones, who promoted Lloyd George's candidature to the hilt. It also claimed, as a Bangor-based publication, that the citizens in that borough were favourable to 'the young attorney of the people'.

As may be predicted, Lloyd George was more than pleased with these machinations to utilize ruthlessly the press for his own ends and to broaden his support in the Caernarfon Boroughs constituency. He wrote to D. R. Daniel: 'Have just perused "Demos's" truly masterly letter in the *Herald*. Ardderchog fachgen! [Marvellous, my boy!] It will, or at least it ought, to produce an excellent effect.'[20] A week later, in another letter to Daniel, he claimed, perhaps over-optimistically, that Caernarfon and Bangor were favourable to him, with leading Bangor Liberals like John Price, vice-principal of the town's Normal College, supporting him. Moreover, at Caernarfon he had the support of Liberals like J. T. Roberts (his first election agent), R. A. Griffith, the poet Elphin and J. R. Hughes, both advocates of the Young Wales cause. The letter ended on a triumphant note:

> Just received telegram from Morgan Richards (Bangor). Certain to be selected at Bangor. So you see my most sanguine expectations are being corroborated by my friends . . . saw old Morgan, Cadnant, on Sunday. He came up to me for an introduction. Said I was just the man for the Boroughs. Could you not induce him to write a letter to the *Herald* to that effect? I did not like to ask him as I have made it a point not to canvass support, except through my intimate and loyal friends.[21]

No holds were barred, therefore, in Lloyd George's press campaign to secure his goal and win support throughout the constituency. Yet although he had claimed in his correspondence with D. R. Daniel that it was only a formality before he was adopted by the northern boroughs, this was far from being the case, for he had major hurdles to clear before celebrating such an event. By the end of July 1888, he had another plan for a second blitz of articles to be published to reach the far ends of the constituency, this time centring his aim on the working-class readers of *Y Werin*[22] (The People), which its proprietors claimed that it had a weekly readership of 10,000. There duly emerged several contributions in the paper, again using pseudonyms, extolling his virtues as a candidate chosen from among the people and stressing his concern for the welfare of workers in the constituency.

In July 1888, too, the second stage in the hearing of the Llanfrothen Burial Scandal was held at Porthmadog. In a dramatic development, Judge Bishop this time declared in favour of the rector, amidst an uproar of disbelief, which led Lloyd George to protest vehemently in court and to state that he would take the issue to the highest court in the land, namely the High Court in London.[23] Though he had suffered a setback with this remarkable verdict via Judge Bishop's volte-face, he received praiseworthy publicity in the press and the case was by no means finished. There was also the bonus that he could milk publicity from a further hearing – which would coincide, at the end of 1888, with the time when the Caernarfon Boroughs were finally ready to select a candidate.

By the end of July 1888, however, the tide seemed to be flowing in his favour in the boroughs; the *North Wales Observer and Express* noted: 'There is a strong and increasing expression throughout the constituency, favourable to Mr Lloyd George's candidature.'[24]

By August, the *Genedl* press, with the 'Quarrymen's Champion', W. J. Parry, in control, was orchestrating, with David Edwards, managing editor of the company, another propaganda exercise for Lloyd George. This bare-faced campaign led A. C. Humphreys-Owen to write to Stuart Rendel complaining that Lloyd George and his friends were carrying out a shameless press campaign to secure for him the nomination at all costs. With some justification, he informed Rendel bitterly: 'I have just read the Caernarfon papers. Their rowdiness is sickening: they are just as bad as the worst Tories.'[25]

At the end of August, in another letter to Rendel, A. C. Humphreys-Owen said he was considering withdrawing from the nomination race, but everything was not in Lloyd George's favour in the summer of 1888. Indeed, in August the redoubtable editor of the *Cambrian News*, John Gibson, wrote a leading article which was scathingly critical of Lloyd George, reminding his readers, with much justification, that Lloyd George had not always been faithful to the Liberal Party. He told his readers, many of them from Cricieth and Pwllheli, that the Porthmadog attorney had flirted with Chamberlainism in 1886. Gibson commented pithily: 'George in 1886 was nothing more than a Paper Unionist . . . where was David Lloyd George at the last election and what was his political creed then?'[26]

This barbed criticism, referring to his espousal of Chamberlain's 'Home Rule All Round' policy, must have caused Lloyd George some trepidation, but it did not curtail him from further energetic activity to secure the nomination. In August 1888, he addressed a public meeting at Bangor, alongside the Irish Nationalist MP, T. D. L. Sullivan. At this meeting, he called for a Welsh Federal Parliament as the only means of facilitating social and economic changes in Wales. Referring to the Irish example, he stated that the Welsh Liberals should give priority to Welsh demands and aspirations and not be, first and foremost, loyalists to the British Liberal Party. He was undoubtedly, therefore, putting himself forward as the nationalist candidate for the Caernarfon Boroughs.[27]

By 27 August, he could take heart that the Boroughs Liberal Association general meeting once more postponed selecting a candidate and he was further heartened when the association was informed that Humphreys-Owen had officially retired from the contest. However, at the meeting, there emerged another dangerous opponent in the shape of the barrister from Cricieth, R. Pugh Jones, local born, Welsh-speaking, but a fervent critic of Lloyd George's brand of radicalism and nationalism. Moreover, at the meeting, the Gladstonian moderate secretary of the association, R. D. Williams, put a further spoke in Lloyd George's wheel by announcing that, in addition to R. Pugh Jones, he was expecting other candidates to enter the lists.[28] Lloyd George's confident belief that the candidature was in the bag was far from being cut and dried.

Undercurrents of hostility towards him were further evinced in September in a letter from Michael D. Jones, the Independent in religion and nationalist in politics, to D. R. Daniel. He bemoaned the slowness of the Caernarfon Boroughs Liberal Association in choosing a candidate, and claimed it was the Calvinistic Methodists in the constituency who were delaying the selection because they did not want a Baptist and an extremist representing them. Michael D. Jones also added that their opposition was not denominational alone, but based on hatred towards Lloyd George's nationalist stance.[29] Tension was further heightened when R. Pugh Jones wrote a poisonous and controversial letter to the editor of the *Carnarvon and Denbigh Herald*.[30] The letter claimed, with considerable justification, that Lloyd George's campaign in the press had been deceitful. Jones alleged that: 'Not infrequently the letters published in his favour have been written by the same hand under different nom-de-plumes.' The Conservative weekly, *Y Gwalia*, pounced upon the letter to pour scorn further upon Lloyd George's efforts to win the parliamentary nomination, claiming his campaign was hypocritical and deceitful and that the whole campaign had been orchestrated by his own hand.[31] The press onslaught was not entirely successful, but could well have rebounded against him. Undaunted, however, he pressed on with the campaign and by October the southern Boroughs, which had expressed their preference for him, now came out explicitly in his favour as the official choice. This was followed by Conwy, whose members chose him as their nominee by the end of the month. In November, Lloyd George arranged a series of public meetings in the six boroughs to seek to press home his advantage. He knew that the next AGM, of the Caernarfon Boroughs Liberal Association would be held in January 1889 and that his long campaign needed to be solidified in November and December.

Perhaps the main clinching factor for him was that the final phase of the long drawn-out Llanfrothen Burial Case came to a climax in the High Court in London before Justice Manisty in December.[32] He ruled that Judge Bishop in July had returned the wrong verdict, overruled him and found in favour of Lloyd George's clients. The judge ruled that the rector had had no right to undertake a new agreement with the donor of the additional burial plot in 1881 and that the verdict should be in favour of Robert Roberts's family. The newspapers throughout Wales, including the three morning dailies, the *Daily Post*,[33] the *South Wales Daily News*[34] and the *Western Mail*,[35] gave the verdict extensive publicity and, according to the *Genedl* papers, circulating in the boroughs, the verdict was bound to clinch for Lloyd George a parliamentary nomination there.[36]

That certainly was a dominating factor when the Caernarfon Boroughs Association met on 3 January 1889 finally to choose a candidate for the constituency. After much deliberation, they decided to select 'the people's attorney' – a decision which gave Lloyd George immense satisfaction, as he recorded in his diary that night: 'Selection of candidate last thing on programme so I had to wait for two hours. Had excellent reception. Delegates got up and cheered me. Felt position keenly. Could not speak with much verve.'[37]

Although the delegates cheered him, and although he was overcome with emotion, the press response to his selection was more cautious and mixed and from several directions was caustic. He received a favourable reception from some Liberal papers, especially from the Baptist paper, *Seren Gomer*.[38] But the Independents' denominational weekly, *Y Tyst a'r Dydd*, was anxious to project the view that he would have to be wise and responsible in his public pronouncements in the future and should not press too forcefully his 'nationalist standpoint'.[39] Indeed, even the *Genedl* stable of papers were nervous of his extreme views, with the *North Wales Observer and Express* calling for compromise and reconciliation if the seat was to be won at a forthcoming election. The paper noted: 'Liberals of all shades and degrees, old and young, moderate and advanced, need to recognise his choice and rally around him.'[40]

This careful and circumspect reaction was, perhaps, not surprising, for his campaign to win the seat had been arduous and controversial, bordering on the duplicitous, as the Tory paper, *Y Gwalia*, was quick to declare in early January. The paper asserted that his choice would lead to a split in the Liberal ranks in the constituency between old and new Liberals and that he had been chosen by 'the noisy and most inexperienced faction of the party in the constituency' – the new radical nationalist group led by Lloyd George himself.[41]

After reaching a crucial milestone in his career, where failure could have ended it prematurely, Lloyd George, despite the entreaties from his own party, was not prepared to play a pragmatic, moderate role after his selection. He believed in January 1889 that he could well have another three years before a general election was called – ample time, he felt, for him to make his advanced views acceptable to the electorate and to cultivate further his identity as a 'breakthrough' radical and nationalist.

He had certainly won the constituency's Liberal nomination on a nationalist ticket and his victory had been a triumph for the new politics coursing through Wales in the late 1880s. His securing of the nomination had also been achieved thanks to his single-minded zest and energy and his masterful use of the press and his impressive oratorical powers, in both English and Welsh.

However, despite warnings from several sectors of the Liberal press, that he should tread warily in future, the disciple of Michael D. Jones and Michael Davitt was not likely to retreat into the moderate Gladstonian fold after January 1889. He was, indeed, determined to promote further his radical agenda in the press and on public platforms, and particularly as 'the Boy Alderman' on the new Caernarfonshire County Council in 1889, where he did not flinch from further escalating his radical and national profile. He was intent on showing that he was 'the Nationalist candidate for the Caernarfon Boroughs'.

VI

THE NATIONALIST HOTHEAD,
1889–1890

After winning the parliamentary nomination of the Caernarfon Boroughs in January 1889, Lloyd George believed he had another three years before he would have to challenge his Tory opponent, Edmund Swetenham, in a general election campaign. This would be a comparatively comfortable period, he believed, which would enable him to make his controversial, radical and nationalist ideas more acceptable in a constituency which was, after all, a marginal one and, most certainly, one with an electorate which was far from being amenable to his pioneering and advanced political standpoint.

As a parliamentary candidate, Lloyd George would have the status and influence within the corridors of power of Welsh Liberalism in the meetings of the North and South Wales Liberal Federations. At these gatherings, he could promote the objectives of Cymru Fydd, but he also needed a platform closer to his own constituency so as to seek to secure the support of the electors of the Caernarfon Boroughs constituency and attract them to his new Liberalism and emergent nationalism.

That platform was the new 'people's parliament' – the county councils established by the Local Government Act of 1888. Before Lloyd George was selected as the Caernarfon Boroughs prospective parliamentary candidate in January 1889, he had been ubiquitous in the latter months of 1888, before the county councils' first elections, in leading a crusade throughout north Wales alongside leading Liberal figures, like the Revd Dr Herber Evans, the Independent 'Pope', and the newspaper proprietor, Thomas Gee, to emphasize how vital the new bodies were in promoting democracy and Welshness. In addition, during the election campaign to the new authorities, he and his close friend, Tom Ellis MP, had addressed crowded meetings supporting like-minded, radical-nationalists standing in the constituencies in Merioneth and Caernarfonshire. These efforts were to reap rich dividends for him personally and politically, ensuring that localities within his prospective constituency would be represented by politicians of the same leanings as himself. As one of the most influential newspapers circulating in the constituency, the *North Wales Observer and Express*, noted, at the end of the election campaign, that Lloyd George's participation on the hustings had been of considerable significance in consolidating his hold on the electorate:

> The County Council elections have assisted to bring Mr. D. Lloyd George closely in touch with his future constituents. He has been ubiquitous and not a few of the Liberal members on the Council will owe their return to his services on the platform.[1]

Local government democracy was not a trivial matter for Lloyd George, as K. O. Morgan has asserted in his lecture, 'Lloyd George and Welsh Liberalism' (1995). Rather, it was central to his beliefs at the time. He believed that the 'County Parliaments' were vehicles of democratic change, which could themselves provide, in unison throughout Wales, the basis for a Welsh Federal Parliament. An opportunity was, indeed, provided for him in the first pre-preparatory meeting of the Caernarfonshire County Council, to be given a platform from within the county chamber to promote his radical views and to press the Cymru Fydd case.

As was the case throughout Wales, the Liberals emerged triumphant from the first county council elections in the county of Caernarfon, securing 32 seats in comparison to the return of only 16 Tories. Having made such a considerable impression at the election meetings, he was 'invited' to join the new council (through the back door) as an alderman. His elevation as the 'Boy Alderman', as he was dubbed slightingly by the Tories, elicited fierce criticism from Ellis Nanney, the Gwynfryn squire and his future opponent in his first election for the Caernarfon Boroughs constituency, who had been elected as councillor for the Llanystumdwy constituency. Similarly, the county's leading industrialist/landowner, Lord Penrhyn, led a vociferous attack on what he regarded as a fix and a corrupt and dirty appointment. The leading Welsh-language Tory weekly, *Y Gwalia*, also thundered against his nomination, claiming that the county council's Liberal caucus had discredited the supposedly democratic new body by fixing an aldermanic post for the young and inexperienced agitator, Lloyd George.[2]

Therefore, Lloyd George became a county councillor in the midst of much furore, controversy and allegations of corruption. Typically, the 'Boy Alderman' was not unduly troubled by such allegations and enjoyed the publicity his appointment secured. He was delighted with the opportunity his elevation provided to project his advanced views within the county and his provisional constituency, but he was also well aware that his activities there would bring forth much valuable press publicity and a reputation enhanced well beyond Caernarfonshire. In a tumultuous year, therefore, before he had to face a totally unexpected by-election in April 1890, the 'Welsh nationalist of the Ellis type' (and perhaps more of a nationalist than Ellis) was ready within the new county council to fan the flames of Welsh public opinion. With the activities of the new council firmly in the public eye, Lloyd George wasted no time in creating a controversial reputation in 'the County Parliament', fearing neither Tory foes nor humdrum Liberals, who were unprepared to spend public finances on welfare issues. His appearances at County Hall were to bring him widespread publicity – both hostile and favourable.

Indeed, before the first real meeting of the council began in April 1889, at a hugely packed gathering of Liverpool Welsh people at Hope Hall in that city – a meeting which secured publicity even in the London press – he expressed his vision of what the new councils could achieve for social reform and for nationalist aspirations in Wales.[3] Contrary to orthodox British and Welsh Liberal public opinion, he claimed that the new councils could come together on a nationwide Welsh basis to form an all-Welsh National Council – the precursor for a powerful, federal Welsh parliament. This was a vision shared by Tom Ellis and other Cymru Fyddites but not by the old Liberal hierarchy in his provisional constituency in the county, in Wales and certainly not in the Gladstonian temple of high politics.

Lloyd George in his Hope Hall speech and on the hustings preceding the county council election, foresaw the councils' promoting policies to raise rates on the rich and privileged, securing measures such as leasehold reform and municipal socialist policies – policies he had championed since the mid-1880s. He was anxious to bring land and rivers and fisheries under public control and to see the new authorities increasing spending on public work schemes for the underprivileged and the unemployed – measures which would not be welcomed by laissez-faire Liberals. In the peroration of his speech at Hope Hall, he also hailed the 'new democracy', which the county councils signified, as it brought to an end the previous dominance of local authorities by the Tory and Anglicized landowners and monopoly capitalists of his area and of Wales. He was to claim that: 'The day of the Squire was gone, the sun of the aristocracy had set and the grand tomorrow had dawned upon Wales.'[4]

After this opening salvo in his crusade to make the new 'County Parliaments' a vibrant force in Welsh life, he immediately plunged into controversial waters in the County Chamber. At the first ever full meeting of the council in April, he was elected to sit on one of the leading committees alongside the formidable English-born, new radical politician and social reformer, A. D. Acland MP, who had a house at Clynnog, near Caernarfon, and who had been selected on to the council, he too as an alderman.[5] He was, in 1890, on the threshold of becoming a reforming minister of education in the next Liberal government of 1892. He was a close friend of Tom Ellis, a champion of the Welsh Intermediate Education Act of 1889 and an agitator for increasing income taxes and using death duties to redistribute wealth. Lloyd George, sometimes accused by Welsh historians of not being interested in education as a lever of social change, savoured his company, and indeed, in April 1889, seconded Acland's call in the Caernarfon chamber for a measure of leasehold enfranchisement to help the working class secure freeholds on their properties.[6] Lloyd George's relationship with Acland showed, even as early as 1890, that his thinking was being permeated by new, collectivist labourist values – underlining that an artificial distinction has been drawn by historians between Lloyd George's supposed 'old' and 'new' Liberalism, pre- and post-1906. He was, before he became a parliamentarian and in his early political parliamentary career, not only the advocate of old Welsh radical Nonconformism, but on both rural and urban reform issues he was an interventionist. Moreover, at this stage, he believed that such measures could be facilitated more quickly by a Welsh parliament than by a House of Commons, dominated often by Tories or laissez-faire Liberals and a London government, where radical measures would almost invariably be torpedoed by the House of Lords – the chamber he had castigated in his pioneering columns in his *Udgorn Rhyddid*.

Naturally, he was also quite prepared to push the Nonconformist measures of land reform, disestablishment of the Anglican Church and anti-brewing issues in the Council Chamber, but allied to new, social issues. Indeed, at his second council appearance, he secured much publicity in the local press when the council discussed what evidence to provide for the Royal Commission, then inquiring into the need for further temperance reform to amend the Sunday Closing Act of 1881. Lloyd George suggested that the 'man on his travels' clause in the act should be amended, as licensees and hoteliers were using this loophole to provide alcohol for Welsh people on a Sunday, under the pretence that they were travellers or tourists.[7] He also spoke against the emergence of clubs in Wales where strong drink could be obtained on a Sunday. He called for all clubs in Wales which sold alcohol on a Sunday to be closed down, although he himself was far from being a strict Sabbatarian. However, by plucking the temperance strings, Lloyd George knew he would please much Liberal opinion in his constituency and court support amongst older Liberals. The temperance tune was again to be replayed in the Council Chamber in January 1890 and it aroused what can only be described in Welsh as *cythraul canu* – a real hornet's nest being raised by him at the meeting of the county's Police Committee.[8]

The chief constable, Colonel Ruck, father of the eminent novelist Berta Ruck, delivered his quarterly report and informed the members that cases of drunkeness had increased in the county and that only four licensees had been prosecuted for supplying liquor to drunken customers. Lloyd George then condemned the chief constable and his force. He accused him and them of being servile to the licensing trade and to the capitalists and landowners who owned many hotels and public houses in the area. He criticized the police force for their inactivity, but also caused uproar in the chamber when he insisted that the police should wear plain clothes and enter public houses to spy on licensees and, while drinking ginger beer themselves, should then bring the taverners to justice for supplying drink to inebriates. At the meeting, reported widely in the press, he even condemned the Tory members for alleging that the police were prejudiced, while also arousing the spleen of moderate Liberal members, such as D. P. Williams JP, of Llanberis, who regarded his hectoring of the forces of law and order as being unjustified. This would not be the only occasion for the respectable Liberal businessman and magistrate and 'the people's attorney' to come to blows in public. Nevertheless, Lloyd George, never an orthodox party man, was well pleased with the raucous intervention he had made at the Police Committee. Indeed, it became a tactic for him to attack the legal establishment in the county during his pre-parliamentary career, not only in the Council Chamber, but also in the local courts.

Indeed, while a county alderman, he made a sensational attack upon the Caernarfon magistrates, both Tories and Liberals, during his defence of poachers in May 1889.[9] They were slate quarrymen from the Nantlle Valley who had been brought before 'their betters' for alleged poaching at Llyn Isaf, Nantlle. The chairman of the bench was a local Tory squire, Captain J. G. Wynn Griffith of Llanfair Hall, renowned for his merciless punishment of poachers, whilst the leading Liberal, D. P. Williams, Colonel Ruck's defender, was vice-chairman. After the bench had delivered a guilty verdict against the quarrymen, although Lloyd George had claimed they had a right to fish in the lake without a licence, he then alleged that the bench was completely prejudicial to the rights of the common people and that his clients would never have a fair hearing in such a court. Using the ruse he had deployed in the Llanfrothen Burial Case, he threatened that he would later take the case to a higher legal authority where justice would be dispensed equitably, adding that the magistrates were corrupt. Amidst scenes of turmoil, the bench, with the exception of W. J. Parry, the 'Quarrymen's Champion', condemned his actions. His protests on this occasion were not followed by recourse to a higher court, but the case was printed verbatim in both local Tory and Liberal journals and brought him much publicity.

The Tory weekly, *Y Gwalia*, was especially vindictive, claiming that he had libelled a leading Liberal moderate in D. P. Williams, adding that the sober, respectable electors of the Caernarfon Boroughs constituency would be antagonized by his behaviour. The paper dubbed him 'an apprentice in insolence', more vividly captured in Welsh as 'Y Prentis mewn Haerllugrwydd', whose behaviour in a court of law was 'a disgrace' – *gwarth*. The case, confirmed, however, that he was prepared to resort to extreme tactics to secure widespread publicity.[10]

Much has been made, by many Welsh historians, of the assertion that Lloyd George purportedly had no labour sympathies, but he was to show in his defence of the Nantlle quarrymen in this case, that he understood their plight and poverty and, indeed, as later chapters in this book show, in the mid and early 1890s he took a leading role on several occasions in defending Welsh slate quarrymen while also championing their trade union rights and their right to strike. His commitment to industrial and urban workers was not just lip service, as many Welsh historians have argued, nor was the Cymru Fydd League from 1894–6 without a working-class message. Much to the chagrin of his brother, William George, despite his firm's impecunious state, he often took such cases as the Nantlle poaching defence, without securing payment from their clients.

His concern to free the fisheries and rivers of Wales to public access and to stimulate public investment in sea fisheries, especially to aid the sea-going fishermen of his prospective constituency, was also much in evidence in another initiative he undertook in the county council in this period. Since the council's inception, he had ensured a place for himself on the Rivers and Fisheries Committee. In November 1889, during that committee's hearing, he proposed the establishment, together with other Welsh councils, of a Fisheries Board for Cardigan Bay, reflecting his collectivist views and his emphasis on public investment to raise poverty levels amongst his less privileged constituents.[11] Public money, he claimed, should be invested to improve the fisheries and to safeguard the welfare of local fishing fleets and the workers employed in the industry. Long before his supposed 'new Liberalism' and measures for sailors, dockers and fishermen, as president of the Board of Trade (post-1906), the young politician, aware through personal and family connections of the deprivations suffered by ordinary seafarers, was blazing a pioneering, radical, interventionist trail in Wales. His calls for joint regional and Welsh national bodies, such as the Cardigan Bay Fisheries Authority, also reflected his attempt to synthesize Welsh national self-determination and social and economic change.

Also, in November 1889 at the county council, he took another opportunity to highlight the cause of Welsh Home Rule. He seconded W. J. Parry's resolution demanding that all Welsh county councils should unite to establish a Welsh National Council, which could prioritize Welsh national demands, including linguistic equality for the Welsh language.[12] The National Council would not only spend the Anglican Church's endowments on Welsh social and economic needs, but would also be an evolutionary step towards the establishment of a Welsh parliament, with powers to control the Welsh economy and to promote social welfare and education.

He also used the council chamber to attack personally and with much vilification the landowners and industrialists who dominated the life of the area, reserving his most hostile jibes for the most wealthy and prominent of them all – the slate-quarrying magnate of the Penrhyn estate, Douglas Pennant, against whom he had carried the Liberal banner during the 1868 general election, during his infancy at Llanystumdwy. He was to attack Douglas Pennant (who became Lord Penrhyn in 1886) personally, his boyhood anti-hero Ellis Nanney and the Wynns of the Glynllifon estate in February 1890, when an aldermanic vacancy was caused by the sudden death of the Llŷn Tory landowner, Lloyd Edwards of Nanhoron. Orthodox Liberals on the council, for the sake of courtesy, proposed, together with the Conservatives, that the new alderman should be a Tory. Subsequently, Lord Newborough of Glynllifon's heir, the Honourable Frederick Wynn, was proposed as the new alderman. He was heir to a landlord whose tenants were not well treated and a capitalist who had gained considerable wealth from land, which had been exploited for slate quarrying, providing him with unearned profits, which Lloyd George claimed should be taxed to provide pensions and benefits for the poor and the elderly. Lloyd George, incensed by the servility of the majority of Liberals on the council, rose to oppose Wynn's appointment and, in the teeth of much barracking, proposed instead that a fellow Cymru Fyddite, Pwllheli councillor Isaac Morris, should fill the vacancy. His proposal was highly controversial, but that did not prevent him from protesting at the end of the proceedings that the votes for Morris and Wynn, a contest which Wynn won handsomely, had been miscounted.[14] Further uproar ensued, but in his last foray in the Council Chamber before the unexpected by-election in the Caernarfon Boroughs in April 1890, he had again obtained widespread publicity in the press and amongst his prospective constituents. This last appearance in the Council Chamber had been as controversial as the scandal which had accompanied his sensational appointment in 1889 as the 'Boy Alderman'.

His role in the county council had not been child's play, nor 'parish politics' as John Grigg has claimed in his biography, *The Young Lloyd George*. Rather, he had used his time there to seek to transform Welsh and Liberal politics to the core, as a pioneering radical-nationalist. It is also difficult to understand K. O. Morgan's contention that he had no interest in local politics and local government issues. On the contrary, his activities at the 'County Parliament' and his crusade for these new democratic bodies before the first council elections had underlined how passionately he viewed the councils as instruments to promote social changes and, acting in conjunction on a Wales-wide basis, how they could promote the cause of Welsh self-government.

At a crucial moment in his career, he had used the county platform assiduously to project advanced and dangerous views, in the face of criticism from orthodox Liberals. He could have adopted a much more moderate line, tempering his radical-nationalist standpoint, but his main concern had been to use his aldermanic platform to change the course of Welsh politics and win the support of the newly emancipated voters who had come on to the register after 1885. His actions at County Hall showed that he was he was intent on winning support for new ideas and that he was a new kind of Welsh politician, as had been underlined by his baptizing his own *Udgorn Rhyddid* (The Trumpet of Freedom) – 'a Nationalist and Socialist regenerator in every respect'.

Moreover, he was not only to display his radical-nationalist views on the county council in the political, social and economic sphere alone, but, more sensationally, and perhaps more unexpectedly, he used this platform to call on a pioneering way for the Welsh language to be used fully and officially in the council's activities. This bold initiative was undertaken against the background of much apathy, indeed, hostility, towards the language in Victorian Wales; in the schools, colleges and throughout Welsh public life and even within the chapels and denominations of Wales – especially with the Welsh Nonconformist sects' obsession with 'the English Cause', which led Welsh-language denominations to build English-language chapels, even in predominantly Welsh-speaking areas. (Lloyd George himself had witnessed a hostile split caused in his wife's Calvinistic Methodist chapel at Cricieth in the mid-1880s by a proposal to build an English-language chapel in the town.)

Consequently, Lloyd George's determination that the Welsh language should be the official language of the new Caernarfonshire Council was bound to cause great controversy and opposition and was a bold step to undertake. Though he himself had had an English-medium education and was a master of English oratory, even in his youth, and despite the fact, that according to the fashion of the time, he wrote most of his personal letters and diary entries in English, he insisted from the outset on speaking in Welsh in the Council Chamber. Indeed, before the council's first ever full meeting, in March 1889, he called publicly for equal status for the language in the council's proceedings. He was determined to underline that the Welsh language was just not an ornament nor a homespun medium, but a treasure, which had to be adapted to a new, modern, democratic age in public and government administration.

In mid-October 1889, he was asked by one of the county's leading newspapers, the *Carnarvon and Denbigh Herald*, to express his views as to the possible use of the Welsh language in the new council – both in the chamber and in official forms. Under the heading, 'Should the Welsh language be accorded equality in the proceedings of the Caernarfonshire County Council?', he wrote an extensive and powerful article supporting the language to the hilt. In his opening salvo he iterated: 'The Local Government Act of last year certainly does not designate the English tongue as the only one in which the proceedings of the Council should be conducted.'[15]

Even if the Acts of Union between England and Wales proscribed the Welsh language officially, he added, this should be disregarded, because the newly established councils heralded the dawn of a new, democratically transformed Wales, no longer under the hegemony of the Anglicized, landed gentry over the previous local authorities – the un-elected Quarter Sessions. He claimed:

> Whether there is some antique and long-forgotten Act of the legislature proscribing the official use of the Welsh language, it is scarcely worth the Council's while to enquire. The Act – if such there be extant – was intended to provide for circumstances foreign to those now in being and is so obsolete as the laws against heresy and apostacy and deserves the same respect as those antiquated laws.[16]

After rejecting that there were any legal obstacles in using the Welsh language officially, he resorted to another argument in its favour, a contemporary one: he claimed that its use was justified on grounds of social equality, democratic rights and efficiency in a predominantly Welsh-speaking society:

> Apart from any question of sentiment, the efficiency of the Council requires that free permission should be given to such councillors as prefer Welsh to express their views in that language and for the simple reason that the English language would of necessity be confined to a minority on the Council.
>
> Moreover, an unfair advantage in all debates would thus be given to such of the councillors, as are least in sympathy with the masses of the Welsh people.[17]

As can be seen from the last clause of his article, he was proposing the use of Welsh primarily on class grounds, in that it was the language of the majority of the people in his area and because it was the language of the democratic majority of elected councillors and those they represented. He was not prepared to see the language of the minority elite, the Tory Anglicized local gentry and industrialists, reigning supreme on the council. Neither was he prepared to see the English language, which monopolized the proceedings of the old Quarter Sessions, being accorded the primary role in the activities of the new council – 'the People's Parliament'.

Therefore, it was not because the Welsh language had once been the preferred language of the medieval Welsh gentry, nor primarily for literary and cultural reasons that he supported the use of the Welsh language as an official medium; his main motive in supporting the language was on grounds of greater social equality and democratic entitlement. By championing the language, the 'cottage bred boy' was celebrating the beginning of the end of the supremacy of the Anglicized Welsh gentry and humdrum orthodox Liberals in Welsh public life, although, in so doing, he was flying in the face (and opposition) of a substantial element within the old Liberal hierarchy in Welsh politics. Indeed, some of his Liberal colleagues on the new council were apathetic about the future of the language and were critical of his revolutionary proposals.

It is significant that in all the biographies of Lloyd George, no mention has been made of this linguistic initiative he undertook in 1889, while many Welsh historians of Lloyd George and the Cymru Fydd era have been anxious to show that he and similar like-minded radical-nationalists of the period did not place any significant emphasis on the role of the Welsh language in official circles in the 1880s and 1890s.[18]

Rather, historians have argued that the nationalist impetus culturally was placed on securing Welsh national institutions, such as the university, the National Museum and a National Library, where no prominence was to be accorded to the language in their administration and activities – certainly not during their formative decades. D. Tecwyn Lloyd has also shown how, in the 1880s and 1890s, English was given status and prominence while the native language was accorded an inferior role even in events such as the National Eisteddfod and certainly in the primary and intermediate schools, where teaching was undertaken primarily through the medium of English.[19] Even in the teacher training colleges and particularly in the University of Wales the Welsh language and Welsh literature were taught in English. However, this was certainly not Lloyd George's approach towards the language, in Caernarfonshire County Council before 1890, and in the mid-1890s, when he called frequently for the Eisteddfod to become all-Welsh and for the language to be used equally with English even in union and industrial matters (see chapter IX).

There is no doubt that as a 'Boy Alderman' he had launched the innovative call for the native language to be given full status in governmental business and to re-establish the language as a modernizing force in Welsh life. Equality for the language was an integral part of his strategy to awaken national consciousness in Wales. His aspirations for the use of Welsh in local government were not fulfilled, however, despite the fact that many members there spoke in Welsh at meetings and in committees, mainly because of apathy and hostility locally and because in 1891 the government refused the application of Merioneth County Council to administer that council's affairs in the native language; this was despite the fact that many of its members, as on several other county councils, were monoglot Welsh speakers or, at best, more at home in Welsh.

Lloyd George's championing of the Welsh language contradicts the view of many Welsh historians. They have sought to portray him as one who had only a sentimental sympathy for the language – the language of his childhood, the language of the cottage and the chapel, the language of the hearth and that of the small eisteddfodau, the language of homespun rural Welsh culture. This is Hywel Teifi Edwards's interpretation of his annual address at the Treorci National Eisteddfod in 1928.[20] Here, Edwards asserts, he did not promote the language as an official modern medium of government and administration, but as 'a homely language, a warm language, the language of the hearth . . . the language affecting the deepest and tenderest private thoughts, the language of mysticism, and of the hidden byways of life [*iaith yr encilion, y dirgelion*]'.

No doubt Lloyd George could romanticize eloquently and rhetorically at the National Eisteddfod, especially in his later years, upon the Welsh language 'as the language of the hearth'. Yet, it was he, in the Caernarfon and Bangor National Eisteddfodau of the early 1890s who condemned from these Eisteddfod platforms, the Anglicization of the Eisteddfod and began the call for it to be an all-Welsh-language festival and who, in the 1906 Caernarfon Eisteddfod, sought to modernize the festival by calling, in the teeth of Nonconfirmist, puritan opposition, for dramatic productions in Welsh to be a mainstay of the Eisteddfod week.[21] Although, as he became older and in the 1920s, ensconced with his English mistress, Frances Stevenson, in the Surrey countryside, he would wax sentimentally about the language, he was to instigate the 'All Welsh Rule' in the National Eisteddfod at Machynlleth in 1937 (see chapter XI). There is obviously some truth in K. O. Morgan's view about Lloyd George's somewhat superficial attitude towards the Welsh language and Welsh culture by then, although this viewpoint is exaggerated:

> Lloyd George had relatively scant concern with Welsh literary or musical culture, other than the lusty singing of Welsh hymns. Nor did he have any particular involvement with the moves to protect the Welsh language – although, it should be said that Lloyd George in this respect was typical of virtually every Liberal

of his time, since there was not the same anxiety about 'the fate of the language' of the kind that emerged in the inter-war period.

Lloyd George's approach to Welsh culture was genuine enough, but it was the knowledge gained by upbringing, personal contact and conversation. It was instinctive and intuitive, rather than intellectual. At times, it was even sentimental.[22]

This is surely a half truth, as he was not only close friends with leading Welsh historians and literary critics like W. Llywelyn Williams, John Edward Lloyd, John Morris-Jones and many others, but in his late youth and early political career he read extensively Welsh historical works and knew a great deal about contemporary and earlier works of Welsh poets, particularly the strict-metre works of Eifionydd poets. And there is no doubt that in championing the language officially, at the inception of the new county councils, he was displaying the need for a modern, new and dynamic pioneering role for the native language in Welsh public life, at a time of crisis for the Welsh language, when, indeed, many Welsh Liberals, but not all, were apathetic towards the native tongue.

He was to call for equality for the language at a time when it was not fashionable to do so. This he did at a potentially high political cost to his career, when he was aware that sooner or later he would have to fight an election in a marginal, 'cosmopolitan' constituency such as the Caernarfon Boroughs, where there were a significant number of non-Welsh-born electors and where a sizeable section of a snobbish, Welsh middle class were attracted by English attitudes and mores.

As the innovative 'Boy Alderman' in 1889 and 1890, in the 'People's Parliament' of Caernarfonshire County Council, he had shown great courage in promoting radical-nationalist views. It was by no stretch of the imagination an exercise, as John Grigg has suggested, in 'parish pump politics' and in this period there is hardly any basis for Grigg's assertion that 'he always cared for Wales but only in the much bigger context of United Kingdom and Imperial politics'.[23] This assumption is a misguided interpretation of his career in the decade spanning the Cymru Fydd era, both pre- and post-parliamentary periods. True, he had to work within the framework of a British Imperial Parliament in pushing his views and, of course, despite being an advocate of a Welsh Independent Liberal Party, in this period, he had to use the British Parliament as a platform to espouse his extreme views. But, in this period, there is no doubt that his priority was to promote Welsh national aspirations, including securing Welsh Home Rule with its unique social, economic, linguistic and cultural agenda. He placed those aspirations above obedience and servility towards the British Liberal Party. He regarded himself as being a nationalist.

In this period, too, it was not only via the medium of the county council alone that he was to press his ground-breaking agenda. After being chosen as the prospective parliamentary candidate for the Caernarfon Boroughs in January 1889, he was also co-opted on to the committee of the North Wales Liberal Federation (NWLF) and had access to the public deliberations of its south Wales counterpart. By February 1889, he was an active member of the North Wales Federation, while, at the same time, two like-minded nationalists, the union leader, W. J. Parry and R. A. Griffith (the bard, 'Elphin'), the solicitor and nationalist, were elected members. These new members especially Lloyd George and R. A. Griffith, were regarded as being upholders of dangerous and flamboyant ideas by the mandarins and patriarchs who had dominated the federations and kept them as bodies subservient to official British Liberalism – some of whom were also still prominent in Caernarfon Boroughs politics.

Despite this inhibiting factor, Lloyd George, from the outset, used these avenues of influence to seek further to arouse radical and nationalist passions and, primarily, to seek to reconstruct and radically change Liberal organization in Wales – while, at the same time, espousing the need for unity between north and south Wales and priority for Welsh measures and, of course, Home Rule. He believed that the federations could coalesce to form a Welsh national organization, which would establish Welsh Liberalism as an independent movement in British politics.

His first attempt to transform Welsh Liberalism's British-centric attitudes and organization came at the NWLF's meeting, in the centre of his own constituency, the town of Caernarfon, in June 1889. The borough, the headquarters of the advanced radical weekly papers, *Y Genedl Gymreig* (The Welsh Nation), *Y Werin* (The People) and the *North Wales Observer and Express*, had played a significant role in securing his parliamentary nomination in January 1889. Now he hoped that at the widely publicized June meeting of the North Wales Federation, he could make a telling and crucial impact on the Caernarfon Boroughs. At the meeting, he delivered a highly controversial motion, covered in detail by the *Genedl* papers, where he criticized personally the Liberal leader, W.E. Gladstone, because he had recently absented himself from the parliamentary debate in 1889 on the proposed disestablishment and disendowment of the Anglican Church in Wales.[24] He also condemned the Liberal hierarchy at Westminister because of their opposition to the measure. He claimed that only a Welsh parliament could legislate on such matters and redistribute the Church's wealth towards the more egalitarian social needs of the Welsh nation. He insisted that the Liberal Party in Britain was overly concerned about giving priority to Home Rule for Ireland at the expense of Welsh needs, as he had done during the 'Home Rule' All Round crisis of 1886. He also threatened that many new, radical, Welsh members would be returned at the next election and that they would not support Gladstone if he gave priority to Ireland over Wales.

These were rebellious utterings in the centre of his own marginal and Conservative provisional constituency, but he was determined to set Welsh Liberalism on a new course and for his constituents to accept what he believed were new forces of change enveloping Wales. His extreme speech was to elicit a mixed response both amongst the audience and in the press. With W. J. Parry at the editorial helm, *Y Genedl Gymreig* welcomed his condemnation of the English odour (*Seisnigrwydd drewllyd*) of the NWLF.[25] On the other hand, other Welsh papers were more circumspect, whilst the Tory papers circulating in the constituency, *Y Gwalia* and the *North Wales Chronicle*, remained quiescent, temporarily, at least.

His resentment towards the north Wales Gladstonian British-centric caucus came to its climax, however, at the end of the summer and in early autumn of 1889, when the second reading of the contentious Tithe Bill was reaching its crescendo in the House of Commons. At Llandrindod Wells on 3 September, at an executive meeting of the National Council of the two federations, which he believed was a totally ineffective and unrepresentative body, Lloyd George did not deliver a speech, but seconded Thomas Gee's resolution that the tithe was an insult to Wales and an immoral iniquity and that every means should be used to prevent its collection. In a letter from Llandrindod Wells to his wife, Margaret, he noted 'that the meeting had been extremely lively and that resolutions had been passed, which would be a shock to the weak Welsh Liberals and tepid Liberal M.P.'s of the Principality'.[26] The Liberal hierarchy at the meeting, however, refused to accept Gee and Lloyd George's resolution, indicating that acceptance of such a resolution would be a personal insult to Gladstone, who was himself an Anglican and ill-disposed to the question of Welsh disestablishment. However, at Llandrindod, Lloyd George secured a place for himself on the National Council, hoping that he could reconstruct it into a thorough and radical nationalist body, which would also organize a campaign of civil disobedience against the collection of the tithe to the Anglican Church. Following this meeting, a leading article appeared in the 18 September edition of *Y Genedl Gymreig*, criticizing the moderate and lukewarm structure and representation of the Council of the Federations and their reluctance to support tithe and Church reform.[27] Lloyd George's close friend and co-Cymru Fyddite, R. A. Griffith, was the author of the article.

R. A. Griffith and Lloyd George were further incensed at the end of the same month, when the NWLF, at a Blaenau Ffestiniog meeting, confirmed its support for the reactionary resolutions proposed earlier at Llandrindod. The mainspring of orthodox, anti-nationalist Liberalism on the NWLF and the council, A. C. Humphreys-Owen of Glansevern, who had been defeated by Lloyd George for the Caernarfon Boroughs nomination, was particularly pleased with the Blaenau Ffestiniog meeting. He wrote to Stuart Rendel, the leading Gladstonian, MP for Montgomeryshire and Gladstone's confidant:

> This is a triumph for us, because as usual the emptiness and futility of George and his policy were exposed and beaten in a fair discussion . . . The men who lead Wales are the moderates . . . not the young fire-eaters. Lloyd George was soundly routed by J. E. Powell and had not a word to say for himself.[28]

However, the resolutions passed both at Llandrindod and at Blaenau Ffestiniog, which negated Lloyd George's initiative to transform the Welsh Liberal organization into a militant movement, were a further incentive for him and his nationalist sympathizers to continue to press for Liberal reconstruction nationwide. That further initiative came in October 1889 at Caernarfon, at the AGM of the NWLF and at a Welsh National Council meeting held at the same time. At the centrepoint of his prospective constituency, Lloyd George took the, as yet, boldest initiative of his political career, challenging not only the leaders of Welsh Liberalism, but also the London hierarchy of the party. He was determined that he was, above all, a Welsh nationalist radical, intent on making a revolutionary breakthrough in Welsh politics and, by so doing, convincing his future electors that it was necessary to reconstruct and democratise Welsh politics in the direction of Cymru Fydd.

Typically, Lloyd George, the consummate professional politician, had prepared carefully prior to the meeting, before delivering his call to overthrow the Welsh Liberal organization. A day before the meeting, he and his fellow agitator, R. A. Griffith, had published a long and detailed letter in the powerful Welsh Liberal newspaper, the *South Wales Daily News*, outlining their plan of action to transform Liberal politics in Wales.[29] In this article, Lloyd George condemned bitterly both the Welsh National Council and the North Wales Federation, by calling for their replacement by a new movement; in the Welsh-language weekly, *Y Werin*, preceding the meeting they published a similar article.[30] A Welsh National League would be established in place of the council with the following aims: (i) disestablishment; (ii) nationalizing the tithe for public spending; (iii) reforming the land laws; (iv) a federal parliament for Wales; (v) promoting new Liberalism in Wales with a labourist agenda; and (vi) returning to parliament representatives of the common people of Wales to secure above all the aims of the league. In many respects, this proposed league mirrored Lloyd George's future new and controversial Cymru Fydd League of 1894–6.

The plan also included the democratic election of the new council and executive of thirty-nine members, which would be chosen by committees in every parliamentary constituency, those committees having been elected by ordinary members in every branch. The details of the proposed new structure had, therefore, been prepared in detail beforehand, with a view to undermining old laissez-faire Liberalism in Wales and seeking to distance Welsh politics from London control.

On 17 October, the new proposals were placed before the National Council at Caernarfon, with that meeting presided over by the leading British Liberal (hostile to such widespread changes), William Harcourt. R. A. Griffith proposed the motion, seconded by the loquacious young Cymru Fyddite, William Jones of Bethesda, who would by 1895 replace the moderate, English-born Gladstonian, W. A. Rathbone, as the new member for the Arfon (north Caernarfonshire) Consituency.[31] While addressing the meeting, William Jones stressed the main priority of the new movement was to acquire Home Rule for Wales – an initiative, which raised a storm of protest. Even Thomas Gee was unprepared to accept such a revolutionary proposal and insisted that, though he had some sympathy for Lloyd George and his faction, the proposals were over-ambitious and that precedence should be given to tithe and Church reform. Thomas Gee was not always the uncompromising advocate of self-government that some historians have claimed and, indeed, he had quietly withdrawn from pressing the case for 'Home Rule All Round' in 1886, when such a proposal had resulted in lowest sales figures for his *Baner ac Amserau Cymru*.

Other leading Liberals at the Caernarfon meeting also raised fervent objections to the Cymru Fydd proposals, which were certainly led by Lloyd George. In their midst was the redoubtable figurehead of the Welsh Independent denomination, the Revd Dr Herber Evans, who had been asked in 1888 to stand as the parliamentary candidate for the Caernarfon Boroughs by a coterie of orthodox Liberals, in order to stop Lloyd George's charge for the constituency.[32] At the tempestuous Caernarfon meeting, Herber Evans, regarded as being one of Wales's premier orators, even by Lloyd George, attacked the Cymru Fydd proposals, claiming that they would cause a split in the Liberal ranks in Wales, especially in the Caernarfon constituency. He pressed for a committee to be established forthwith to inquire into Lloyd George's proposals – a clear stalling tactic to spike his aspirations and those of his nationalist colleagues.

Lloyd George undaunted, however, by Herber Evans's intervention, rose, and in an inflammatory speech, not only attacked Caernarfon's most prestigious minister of religion, but also accused vehemently Welsh Liberal leaders of prevarication and, indeed, cowardice. He further claimed that the hierarchy was seeking to keep the Welsh working class from participating in Liberal politics, as they feared that a new, self-governing Wales would bring about new taxation measures to effect social and economic changes.[33] According to widespread press reaction, this attack was constantly heckled, but Lloyd George proceeded, in the most extreme oration he had ever delivered up to that stage in his career, to insist that the new proposals were the only way forward for the future of Welsh radicalism. The meeting, however, refused to ratify his proposals and postponed any further discussion of the issues raised in a pioneering and highly controversial step – long before the Cymru Fydd League was set up in 1894. Despite the failure of the venture, however, which had caused such hostility at Caernarfon, Lloyd George had gained considerable publicity for the Home Rule cause and was determined that his proposals would again be aired.

Some Liberal newspapers responded to the fracas by supporting his new scheme: weeklies such as the *Genedl* papers[34] and the nationalist and socialist journal edited by E. Pan Jones and supported by Lloyd George's nationalist mentor, Michael D. Jones, *Y Celt*. It claimed that the Caernarfon meeting had been a 'moral victory for the reformers' – emphasizing that Home Rule for Wales was of far greater importance for Wales than disestablishment of the Anglican Church.[35] However, the majority of Liberal papers, such as Gee's *Baner ac Amserau Cymru*[36] and the Independent sect's weekly, *Y Tyst*,[37] were hostile. The latter, closely supervised by Herber Evans, alleged on 25 October that 'extremist young men' represented Lloyd George's militant faction, while, not unexpectedly, the Conservative-leaning, influential, Liberal Calvinistic Methodist weekly, *Y Goleuad*, vented its spleen upon the plan.[38] The Conservative local weeklies were overjoyed at the split in the Liberal ranks, whilst the Tory daily paper, the *Western Mail*, on 19 October, was especially vindictive, alleging:

> Parnellism is the model after which Mr. Lloyd George and his friends would form Home Rule – no discussion but strict obedience to the dicta of a clique.[39]

Indeed, in the 1880s Lloyd George had certainly been ready to push further than any other Welsh politician, including Tom Ellis MP, the thorny issue of Home Rule, hoping then that he had three more years for this advanced view to become acceptable to his electors before he faced a general election. A few months later, he proceeded to raise the temperature further on the question of Home Rule for Wales.

The climax of this agitation, before the unexpected by-election in the Caernarfon Boroughs in March 1890, came at a highly contentious meeting of the South Wales Liberal Federation, at Cardiff in February 1890. Here he was to take his crusade for self-government on to an even higher plane than that at Caernarfon. At his first ever public meeting in south Wales, and against the background of greater public attention than he had ever previously secured, he placed the emphasis in his speech before a crowded meeting upon the need for Welsh Liberals to give priority to Home Rule. He insisted that this was the only course to take, in view of frequent Tory or insipid Liberal governments (and the inevitable opposition of the House of Lords to any reforming programme), to bring about the fulfilment of Welsh national aspirations, including matters of industrial and social reform. The *Carnarvon and Denbigh Herald* noted that his oration at Cardiff was of momentous, historical significance: 'It was the first important political gathering at which the principle of Home Rule for Wales, as a fundamental plank of the Welsh Liberal Federation was adopted.'[40]

The paper added, though, that despite the seeming acceptance of Home Rule there, the majority of those present at the meeting appeared to be lukewarm in their response to such a pioneering objective. Nevertheless, Welsh Liberalism's most widely read daily paper, the *South Wales Daily News*, reported that never had a more reasonable case for Welsh self-government been conveyed publicly in modern Welsh history by such convincing advocates as Lloyd George and by two other speakers, the trade unionist, W. J. Parry and the labourist Liberal member from Swansea, David Randell (who later became a Labour member) and whose presence (and friendship) alongside Lloyd George, showed that the case for Welsh Home Rule was underpinned not only by Nonconformist issues, but also by working-class social, economic and welfare considerations.[41]

Not surprisingly, Lloyd George's efforts at Cardiff were also praised in the Caernarfon *Genedl* papers, with the *North Wales Observer and Express* carrying the arresting headline: 'North Wales Liberal Federation – The Timid: South Wales Liberal Federation – The Bold.'[42] Then in an editorial article *The South Wales Daily News* singled out Lloyd George for special praise: 'We believe he belongs to that class of young and rising Welshmen who will in the future prove to be the pride of the Welsh people.'[43]

The Liberal *Cambrian News*, circulating in the southernmost boroughs of his prospective constituency, though antagonistic to his 'Home Rule All Round' foray in 1886, was equally supportive,[44] while, more predictably, the monthly journal *Cymru Fydd*, was more euphoric in its comments, claiming somewhat optimistically that: 'Glamorgan and Monmouth have already raised the cry in favour of the Welsh people.'[45]

However, the Liberal press was far from being wholeheartedly enraptured by the Cardiff meeting, nor enamoured of Lloyd George's pioneering vision for Wales. Though the *Carnarvon and Denbigh Herald* that week praised his south Wales debut, it emphasized that Welsh Liberalism should pause and take stock before embarking on such a contentious initiative: 'Wales needed time to develop before attaining Home Rule. She should, at first, be content to demand as a first instalment – a National Council with only administrative functions.'[46] The paper then added in another article the following day: 'Home Rule should not be pushed forward so as to obstruct the movement for the disestablishment of the Welsh Church and the reform of the Land Laws.'[47]

Tom Ellis, who was recuperating from illness in Egypt during this period, was privately pleased at the innovative initiatives taken by Lloyd George, W. J. Parry and Randell at Cardiff, writing to the 'Quarryman's champion': 'The momentous adoption of Welsh Home Rule was a striking indication of the ripening of public opinion on the issue.'[48]

However, this view was not shared by all: the *Western Mail* claimed that Lloyd George intervention at the Cardiff conference had been a failure, stressing that 'Lloyd George and W. J. Parry must have felt themselves out of their element in the atmosphere of Cardiff.'[49]

Despite the fact that there was a mixed reception and cross-currents of public and press reaction to the historic meeting at Cardiff, and despite the implicit assertion in several newspapers, and Liberal circles, that Wales was not yet ripe for Home Rule, Lloyd George had certainly succeeded in winning much publicity for his crusade and had secured much favourable personal attention as an effective and fearless politician. With Tom Ellis ill, Lloyd George had taken over the leadership of the emergent nationalist movement. In the peroration of his speech at Cardiff, he had sounded the clarion call of his nationalist stance: 'That would self-government be granted to Wales, she would be a model to the nationalities of the Earth of a people who had driven oppression from their hillsides and initiated the glorious reign of freedom, justice and truth.'[50] Though couched in a rhetoric flourish, these words reflected a passionate commitment to Welsh nationalism within a federal context, with its own parliament acting as a visionary legislative body, as he emphasized:

> You have pledged yourselves to Disestablishment, Land Reform, Local option and other great reforms. But, however drastic and broad they may appear to be, they after all simply touch the fringe of that *vast social question*, which must be dealt with in the near future.[51]

This 'vast social question' was obviously a reference to the need for a self-governing Wales to effect fundamental social welfare changes with Lloyd George, even at this embryonic stage, becoming increasingly aware of the needs of both the rural and urban working classes – a factor given dubious credence by many historians of his first decade in politics from 1886 to 1896 (see in particular chapters VIII and IX). W.R.P. George has commented that this awareness of the social question signified clearly that 'his political concern and vision extended beyond granting self-government for Wales'.[52] But this surely is misleading. Rather, it can be contended that he was envisaging a devolved parliament not only fulfilling Nonconformist aspirations, but also effecting itself widespread social welfare changes for the people of Wales, especially its least privileged class. And, undoubtedly, when he came to lead the Cymru Fydd League campaign in 1894–6, this new organization, as distinct from the earlier Cymru Fydd Society of the late 1880s and early 1890s, was committed to labour and social welfare reforms – a parliamentary model of what he had termed in Cardiff in 1890 as a system empowering 'a people who had driven oppression from their hillsides and initiated the glorious reign of freedom, justice and truth'.

Nevertheless, his crusade for self-government, as evinced at Caernarfon and Cardiff in 1889–90 (within both the Liberal Federation and the County Council Chamber), met many obstacles and opposition from within the less progressive elements in his own party ranks. Yet, after the Cardiff SWLF meeting in February 1890, at a Pwllheli meeting and then at a packed Caernarfon gathering, he delivered powerful speeches on the theme 'Lessons from Welsh history', drawing upon the Irish example of an independent Irish nationalist party which Wales should follow, while calling for Welsh self-government to be accorded equal status and priority as Irish Home Rule.[53] Perhaps Lloyd George was no academically trained intellectual from an university ivory tower, as K. O. Morgan has intimated, but he drew political parallels from Wales's past, while delivering these orations on Welsh history and there is some evidence that he spent part of his scarce spare time in reading up on Welsh history and gleaning support for his nationalist standpoint from such sources and from his more widely educated Cymru Fydd colleagues.

As he was delivering these orations upon radical and nationalist aspirations, he had had only fourteen months since his election as a prospective parliamentary candidate in which to cultivate his constituency and, no doubt, felt that more time was needed for his aims to be made more acceptable. However, at the very same time that this campaign was developing, he was faced with the far from welcome and sensational news that he would have to face an immediate by-election in the Caernarfon Boroughs. In March 1890, the sitting Conservative MP, Edmund Swetenham, suffered a fatal accident, perhaps significantly while out hunting, dying from pneumonia after a heavy and lethal fall while hounding the fox.

Therefore, Lloyd George had to face a premature campaign, which would focus considerable attention on him even in the London press, as many local by-election candidates experienced. The campaign, as the Conservative government entered upon its fifth year in power, would be of considerable concern to the Liberal Party, especially at its London headquarters, which naturally hoped that every single by-election victory for them would weaken and undermine Lord Salisbury's administration. Such concerns would bring massive pressure to bear on Lloyd George from the Liberal hierarchy in the constituency, in Wales and in Britain to toe the party line in a marginal, cosmopolitan constituency where an outspoken and controversial radical nationalist, only fourteen months into his prospective parliamentary candidature, was felt by many to be a dangerous loose cannon who had created for himself an extreme public image.

One factor was certain. The by-election would be engrossing and explosive and would prove to be a memorable and contentious battle, an extraordinary contest in Welsh history, made even more exciting by the fact that his suddenly chosen opponent would be none other than the Llanystumdwy squire, Ellis Nanney, whose presence and wealth dominated Lloyd George's boyhood village and the person he had staged a childhood rebellion against at the village's Anglican elementary school. The self-baptized 'Nationalist' candidate for the Boroughs in 1888 now faced the first great crossroad in his public career; with enemies within his own party in his locality, failure would surely mean potential political extinction at the age of twenty-six. Not only Tories, but many Welsh Liberals no doubt, hoped for such an outcome as he entered upon a campaign, which could cast him, perhaps terminally, into the political wilderness.

In March 1890, he faced the greatest political dilemma of his yet unproven career. Would he stand in the election on a high-risk nationalist-radical platform, or would he have to bow to political pressures and adopt, if only temporarily, a more pragmatic role in the election, as the public spotlight on a widespread scale was turned upon him?

VII

THE CAERNARFON BOROUGHS BY-ELECTION, 1890: THE NATIONALIST-RADICAL PRAGMATIST

Lloyd George was placed in an invidious position as he faced his first ever parliamentary election because the constituency was Tory held and had in its composition, socially, economically and in its religious sphere, a far from promising scenario for an advanced radical-nationalist. The six constituent boroughs of the Caernarfon Boroughs – Cricieth, Pwllheli, Nefyn, Conwy, Bangor and Caernarfon, particularly the latter three – were far more Anglicized than the two other Caernarfonshire constituencies, Eifion and Arfon – created after the Third Reform Act of 1884 and the Redistribution Act of 1885. It remained after the extension to the suffrage by these acts a comparatively small electorate, with Anglicanism and landlord-capitalist interests particularly strong in Caernarfon and Bangor and with the Conwy borough becoming increasingly Anglicized.

In the general election of 1886, the Tories had won the seat, in contrast to the huge majorities gained by the Liberals in the quarrying, agricultural constituencies of Arfon and Eifion – with their substantial slate and quarrying electorates of both granite and slate quarrymen voters. Moreover, since 1886, divisiveness and prevarication had characterized Liberal politics, following the loss of the seat by the maverick Liberal, Whiggish landowner Love Jones Parry (Madryn), whose raucous and wild lifestyle of womanizing and drunkenness had antagonized the predominantly Nonconformist Liberal electors.[1] In addition, long before 1886, though the Liberals, in name, at least, had held the seat since the 1832 Reform Act, the constituency's parliamentary representatives had been Whigs or had been turncoats from the Tories, such as Bulkeley Hughes of Plas Coch, Love Jones Parry's predecessor. Apart from a brief interval in the 1860s, he had held the seat between 1837 and 1882, as his own personal fiefdom, and was hardly a radical in any sense. He had, moreover, been a colourless and quiescent member who had made little impact at Westminster. Indeed, since 1868, he had not been challenged in any election and thus had not been impelled to adopt any significant radical policies during his long and humdrum tenure of the Boroughs. After Hughes's death in 1882, Love Jones Parry had inherited the seat and likewise took no radical steps to galvanize the electorate – his one and only contribution to Welsh public life being his early involvement, which was not entirely satisfactory, in contributing to Y Wladfa, the Welsh colony in Patagonia. He secured the seat in the 1885 election, by the skin of his teeth, despite the extension to the suffrage, his majority minority reflecting how Conservative were many Nonconformists in their political allegiance, particularly many Calvinistic Methodists, the predominant sect in the constituency.

It was thus no easy task for Lloyd George, coming from a completely different socially and religious background to Bulkeley Hughes and Love Jones Parry, to capture the seat – despite the enlargement of the electorate since 1885. The voters of the boroughs had been used to landowning Liberals (or a Tory estate agent and barrister in Edmund Swetenham after 1886) rather then a new-style breakthrough politician. The onset of a more democratic electorate after 1885 must not be exaggerated, moreover, as the extension to the vote was particularly insubstantial in the borough electorates generally, and in the Caernarfon Boroughs in particular. By 1890, the Caernarfon Boroughs electorate had increased only marginally since 1885. In 1890, the electorate numbered only 4,628 voters, an increase of only 152 voters since 1885 – a rise of only 3.6 per cent and a rise of only 12.6 per cent since the 1880 election. For a democrat and radical like Lloyd George, these figures did not give much ground for optimism as the champion of the newly emancipated.

Indeed, a survey of the electoral registers of the boroughs, which have survived in historical archives, reflect how much of a middle-class constituency was Lloyd George's hoped-for base, with many electors dependent for their livelihoods in professional and business ranks on the largesse of the Tory landowning-industrialists of the area, with their financial/business and property interests in the boroughs. Moreover, the registers reveal how small was the percentage of those who voted in the working-class areas of each borough.[2] For example, in the borough of Caernarfon, according to the electoral register of 1891, only 1,476 voted out of a population of 9,804 people aged over twenty-one, with only 15 lodger voters on the register. In the poorest streets of the town, the back-to-back 'courts', very few had the vote, in places such as Palace Street 'Court' (one vote) and Elisa's 'Court' (one vote). Conversely, in a more respectable working-class street, such as Assheton Terrace, although the majority there possessed no vote, 16 voted. However, in the middle-class areas of the town, the voters were much more numerous, for example in North Road – where leading Tories such as Issard Davies lived alongside the prosperous businessman and moderate Gladstonian Liberal, Henry Jonathan – every one of the 37 householders had the vote. Similar voting patterns were to be found in the middle-class streets of professional and businessmen householders, such as South Road, Bangor Street and St David's Road. The town also had military voters on the register in 1891, the service voters associated with the town's barracks. Nine officers at the barracks had the vote, almost invariably Tories, while 37 servicemen also voted – no doubt following their officers in their political sympathies.

A similar mix of voters was revealed by the Cricieth register of 1891, with only 249 of the adult population voting out of a total of 1,410 aged over twenty-one. As in Caernarfon, the local outlying gentry had property votes in the borough, while the town had several businessmen, craftsmen and self-employed fishermen on the register. But a minimal number voted in the poorest areas, such as Lon Bach and Dinas Terrace and, perhaps significantly, as Lloyd George in 1890 lived with his in-laws at Mynydd Ednyfed, even he did not feature on the electoral roll. Several farmers who lived within the borough confines also had the vote.

Similarly, Nefyn had a limited electorate in 1891, where only 366 voted out of an adult population of 1,798 and at Pwllheli where there were only 587 with the vote out of a population of 3,231. The majority of the male working class were voteless, with the vote concentrated in the hands of the town's businessmen and professionals; voters were sparse in streets such as Sand Street, where many granite quarrymen lived.

It can be gleaned from this brief survey of electoral rolls (because the evidence for Bangor and Conwy is not available)[3] that the electorate consisted, in the main, of a solid middle class, craftsmen and the self-employed and a modicum of working-class voters, who had secured the vote after 1885. Indeed, as only 33.7 per cent of males over twenty-one had the vote, in 1891, it was obvious that the Caernarfon Boroughs electorate was a very limited one – despite several personal initiatives by Lloyd George, after his selection as a parliamentary candidate, to get entitled voters to register their right to vote. The electorate was also far from being fertile territory for Lloyd George to cultivate on a socio-linguistic basis. The census of 1891 revealed that the vast majority of the 8,118 of monoglot English speakers who lived in Caernarfonshire, out of a population of 119,349 would be citizens of the boroughs, rather than living in the overwhelmingly Welsh-language Eifion and Arfon constituencies.

The constitution of the Caernarfon Boroughs thus presented great obstacles to the militant Lloyd George as he faced his first election – with a population who were hardly in tune with his radical-nationalist stance. In addition, the minority element of the working class who were emancipated had been conditioned and influenced by their economic dependence on the large, landowning, industrial monopolists of the area, to vote Tory during Salisbury's administration, while many such voters, particularly in the Bangor borough, were under the influence of Anglicanism in the cathedral city, with its economic life dominated by the Penrhyn interest. Indeed, as at Bangor, so, too, throughout the boroughs, Conservative clubs flourished. Bangor had three such establishments, in addition to a flourishing branch of the Conservative Ladies' Primrose League, rendering the university city the most Anglican and Conservative of the six boroughs. As the results of the first Caernarfonshire County Council elections in 1889 had demonstrated, too, the Tories had secured a majority of seats, not only at Bangor, but also, significantly, at Caernarfon, where there was strong Tory support, and at Conwy. Conwy and Caernarfon were garrison towns, renowned for their British jingoism and Conservatism, with Caernarfon boasting since the mid-1880s a new, grand and imposing Conservative Workingmen's Club, patronized by the Faenol and Glynllifon landed gentry and industrialists; Caernarfon also had two English-cause chapels, built by 1890, with many middle-class Welsh-speaking members of their congregations. Criccieth and Pwllheli, too, had their 'English cause' establishments – hardly centres of goodwill towards the pioneering initiatives undertaken by Lloyd George to bring status to the Welsh language in Wales's public life. In his own borough of Criccieth, he had to contend not only with two Anglican churches, but also with the members of 'the English cause' chapel established so controversially there. Neither would he find favour amongst the elite who patronized the town's flourishing tennis club, nor the local Conservative Club, which was as active as similar establishments at Pwllheli and at Nefyn.

Sectarian jealously was also rife within the boroughs – the denominationalist hostility which Lloyd George had encountered while he courted his Calvinistic Methodist sweetheart, Margaret Owen. The Calvinistic Owen family regarded the 'Little Baptists' with derision because they were poor and radical in politics and theology. This hostility towards them was shared by other denominations throughout the area, but not to the same degree by the Independents. The Campbellite Baptists had undoubtedly contributed to Lloyd George's political radicalism and egalitarian views as they used their Sunday collections to care for members sticken by illness and unemployment. Nevertheless, his denomination was by far the least numerous, in the six boroughs, as Thomas Gee's unofficial religious census showed in 1889, with the conservative-inclined Calvinists by far the majority, while Anglicanism was powerful at Conwy and especially at Bangor. This religious make-up stood in sharp contrast to the situation in the Eifion and Arfon constituencies, with their large

Nonconformist followings; in the more urban and snobbish boroughs the Campbellite Baptist was at a distinct disadvantage, despite his marriage to Margaret, who remained a lifelong Calvinist. Lloyd George's friend and Cymru Fydd League colleague in the early 1890s, the quixotic and colourful newspaperman and dramatist, Beriah Gwynfe Evans, emphasized in his biography of Lloyd George how much of a handicap his Campbellite Baptist background was to him in the constituency in 1890:

> That of the four dissenting sects in the constituency, that to which he belonged was the weakest in numbers, in influence and in worldly wealth and when he entered the lists, the various non-conformist bodies, each aspiring to political power, regarded each other with almost as great distrust as that which they regarded the Established Church.[4]

Indeed, Beriah Gwynfe Evans claimed that even in the westernmost borough of Nefyn the Tory influence was strong amongst Nonconformists and that the orthodox Baptists there (as distinct from the Small Baptists) were not supportive of him. He claimed somewhat exaggeratedly that 'not one Baptist there supported him in the by-election of 1890'.[5]

In addition to sectarian difficulties and the other socio-economic and political disadvantages facing him on the eve of the election, Lloyd George also possessed many plus points as he faced the challenge before him. In particular, he was the first in the race, with his presence as a candidate since late 1889, who had striven ubiquitously to cultivate the constituency. On the other hand, due to Swetenham's unexpected demise, the Tories not only were shaken but had to decide suddenly, without having a potentially strong Welsh-speaking contender as a readily available candidate, to choose a successor to Edmund Swetenham, who had created no reputation as a parliamentarian. Lloyd George's advantage in this respect was highlighted by the *South Wales Daily News*, which intimated that he had begun campaigning even before Swetenham's funeral: 'Mr George has not let the grass grow from under his feet . . . he has already met with an enthusiasm which augurs well for his chances . . . In marked contrast is the frantic flutter of the Conservatives.'[6]

It was certainly no easy task for the Tories to choose a candidate in a state of some considerable panic in their ranks. Only after much soul-searching was Ellis Nanney prevailed upon to fill the breach, after he had refused publicly to stand at the first time of asking. Rumours also circulated in public and in the press that fervent and widespread efforts had previously been made by the Tory hierarchy locally to secure a more renowned and more talented politician than the Gwynfryn squire. However, all such entreaties had fallen on fallow ground, as those approached had no great desire to stand in a marginal constituency during the Tory government's mid-term unpopularity. Moreover, Ellis Nanney had failed to shine (and win) in other previous elections in the county, with the Welsh Tory daily, the *Western Mail*, revealing that on the day after his enforced selection, the paper's editorial team had little faith that he was a favourable candidate. Its editorial concluded: 'Surely, there is no lack of good men and true in the County of Caernarfon who could have been prevailed upon to stand.'[7]

Lloyd George had other clear advantages from the outset. He had at his disposal, despite insufficient time since 1889 to register all 'newly emancipated voters', an efficient election machine with his brother an effective and enthusiastic activist. The *Western Mail* had to admit, despite Lloyd George's worries on the registration front, that his campaign machinery was in good order. The paper was alarmed that:

> The Separatists (Nationalists) have their candidate well before the constituency . . . the greatest attention has been bestowed upon the registration and organisation of the Liberal Party, so that the Unionists cannot count upon the un-preparedness of their opponents.[8]

Indeed, as early as 26 March, the *Genedl* stable of newspapers – with its three separate influential organs of public opinion – had published separate, special, election editions to champion Lloyd George's candidature and deliver an explosive opening salvo to the campaign. He had a real head start with the Conservatives in initial disarray.

Moreover, the tide of electoral opinion in Wales and Britain was flowing in the Liberals' favour by early 1890. Since the general election of 1886, the Tory majority throughout Britain had fallen by March 1890, to 70 seats, after a series of by-election losses, especially in Wales.[9] Also after the 1886 election, six new, young members, the majority of them representing the Cymru Fydd interest, had been returned in Welsh constituencies, although they were far less marginal seats than the Caernarfon Boroughs; amongst these were S. T. Evans for Mid-Glamorgan and David Randell – a labourist nationalist with close connections to the tinplate workers union – for one of Swansea's constituencies.[10]

Lloyd George could take great heart from these successes, while he could obviously take advantage of the inevitable protest vote in a by-election against the governing party. He could benefit, too, from external help from Cymru Fydd sympathizers outside the boroughs and from Liberal politicians within Wales, while from further afield, politicians could be drafted into the seat to maximize the effectiveness of his campaign – despite the fact that many orthodox Liberals were wary of supporting a 'Separatist' national, radical candidate with his embryonic collectivist views.

Certainly, at the beginning of the campaign, the Liberals were quite confident of securing a victory, with the *South Wales Daily News*, as early as 25 March, declaiming that 'the Seat was in the bag',[11] while the Baptist journal, *Seren Gomer*, was smugly contending, with much exaggerated exhilaration, 'Caiff y sedd ei hennill yn hawdd' – 'The seat will be won with ease'.[12]

These highly optimistic early forecasts, however, hid the real truth and the underlying fear amongst the more staid and respectable, orthodox, Gladstonian leaders in the constituency, and at the Liberals' London headquarters, that Lloyd George's radical-nationalist views could well rebound against him and fail to secure a Liberal victory. On the eve of the poll, the Gladstonian moderate Arfon member of Parliament, the wealthy Liverpool businessman, William Rathbone, fearful of Lloyd George's 'Separatism', wrote confidentially to R. D. Williams, the long-serving and equally moderate secretary of the Caernarfon Boroughs Liberal Association, that he feared a defeat. He confessed: 'I am afraid that with Lloyd George as your candidate, he will, as you say, cause the loss of the seat'[13] – a fear obviously shared by R. D. Williams himself, whose knowledge of the highly conservative nature of the constituency was extensive and profound. R. D. Williams in 1888, too, at the height of Lloyd George's sensational and controversial attempt to win the Boroughs' candidature, had certainly sought to forestall him and, indeed, to seek a more moderate Liberal representative for the nomination and was known to have prevailed secretly upon the moderate Herber Evans to stand.

There was much hidden friction and unease within the Liberal ranks, which would become more open and strident as the campaign progressed, and, even from the outset, the local Tory press was aware of the tension between the old and new factions in the enemy's camp. *Y Gwalia*, for example, was ready to exploit the inherent differences between the Gladstonian and nationalist elements in the Liberal fold, remarking that:

It is obvious in every one of the boroughs that a majority of the Liberal Party do not want Lloyd George, because he has been pushed to the forefront by inexperienced and ambitious youngsters [*bechgynnos di-brofiad ac uchelgeisiol*], while cautious people wish to express their views freely, that while admiring Liberalism, they do not like Mr George's principles.[14]

As Lloyd George sought to cross the most challenging threshold of his career, he faced the daunting task, as a recognized leader of Young Wales, of winning a seat with its possible, if not probable, preponderance of Gladstonian Liberal supporters. With that in mind, he faced a serious and fundamental dilemma – would he bow to the official party line and trim substantially those radical-nationalist policies he had, prior to this stage, projected so prominently? And, if he followed such a course, would he be portrayed by his enemies within and without his party, as not only a pragmatist, but also, indeed, an opportunist ready to sacrifice his principles in the face of intense political pressure? This dilemma was the central problem facing him in a highly publicized campaign, when the contradictions enveloping him would be increasingly spotlighted by the Tory press, but would also be subjected to the increasing scrutiny of influential Liberal moderates, as well as the electorate as a whole.

The election campaign, which secured widespread publicity throughout Britain, started officially only two days after Swetenham's funeral, when Lloyd George published his election manifesto. This document incurred the hostility of many of his own party immediately, let alone the Tory press – hostility which characterized the whole campaign and created a split within the Liberal ranks. Two days later, Ellis Nanney's election manifesto was published, clearly couched in moderation – 'To the free and independent electors of the Caernarfon Boroughs'.[15]

Moderate in tone and content, with an element of progressive politics aimed at the working class, it brought concern and consternation to the Liberal camp. Although the manifesto emphasized his sympathy for Balfour's Irish policy and 'the Unity and Integrity of the British Empire', the document praised the Tory government's support for the Welsh Intermediate Education Act of 1889 and called for more powers for the new county councils, especially in the sphere of education. Nanney also promised further legislation to provide greater religious freedom, although noting his opposition to disestablishment of the Anglican Church in Wales. He further claimed that Salisbury's government had boosted employment and prosperity while also, surprisingly, calling for the then sitting parliamentary committee to press ahead with leasehold enfranchisement. In addition, he was in favour of reforming the Cardigan Bay fisheries and claimed that 'local economic initiatives would not be thwarted under his influence'.[16]

Nanney's manifesto, therefore, not only aimed to secure local Tory support, but was also directed craftily at Nonconformists and that element of the working class which had the vote. Not surprisingly, the Liberal press, betraying a great sense of anxiety, mercilessly attacked Nanney's moderate manifesto; the *North Wales Observer and Express* claimed that it was deceitful, 'decked in the most becoming of cast-off Radical clothing', a comment which reflected their fear that his programme could entice moderate Gladstonians and the working class, while also seducing the uncommitted voters.[17]

Lloyd George's own manifesto, carefully and pragmatically drawn up, after much soul-searching,[18] was to prove to be much more controversial and damaging than that of his opponent from Plas Gwynfryn: indeed, its contents not only were to cause ire amongst both extreme and moderate Liberals, but were also open to criticism that they were both insincere and hypocritical. Indeed, the manifesto bore no resemblance to the radical-nationalist programme he had been enunciating since 1889, but rather followed, in most respects, the Gladstonian party line. It is not possible to see how John Grigg could interpret it in the following light: 'He realised that his best issue would be Welsh Nationalism.'[19] Nor is K. O. Morgan's conclusion remotely credible that Welsh Nationalism was accorded priority in his manifesto; the issue, he asserts, 'dominated his election address in the by-election for the Caernarfon Boroughs in 1890'.[20] Rather, the converse is true. It is obvious that with pressures placed upon him by leading Liberals locally, and beyond, and by electoral considerations in a conservative, marginal constituency, he trimmed his programme considerably. Hiding his true convictions, Lloyd George adopted a highly pragmatic stance, if, albeit temporarily, in the by-election where he stood as a seemingly moderate candidate, not as a radical, nationalist advocate.

His main promise, in contradiction to his previous public statements, was that he would loyally support the Gladstonian policy of priority for Irish Home Rule, rather than for Welsh Home Rule and, indeed, Welsh disestablishment. Then there was an ambiguous reference to land and labour reform – another example of trimming his labour and land views, although he did include in his address the need for the taxation of land rent profits and taxation of the increase in land values, while also calling for an increase in graduated taxation. But the most startling moderating feature of his manifesto was the relegation of Welsh Home Rule to a statement which was couched in ambiguous language on the need for 'the Liberal extension of the principle of decentralisation'; this was a clear example of his hiding his real (and previous) commitment to federal self-government for Wales, as he faced a sudden, unexpected electoral challenge. One of the co-writers of his manifesto was his brother, William George, also a Cymru Fydd advocate, who noted that 'the manifesto embodied the reforms which were nearest to the author's heart'.[21] That is hardly true and is a gross example of history being re-written, as the manifesto had been tailored to hide, indeed, deceive those at whom it was aimed, as to Lloyd George's true beliefs.

The aim of the manifesto was to secure consensus support amongst a divided Liberal Party and several 'swing' voters and also to bow to pressure from leading Welsh and British Liberal big-wigs. Indeed, there is clear evidence in Stuart Rendel's papers that A. C. Humphreys-Owen, Rendel's confidant, had persuaded Rendel to exert pressure on Lloyd George, through the Gladstonian intermediary, J. Bryn Roberts, the Eifion MP, to temper his radical and nationalist views, or else the seat would be lost. A. C. Humphreys-Owen had written to Rendel: 'We must get pledges from Lloyd George for the cessation of the vilification which he has used persistently against the Federation'[22] – implying that he should fight the election on official Gladstonian policy. In another missive to Rendel, an urgent message was also sent to him by A. D. Acland, MP, who assured him: 'The moderate men are in line with us.'[23] It was obvious that much pressure had been placed upon Lloyd George to toe the official line, not only on electoral grounds but, no doubt, on financial grounds, too, for he was dependent, as an impecunious young solicitor, on official Liberal financial support to conduct the campaign.

It was also obvious, from some Liberal press reports, that his moderate line pleased official Liberals. The Gladstonian weekly, the *Caernarfon and Denbigh Herald* (and its Welsh-language counterpart, *Yr Herald Cymraeg*) – both of whom turned against him during the campaign, for financial advertising motives – at the outset welcomed his 'accommodating' election address. The *Caernaron and Denbigh Herald* stated in late March: 'The Manifesto appeals to all sound Liberals and wisely avoids the few controversial topics upon which his enemies and a handful of injudicious friends, would wish to see him impaled.'[24] This comment obviously referred to his previous support for unconstitutional tithe agitation, land nationalization proposals and Welsh Home Rule, although the manifesto did support graduated, progressive taxation.

The London correspondent of the seemingly radical and sometimes nationalist *Baner ac Amserau Cymru*, Y Gohebydd, also welcomed Lloyd George's moderating stance in his manifesto. He welcomed the fact that 'he had the common sense to be responsible by moderating his policies'.[25] However, *Y Genedl Gymreig* – a paper which had done so much to get him selected as the nationalist-radical candidate for the Boroughs in 1888 – had to struggle, in its editorial of that week, to defend his manifesto, by declaring: 'It should satisfy the objectives of the progressive elements in the party without causing problems for the most zealous advocates of traditional Liberalism.'[26] This was a somewhat paradoxical statement, which underlined the dilemma which was to face Lloyd George throughout the campaign.

Indeed, the Tory press immediately began to exploit this dichotomy in Lloyd George's election address and its somewhat duplicitous character, attacking him for his humdrum Liberalism, when he was really a nationalist agitator. For example, the *North Wales Chronicle* poured scorn on his pragmatism, claiming that much pressure had been placed on him to sacrifice his convictions for political gain and that he had dropped Home Rule for Wales from his manifesto when he was 'one of the most pronounced representatives of Young Wales'.[27] The *Chronicle* added, with much truth and venom, 'if he believes in what he preaches in South

Wales, he does not muster sufficient coverage to enunciate the same to the Caernarfon Boroughs.'[28] The paper also noted he had relegated disestablishment to second place in his manifesto, giving priority to Irish Home Rule.

More damning to Lloyd George's prospects of winning the by-election was the fact that this Tory indictment was not confined to the Conservative press. Indeed, criticism emanated, more damagingly, from Liberal quarters desiring Welsh disestablishment to be placed ahead of Home Rule for Ireland in any future Liberal government policy – contrary to Lloyd George's manifesto.

This opposition, from the heart of his constituency, reflected in the Liberal press, came with his first platform appearance at Caernarfon during the hustings. Caernarfon's most notable Calvinistic Methodist minister, the Revd Evan Jones, Moriah, the redoubtable and loquacious preacher, obsessed with the need to diminish the power of the Anglican Church, intervened when Lloyd George was speaking and delivered a stunning attack upon his manifesto – highlighting his affected spineless Gladstonianism and his relegation of disestablishment to a secondary role in his priorities. He added further grist to the Tory mill, when he expressed the view that it was a deceitful stand to take and belied his true beliefs. According to the press, Lloyd George tried, unsuccessfully, to counter his arguments but was shouted down, whereupon Jones left the meeting and disarray ensued. The *Western Mail* correspondent reported with glee the carnage caused by Jones's intervention,[29] while also drawing attention, with much delight, to the fact that the Liberal *Carnarvon and Denbigh Herald* had already given Jones, in a poisonous column, much space to condemn Lloyd George.[30] The Anglican Tory weekly, *Y Llan a'r Dywysogaeth*, revelled in the chaos in the Liberal ranks,[31] while *Y Gwalia*, somewhat hypocritically, but with great effect, claimed that 'Jones was far more principled and consistent than Lloyd George'.[32]

The Liberals' daily organ, the *South Wales Daily News*, sought to paper over the cracks in the Liberal manifesto caused by Jones's intervention, but could only comment: 'Of the nonconformists in the district, the Calvinistic Methodists are the dominant sect . . . and it is somewhat unfortunate that the Rev. Evan Jones should have come into collision with his fellow Liberals.'[33]

A similar line was adopted by the same week's edition of the *North Wales Observer and Express*, which insisted that Jones's remarks had been delivered at a particularly unfortunate juncture and in the vital borough of Caernarfon, while the Methodist's own weekly paper, *Y Goleuad*, tried to calm the ruffled waters by calling on their members to 'cau'r bwlch yn syth' (to heal the rift immediately) between Jones and Lloyd George.[34] However, no compromise emerged throughout the election and much damage was done to Lloyd George's campaign, in which he had many advantages at the outset.

As a consequence of the rift, he had to redouble his efforts to canvass and campaign and to deploy his undoubted oratorical skills in a negative exercise to deflect criticism personally upon his opponent, who was neither a talented politician nor an orator. A survey of the papers of his election agent (J. T. Roberts, a Caernarfon solicitor, who was dropped as his agent after the campaign) reveals considerable canvassing activity and widespread pleas for support for the beleaguered Liberal candidate, with appeals to politicians throughout Britain to come to the Boroughs.[35] Letters and telegrams to politicians, ministers of religion, representatives of pressure groups and trade unions were despatched urgently for aid through personal appearances, canvassing and financial backing and the sending of resolutions in Lloyd George's favour to be read out at public meetings or to be printed in the press.

Moreover, local poets were prevailed upon to send *englynion* – short, strict-metre verses – to be published in the press, praising 'the Cottage-bred boy'. Also, the 'varied' talents of local verse writers were deployed to write songs, which could be sung during election meetings and marches. Indeed, the singing talents of the Liberal trade unionist, William Abraham MP, the miners' trade unionist from Glamorgan, were to become a feature of the campaign, as 'Mabon', an Eisteddfod star, not only came to the constituency to extol Lloyd George's labourism but also to sing his praises. Also, the most redoubtable preacher of the Wesleyan denomination, the Revd John Evans of Eglwysbach, came to praise him as did the moderate but extremely eloquent Independent leader, Dr Herber Evans (loud in his criticism of Cymru Fydd) and Thomas Gee, whose paper took a somewhat ambivalent standpoint during the contest.

Indeed, Dr Herber Evans took a prominent role in the campaign and even went so far as to dismiss allegations that he had previously opposed Lloyd George's selection as the Boroughs candidate and that he shared the same standpoint on disestablishment as Evan Jones – both comments which certainly varnished the truth. Then Thomas Gee resorted, in a public meeting, to a Methodist *rhodd mam* inquisition of Lloyd George, whereby he hoped to persuade the audience that Lloyd George was a loyal Liberal – his presence at the Penrhyn Hall, Bangor, alongside Herbert Gladstone, the Liberal leader's son, being supposedly public proof that everyone was unified in the Liberal cause, according to the *North Wales Observer and Express*.[36] While Mabon was touring the constituency singing 'Unuwch y Blaid' (Unite the Party), the Irish MP, S. T. O'Connor, was also invited to address public meetings, in order to seek to counter the highly effective Tory tactics of bringing Ulster Presbyterian ministers and Unionist politicians to the predominantly Methodist constituency to attack the Liberals' Irish Home Rule Policy and win the Protestant vote. Lloyd George was also to secure the support of S. T. Evans, the newly elected MP for Mid-Glamorgan, but it was clear that several Cymru Fyddites were accorded a minimal role at the Liberal Party's major meetings – a move tailored to prevent the contest from becoming an overtly radical campaign.

During the final days, Lloyd George had organized monster meetings in the two most populous, northern boroughs. At Caernarfon, S. T. Evans, Herber Evans, Mabon and Britain's leading temperance reformer, Sir Wilfrid Lawson, spoke, while the last meeting at Bangor was graced by none other than the symbol of British Gladstonian Liberalism, Stuart Rendel himself, allegedly present after pressure verging on blackmail, according to the Tory press. At this last meeting before the poll, Mabon once more struck the 'Unite the Party' song, betraying considerable anxiety in the Liberal fold, while both during the day and in the evenings meetings were organized in the southern boroughs, where more radical and nationalistically inclined speakers such as D. R. Daniel and Tudwal Davies carried the brunt of speech-making. On the eve of the poll, Daniel informed Lloyd George that after ten o'clock, with the polls closed, he and Liberal supporters 'had a jolly party at the Eifl Temperance, Pwllheli', with Daniel of the opinion 'that great progress has been made since the commencement of the campaign',[37] although, indisputably, it bore no resemblance to the radical-nationalist exercise engineered by Lloyd George, and assisted by Daniel in 1888, to secure Lloyd George's initial nomination for the Boroughs.

The campaign had been far from successful, despite frenetic canvassing and well-attended meetings, especially as Lloyd George found himself lodged between a rock and a hard place. Indeed, he had to manipulate the press as perceptively as he could to seek to justify his pragmatic role in the campaign. Already, as owner of *Yr Udgorn Rhyddid* at Pwllheli, he had had to exert pressure on the Liberal press locally and nationally, to support him fully to counteract the highly explosive exposés of the Tory papers. Certainly, he had the support of London-based Liberal papers while, every day, the *South Wales Daily News* sought to defend him from the *Western Mail*'s frequent jibes. Also, because he had stuck to a moderate line which had been forced upon him after much soul-searching, he gained the support of the ambivalent Thomas Gee's *Baner ac Amserau Cymru* – not always the uncompromising champion of national self-determination and certainly wary of 'labourist issues'.[38]

Perhaps his most trusted and effective support came, however, from the *Genedl* papers, which, despite their discomfiture at his pragmatic pose during the election, nevertheless gave him widespread publicity and counter-attacked the *Herald*'s negative stance towards him in the campaign.

The *North Wales Observer and Express* was particularly supportive, noting, for example, in its eve-of-poll edition that on personal grounds it was 'no contest between the quicksilver dynamic talents of the alleged "Cottage-bred boy" and the Squire of Gwynfryn'. In its editorial, it sailed close to the wind of libel, when it stated: 'So we might say that the present struggle is one between intelligence and . . . well something, which we must leave our readers to designate for themselves.'[39]

Y Genedl[40] and *Y Werin*[41] bordered equally on the vitriolic, attacking vociferously 'The Tory screw', with many allegations that the Tories were plying the poorest voters with bribes of free coal, food and alcohol accompanied by allegations of Tory landlords' threats of eviction to those who rented houses, businesses and smallholdings, who dared to vote Conservative. There were also allegations of religious prejudice and Tory tactics of 'libelling publicly the students of the Bangor colleges', particularly divinity students from the Bala-Bangor Independent College.

The *Genedl* stable's most vital contribution to Lloyd George's campaign, however, was to publish at the eleventh hour three special eve-of-poll editions of their newspapers, aware as they were that the result was too close to call. These editions were also impelled by the publication from the *Herald* company of an edition of the *Carnarvon and Denbigh Herald*, a few days earlier, lambasting Lloyd George's hypocritical stance during the three-week hustings.[43] After the campaign, Lloyd George realized how critical the *Genedl* company's efforts had been, when he wrote a letter to its energetic managing editor, David Edwards, stating that: 'It was I believe of immense help to bring about the Liberal victory.'[44]

The working-class weekly published by the company, *Y Werin*, had been particularly significant, highlighting Lloyd George's support for labour and the underprivileged, while it also had published an array of songs, such as 'Si lasi ba, Si lasi basa, Lloyd George yw'r dyn i ni' (Lloyd George's the man for us), which proved to be highly effective tools of propaganda, even if they lacked true musical or literary merit.[45] *Y Werin* also published numerous letters, telegrams and messages of support for Lloyd George, often with noms de plume attached, such as 'Elector', or more incredibly, 'Owain Glyndwr'. Perhaps more credibly, letters were published from leaders of pressure groups, such as ap Ffarmwr, J. O. Jones founder of the UK Temperance Alliance, and personal letters of support from individuals as varied as Gladstone himself, Michael D. Jones the nationalist leader, Cochfarf, the Cardiff literary figure and nationalist, and Plenydd, H. J. Williams, the temperance leader in the county, as well as many ministers of religion – most notably Independents, Baptists and Wesleyans. There is little doubt that via the press, no stone was left unturned, to win the election. Yet, as the campaign closed, this flurry of press activity had been undermined by the Caernarfon *Herald* company, which had not only given free rein to Evan Jones's damaging interventions, but in mid-campaign had visibly and prominently turned against Lloyd George. In *Yr Herald Cymraeg*, on 25 March, and three days later in the *Carnarvon and Denbigh Herald*, both papers published a lengthy and vituperative attack on Lloyd George by an alleged 'Elector', which also praised Nanney as the candidate who had the wealth, experience and influence to bring, through personal and political activity, concrete benefits to the constituency.[46]

The 'Elector' also claimed that the area needed gifts of land upon which new intermediate schools could be built. This bounty would be provided by landowners such as Nanney. Only Conservatives, in government and with their capital and wealthy connections, could bring industry to the area. Furthermore, the letter writer claimed, Nanney's policy of extending the powers of local authorities was far more practical than Lloyd George's real belief in a federal system of Home Rule, which, it was claimed, would damage Wales economically and would frighten outside investment and Wales's development as a burgeoning tourist centre. The 'Elector' also claimed that Lloyd George was in favour of payment for MPs (as well as for county councillors) – an added burden on taxation and on the rates, in addition to his support for graduated taxes and levies on land profits, ground rents and royalties, to redistribute wealth.

These letters, published prominently by the *Herald* papers, did great harm to Lloyd George, while the company also covered Nanney's meetings in detail and included letters supporting him in every edition as well as placing his photograph and manifesto in a prominent place in their editions. This was undertaken because Lloyd George, bereft of money during the campaign, had, for financial reasons, to advertise his manifesto in only the *Genedl* papers and, consequently, suffered the arrows and barbs of the rival *Herald* weeklies. In addition, the *Herald* company always took a much more moderate Liberal line than the *Genedl* stable.

To add to Lloyd George's woes, he had to contend with a furious daily onslaught from the *Western Mail*, which alleged throughout the campaign that his manifesto was a sham from beginning to end and that he was, in truth, 'A Separatist' and 'A Dangerous Radical' whose policy would create social and economic instability. *Y Gwalia* also continually castigated his image as 'A Country Cottage Bred Boy' by asserting that he was really an ambitious and grasping attorney, with ideas above his station and power-hungry for parliamentary status. In a particularly malicious edition, the paper alleged that the support for him from the Bala-Bangor Independent Theological College (at Bangor) was hypocritical and counter-productive, as Ellis Nanney had already provided a gift of £500 to the college, while 'Lloyd George had not paid, even five pence' into its coffers.[47]

The Tory *Western Mail*, on the eve of the poll, also carried a vitriolic supplement with a stinging personal attack on Lloyd George and his imputed egotism and bravado: 'The only qualification Lloyd George possesses is an inordinate belief in his own powers and in a radical creed so extreme that even his own friends have to apologise for it.'[48]

As polling day loomed, *Y Gwalia* also underlined his ambivalent standpoint in the election, stating in a somewhat unlikely vein that 'we would be ready to support a careful, honest and sober Liberal, but not an ambitious politician, whose only motive was to cultivate a career for himself'.[49] The attacks upon him came to a climax when, days before polling, the Tory government's postmaster-general, Cecil Raikes, visited the constituency to open Pwllheli's new promenade (at the request of the Liberal, D. Evan Davies, who had been prominent in pursuing that project). There, Raikes, in his speech, castigated the unelected 'Boy Alderman' – a vicious attack, which led the *South Wales Daily News* to print a front-page story with the headline 'Mr. Raikes with his Muck-Rake'.[50] The paper added that, in an election too close to call, Raikes had 'scraped the bottom of the barrel', though both sides had participated in far from clean activities.

Lloyd George's campaign in his first ever Westminster election had been far from being satisfactory nor easy as his 'trimming' had enabled his opponents to make much capital out of charges of opportunism by the previously uncompromising advocate of Young Wales. He had fallen between two stools – failing to convince his Cymru Fydd following and the newly emancipated that he was their committed advocate, while, at the same time, hardly assuring the more traditionalist Liberals that he could be trusted. Indeed, in a private letter on the eve of the poll to his wife, Margaret, he contemplated political oblivion and life as a country attorney, confessing: 'I am very much afraid of an adverse verdict.'[51]

In the same vein, R. A. Hudson, the Liberal Party organizer and apparatchik, wrote with much trepidation from the Liberal Party headquarters in London to Tom Ellis recuperating in foreign climes: 'We look to Caernarfon and I trust that our confidence is not misplaced. If we do not win, I fear the poor candidate will have a lot of blame thrown on his young shoulders, whether he deserves it or not.'[52] While waiting for the count to take place, Lloyd George was exceedingly nervous and far from confident that he had secured the seat, fearing that he could well be consigned to an early and possibly premature political grave. There was little doubt, as Hudson's letter to Ellis had implied, that defeat would have led to his forever being consigned to the political wilderness – being blamed by both factions, old and new, of the Liberal Party in the Caernarfon Boroughs and in the rest of Wales.

Indeed, before the hustings were properly underway, the dilemma of which stance he should take – and the pragmatic position he adopted – had antagonized some of his closest most ardent and colleagues, who had striven to secure the candidature fourteen months earlier for a new-style 'breakthrough politician'. For example, a Cymru Fydd associate, Morgan Richards of Bangor, a notable local poet, who had helped to sway that individual borough in favour of the nationalist Cymru Fydd candidate in 1888 (against much opposition there) was deeply upset and angry about his turn-about in the by-election, writing to him a highly emotional letter of stricture after the publishing of his party-line manifesto:

> On carefully reading your address today, with a view to moving a vote of confidence in you at our meeting tonight, I was sorry and greatly disappointed to find that you, in it, truckle to party and electioneering exigencies and make expediency the measure of your political faith. You have been bidding for the last two or three years for political popularity by dangling before the constituencies Home Rule for Wales and nationalization of the land. In vain do I look for the mention of these subjects in your common-phrased-stereotyped address. I presume that you have quietly dropped them these, to conciliate the moderates whom you have always denounced.[53]

Lloyd George had certainly not fought his first ever election, albeit sudden and unexpected, on the Home Rule ticket. Historians such as John Grigg and K. O. Morgan have maintained, that he was portrayed as 'standing to gain by campaigning first and foremost as a Welsh patriot'.[54] Rather, he had yielded to the pressure of party orthodoxy, at least temporarily.

As the count proceeded, Lloyd George was, no doubt, musing on whether his expediency, which Morgan Richards had condemned, would bring him victory or despair – an outcome which generated considerable controversy and much deliberation amongst the thousands who had congregated outside the Guildhall at Caernarfon to hear the outcome of the campaign and witness a crucial crossroad, if not a gallows point, for Lloyd George. Though the electorate was small, with a marginal result almost certain, the count would be lengthy and sensational.

There was recount after recount, with the Tories, after the first count, confident of victory. Eventually, however, after finding a pile of uncounted Liberal votes, Lloyd George secured 1,963 votes to Nanney's 1,945, sustaining a paper-thin majority of 18 votes. The poll had been heavy, the highest in the constituency's history, with 404 more people having voted than in the election of 1886 and 127 more than in the 1885 election. Lloyd George had increased the the Liberal total by 279 votes over the

1886 total while Nanney, too, had increased the Tory vote from that secured by Swetenham in 1886. Lloyd George had won by the skin of his teeth, leading the *North Wales Chronicle* to note in its account of the result that he would have lost his seat had not several alleged Tory fishermen from Nefyn been prevented from voting, as they were caught out at sea in inclement weather.[55]

After the count, the loser, Ellis Nanney, repaired for solace – according to *Y Genedl Gymreig* – to the alcoholic comfort of the Sportsman's Arms, escorted there, it was reported, by 'the drunken rif-raff of the town'.[56] Lloyd George, however, embarked upon a victorious tour of Caernarfon and the other five boroughs, arriving at his Mynydd Ednyfedd, Cricieth home, late in the evening. There, he perused until the small hours, according to *Y Genedl Gymreig*, 'countless telegrams of congratulations from all parts of the kingdom'.[57]

The immediate relief and celebrations were soon muted, however, when the response to the campaign was analysed negatively by the press, especially the Liberal papers, while the radical-nationalist faction soon gave vent to intense and carping criticism of the significance of the result. The Tory press, too, sounded forth intemperately at their loss of the seat, while Lloyd George's closest friends, disappointed at a close victory, which they had believed would be relatively comfortable, went out of their way to seek to justify the narrowness of his win.

Certainly, the *Genedl* papers were exceedingly defensive of his narrow victory – the *North Wales Observer and Express* blaming it on the Tories' 'intolerable influence of the Screw, the bribery, the threats and the boycotting'.[58] In the same edition, Lloyd George's nationalist friend, R. A. Griffith, was incandescent with rage, claiming that he had nearly lost the seat because of the alleged corruption of the Tory campaign – a clear attempt to deflect criticism from Lloyd George's ambivalence during the contest. He alleged that:

> The ladies of the Primrose League canvassed the slums and gave away half-crowns to the children of the poor: to show popularity of the Tory cause, the loafers, blackguards and prostitutes of each borough were forced into a bullying and blastering brigade and their enthusiasm was kept up by a constant flow of beer . . . Indecent pictures were exhibited on the walls of Tory clubs to prove that Ireland is a land of crime and violence.[59]

The *North Wales Observer and Express* also sought to justify the close-run victory, as being attributable to the traitorous intervention of the Revd Evan Jones, while all the *Genedl* papers accused the *Herald* company's papers of treachery and low financial considerations in opposing Lloyd George. *Y Genedl Gymreig* added that the young man had won, 'though he had no influence, no comfortable background, nor social status . . . only the strength of his convictions and the force of his talents and eloquence'.[60]

Thomas Gee's *Baner ac Amserau Cymru* also became involved in a barrage of over-hyped comment, aimed against the Tory press, but also criticized the intervention of Evan Jones and the '*cancerous influence of sectarianism, which brought about the low majority*'.[61] *Y Goleuad* blamed many of its readers for voting Tory, while similar sentiments were expressed by the Baptist journals, *Seren Gomer* and *Y Greal*, and the Wesleyan organ, *Y Gwyliedydd*.'[62]

However, some Liberal journals were less ready to ascribe Lloyd George's near defeat to Tory machinations and Evan Jones's treachery and more than ready to blame him for his disappointing and ambivalent performance in the election. They suggested that the poor performance could well be ascribed to the less than principled campaign he had run, which had brought upon his own head considerable criticism. The *Cambrian News* claimed that 'he was in many respects the weakest candidate that the Liberals could have brought forward'.[63] The *Carnarvon and Denbigh Herald* remarked that his victory could hardly be described 'as a triumph for Welsh Nationalism'.[64] *Y Dydd*, as it did during the election, continued to justify Evan Jones's intervention in the campaign, while criticizing Lloyd George.[65] Indeed, once election pressures were over, the *South Wales Daily News*, which had supported him valiantly throughout the campaign, in the immediate aftermath of self-recrimination, said bluntly that he nearly lost the seat when he should have won comfortably because of his duplicitous manifesto.[66] Not surprisingly, the Michael D. Jones/E. Pan Jones/Keinion Thomas nationalist journal, *Y Celt*, which had lauded his selection in 1888–9, claimed bitterly that he had trimmed his views – an opinion shared by the journal, *Cymru Fydd*.[67]

In its varied reaction and paradoxical response to the result, the Liberal press not only demonstrated how mixed was the reaction to Lloyd George's slim victory, but it also underlined the shortcomings of his campaign; the young Cymru Fyddite had to face up to malicious criticism for having taken a moderate, if not deceitful line in his first election foray. Moreover, the Tory press glorified in his difficulties and claimed it was a hollow victory for the young nationalist – the *Western Mail* alleging after the count: 'It was a dishonourable and inconsistent policy of responding too readily to the wire-pullers of the Liberal Federation.' It added mischievously, 'that Lloyd George would never have had the remotest chance of winning the seat had the Tories possessed nothing other than a weak candidate', and that their campaign had been slow in starting and lacked verve and excitement.[68]

The Anglican journal, *Y Llan*, was equally condemnatory in its response to Lloyd George's victory, claiming that it was of considerable disappointment to Lloyd George, considering that he had had fourteen months in which to nurse the electorate and that his campaign had been shamefully commenced before Swetenham 'was cold in his grave'.[69] The *North Wales Chronicle* also criticized Lloyd George's manifesto for its alleged duplicity and the paradoxical nature of his campaign: 'This campaign was not conducted under his true colours . . . Mr George turned his back on the Young Wales Party and promised to throw oil on troubled waters and to fawn upon moderate and immoderate politicians alike.'[70]

Although the Tory response, through the press, was inevitably condemnatory and slighting about his narrow majority, this interpretation undoubtedly contained a substantial grain of truth, which was also expressed in the more moderate segment of the Liberal press. Condemnation, moreover, came from radical-nationalist sources as well. E. Pan Jones and Keinion Thomas of *Y Celt* had been especially vindictive as no doubt was Michael D. Jones, because Lloyd George had curtailed his previous inflammatory nationalist views; this was also indicated by Morgan Richards's fierce, personal criticism of him as an opportunist. Indeed, his friend, R. A. Griffith, in another post-by-election article in the *North Wales Observer and Express*, added to his woe, claiming that 'in the by-election there was a general feeling that the contest was fought without a distinct issue',[71] and implying that his campaign had relegated the case for federal self-government for Wales to the sidelines. Although Ellis Jones Griffith, later to become the Liberal MP for Anglesey, was an early supporter of Cymru Fydd, he admitted after the election in the *Liverpool Mercury*, that Lloyd George could not afford to place a central emphasis on Welsh Home Rule in a constituency so marginal and so unpredictable as the Caernarfon Boroughs. He noted in his article: 'The present contest was a real triumph for the moderate politician.'[72]

Moreover, Tom Ellis MP, in a letter from Egypt, admitted to W. J. Parry (a fellow Cymru Fyddite), in a highly confessional, private vein: 'The Caernarfon election has very many lessons for the thoughtful nationalist. Welsh Home Rule is in the educative stage.'[73] However, in a letter to Lloyd George after the election, he congratulated him on his victory, noting gladly how much he appreciated comments which Lloyd George was to make at Conwy (once the pressure of electioneering was over) that he would strive might and main in Parliament to bring Welsh Home Rule to the forefront of Welsh politics. In addition, Tom Ellis himself, later in 1890, at Bala, would deliver an ambitious and idealistic speech, claiming that, above all else, Wales needed its own parliament to bring about fundamental, social, economic and cultural objectives – although this speech did not receive the warm reception he desired.

All in all, however, Lloyd George's first election was far from being what one of Wales's leading historians, K. O. Morgan, has called 'a considerable triumph for the tribune of the people'.[74] A close analysis of the campaign shows that it was far from being a triumphant victory, because he nearly lost the election when he had so many initial advantages, and it was hardly a vindication of his previous claim that he was the 'Nationalist candidate for the Boroughs', as he had conducted his first parliamentary election dressed in the most moderate Gladstonian clothing, so unlike his militant career pre-April 1890. Indeed, one can interpret his first election victory as, perhaps, the least successful campaign he fought in the Caernarfonshire Boroughs constituency, throughout his lengthy hold over the seat from 1890 to 1945.

Despite this conclusion, however, and in spite of being on the verge of entering into the political wilderness at his first attempt to enter Parliament, he had gained a foothold at Westminster and a platform to expand his real views. With his chameleon-like qualities, he was not prepared to give up on his radical-nationalist objectives after April 1890. On the contrary, now embarked on a parliamentary career, he was ready to use his London base – a London he had once described as 'a society of contaminating influence' – as a platform to renew his call for Welsh Home Rule and to champion the national aspirations of Wales, which were not without their labour and social welfare objectives.

In truth, after the by-election, however much he had trimmed his views in that contest, he began immediately to put himself – even more than Tom Ellis – in the forefront of a programme, which climaxed between 1894 and 1896, in calling for the creation of an independent Welsh political party, having as its primary aim self-government for Wales. He would not only lead a campaign as a rebel against his own party, but he would also, once more, endanger his own personal, political career by propounding highly controversial views, which he had shunned so clearly and ruthlessly, albeit temporarily, in the fateful Caernarfon Boroughs by-election of 1890.

VIII

THE 'WELSH PARNELL', 1890–1892

In the wake of his controversial by-election victory, it was expected that Lloyd George would have to tread warily in his first parliamentary session before the coming of another general election. Tom Ellis's private warning to W. J. Parry some days after the election, that a parliament for Wales was merely in 'the educative stage',[1] was also a warning to Lloyd George that he would have to be cautious so as not to adopt a controversial and prominent line on the issue as his parliamentary career began. However, he was not to refrain from pursuing the issue continually during his first two years in Parliament and neither was he ready to take the Gladstonian party line in this period. Rather, he was to be dubbed publicly 'The Parnell of Wales'. Indeed, he was to adopt a role as an arch-critic of official Liberalism and anti-Gladstonianism, while creating a name for himself as a supreme parliamentary obstructionist, with the deft and sensational use of parliamentary opposition methods based on the highly successful strategies used by the Irish Nationalists at Westminster in the same period. No wonder he was called by his enemies both in his own party and especially by the Tories, the 'Parnellite Parliamentary Raver' – despite the fact that he wanted equality, if not priority for Welsh issues in parliament vis-à-vis Home Rule for Ireland.

In addition to creating a reputation as a rebel Welsh nationalist parliamentarian in this period with characteristic energy and drive between 1890 and 1892, focusing primarily on south Wales, he undertook frequent speaking engagements across Wales to promote his message of an 'United Wales' (*Cymru'n Un*). The central core of his campaign was that Wales, after many years, required special legislative attention, which also comprised a hidden agenda of securing Home Rule for Wales. He would call for the disestablishment and disendowment of the Anglican Church, satisfying the moderate Liberals, while at the same time pressing for the use of the money from Church endowments to be in the hands of an elected Welsh assembly – the precursor for a Welsh parliament. In addition, both in Parliament and in a nationwide campaign, he would call for 'the tithe money' and the Church endowments to be used in Wales and in a Welsh 'parliament' for social welfare reforms, such as the eight-hour working day. In his first general election manifesto of 1892, he would call for old-age pensions for the Welsh, to be financed from the tithe/endowments money, while also calling for an elected Welsh council to press ahead with taxing the rich industrialists/landowners on their 'unearned' profits and land capital gains and taxing rents and royalties for industrial development and ownership of properties. This latter facet of his campaign between 1890 and 1892 has been given short shrift from historians of Lloyd George, apart from much emphasis placed upon this issue of the taxation of landed/industrial wealth by the historian B. B. Gilbert.[2] It is a myth, which requires debunking, that it was only later in his career, post-1906, that Lloyd George was the champion of 'the new radicalism'. Indeed, by 1892, he was in favour of progressive and graduated taxation; extending income taxes and death duties; demanding secular, free education for all; the municipalization of land and housing; the eight-hour day for workers; and old age pensions. In a word, the redistribution of wealth and collectivist social welfare measures.

In addition to his hidden agenda of Home Rule via a Welsh elected council, he also argued frequently that a Welsh parliament could lead by example, in promoting such labourist/welfare policies in a way which a Tory-dominated House of Commons and an unelected House of Lords would never do – arguing, too, that British Liberal governments were hampered consistently from enacting social welfare reforms by the Upper House.

During his first two years in Parliament the compromising stand he had taken so controversially in the by-election of 1890 was shelved. Lloyd George, above all other Liberal Welsh MPs, including Tom Ellis, was the champion of Welsh radicalism and nationalism. He was to insist, in the teeth of much opposition from his own party, that Welsh Liberals should take an independent line in Parliament and in Wales and that if the Gladstonian British Liberal Party did not respond to Welsh aspirations, the only option for Welsh Liberals should be to form a Welsh Independent Liberal Party, with Welsh self-government at the core of its aims. Indeed, between 1890 and 1892, before establishing the militant and rebellious independent nationalist Cymru Fydd League (The Young Wales League) in 1894, he frequently threatened to resort to independent Welsh action and the formation of an independent, nationalist, Welsh Liberal party. To that end, on the eve of the general election of 1892, he undertook 'a takeover' of the powerful *Genedl* (Welsh National) press at Caernarfon, not only as a powerful propaganda weapon for himself in the marginal Caernarfon Boroughs constituency, but also as a medium to extend, throughout Wales, his nationalist message – for *Y Genedl Gymreig*, under his prompting, would have north and south Wales editions.[3] He hoped to use the paper's south Wales edition, at a time when the great English-speaking influx of workers had not yet taken place in many south

Wales mining valleys, to make a nationwide impact – *Cymru'n Un* (A United Wales). Using the press, nationwide public meetings throughout Wales and his parliamentary platform, he was to stand head and shoulders above all other Welsh politicians in this period, as a radical-labourist agitator, whose views could well endanger and put at risk his parliamentary career in an unsafe and marginal parliamentary constituency. His career between 1890 and 1892 has been described by John Grigg as that of 'The Playacting Rebel' an 'accolade' he hardly merits.[4] Lloyd George was a master of theatrical gestures, even at an early age, but he was not play-acting as the 'Parnell of Wales', but was a committed advocate of Young Wales – socially, economically, culturally, linguistically and politically.

His parliamentary debut, unlike the explosive remainder of his subsequent first two years in the Commons, was slow in coming, but had an immediate impact. His brother, William, and his Uncle Lloyd pressed him to make an immediate debut by speaking on their concern for the temperance cause, then being debated in Parliament. They wrote him several letters, to press for an immediate maiden speech. But, perceptively, he waited for his chance to deliver his first Commons speech in order to prepare meticulously and to ensure his debut was well-received. However, it was on the thorny issue of compensation for licensees, then a controversial piece of legislation, that he launched his parliamentary career, making sure that his proposal would have a Welsh and social welfare message. He informed Uncle Lloyd and William, on 16 May, that he was waiting for an opportunity before making his debut: 'I shan't speak in the House this side of Whitsuntide holidays . . . let the cry against compensation increase in force and intensity: then it is the time to speak.'[5]

His opportunity came on 14 June, when he rose to speak against the Tory government's measure to provide substantial compensation to licensees, who had been 'deprived' of their licences to sell alcohol. He broke the parliamentary tradition of delivering a non-controversial maiden speech, urging an amendment to the bill, that the compensation money to taverners should rather be given to a fund to provide 'free, and secular education to Welsh children'. K. O. Morgan has claimed that Lloyd George had no interest in educational reform to change society.[6] Yet, his maiden speech was deployed to that purpose and he was to make frequent speeches on education during his first two years in Parliament, with his message that it should be secular, free from Anglican control, free to all and a lever of social and economic change.

His maiden speech had considerable press publicity in Wales and beyond, ranging from papers such as *The Times* in London to the *Genedl* company papers at Caernarfon. *Y Genedl Gymreig* called it 'masterly' and, though Lloyd George was never a great self-critic and was far from being a shrinking violet, he believed, quite euphorically and perhaps exaggeratedly, that his maiden speech had been an outstanding achievement, as he related to his wife in a letter the following day: 'There is no doubt that I scored a success and a great one . . . I have been overwhelmed with congratulations both yesterday and today . . . There is hardly a London Liberal or even provincial paper which does not say something commendatory about it.'[7]

He had not only struck a Welsh, Nonconformist note in his first speech, but had also coupled his Liberalism to a secular social welfare issue – free education. But before his first debut as a speaker he had penned a significant parliamentary question, which was again a populist labourite issue with which he had been concerned since the beginning of his pre-parliamentary career. This was the vexed question, which struck at landlords and industrial capitalists in north Wales in particular, of the enfranchisement of leaseholds. He asked whether the Tory government had any intention at all to fulfil proposals, just made, by an all-party Parliamentary Committee looking into the issue. The committee had reacted favourably to leasehold reform and the young Lloyd George then pressed them to implement the proposals. He received a negative reply, but the subject was significant because it was a contentious issue from Cardiff to Bangor, where large landowners and industrialists from the Bute family of Cardiff and the Penrhyn family of Bangor derived massive gains from leased land on which workers' houses had been built. This first parliamentary question underlined the fact that it was not only on the old Welsh Liberal issues of Nonconformity that his mind was set, but on labourite issues.

As soon as he arrived in London, after a much publicized by-election, considerable pressure was exerted upon him to address massive London Welsh audiences and other Welsh expatriate societies in English cities. Indeed, in mid-April, the Tory daily, the *Western Mail*, was pouring scorn on the continual round of meetings and parties in London, where he obviously received much adulation. It reported vindictively: 'His invaluable services are indispensable towards ensuring the success of certain London Welsh tea parties and he has cheerfully accepted the onerous duties at sundry of these convivial gatherings, . . . such are some of the penalties of greatness.'[8]

The adulation and attention that he received in London during his first months did not mean that his life there was completely congenial. Indeed, the impecunious young politician, who had called London society 'contaminating' during his pre-parliamentary career, faced periods of loneliness and hardship in his new surroundings, far from his family and close friends. He had to stay, for financial reasons as he had no parliamentary salary, in an uncomfortable one-room flat in Craven Street, without company, while his wife, Margaret, remained at Cricieth with two young children, Mair Eluned and Richard. She was extremely reluctant to leave her beloved Cricieth and move to grimy London to live there with him. In frequent early letters, he pleaded with her to join him there, for example, in a particularly harrowing letter on 12 June:

> I can't stand this solitude much longer. It is unbearable. Here the House adjourns in a few minutes, that's it at 6 and I go to my lodgings like a hermit or a prisoner to his cell. Dark, gloomy dungeon, my room is. I do not know what I would do now for an hour of your company. It would scatter all the gloom and make all the room so cheerful.[9]

For a highly sexed young man, deeply attractive to women and spoiled since childhood by a host of female relations, being in London, apparently alone, was obviously unwelcome and an early indication that long separations from his wife and her reluctance to move to London would in the long term cause considerable sexual and scandalous episodes in Lloyd George's life and, ultimately, estrangement from Margaret. However, even at this early stage of his parliamentary career, despite his unrequited pleadings to his wife to join him in London, he was privately not prepared to live the life of a hermit there. He frequented fine restaurants in the city, such as St James's Piccadilly and Frascati's, to smoke cigars and probably drink wine with his friend the barrister and nationalist Liberal MP for Mid Glamorgan, the bon viveur, S. T. Evans, who no doubt contributed more to the bill, as he was a successful barrister. On Sundays, the two would visit places of interest on the Thames, which led Margaret to castigate her husband not only for keeping so much company with S. T. Evans, but for going on Sunday jaunts, rather than attending chapel at Castle Street. On 13 August 1890, in characteristic style, he answered her letter of admonition to him by blaming her for her Calvinistic Methodist strictures, underlining the fact that he was far from being a Welsh, puritannical Nonconformist. He dismissed the visit he and Evans had made to Kew Gardens:

> There is a great deal of difference between the temptation to leave your work for the pleasure of being cramped up in a suffocating, malodorous chapel, listening to some superstitions I have heard thousands of times before and, on the other hand, the temptation to have a pleasant ride on the river in the fresh air, with a terminus at one of the loveliest gardens in Europe.[10]

However, despite his bitter-sweet experiences in London and occasional jollifications there in Sam Evans's company, politics was his true delight. From the outset, he was set on a militant, independent course. He began his anti-official Liberal stance alongside a paradoxical partner (but one of similar egotism), the millionaire south Wales coalowner, D. A. Thomas, the MP for Merthyr and for a time something of a quixotic nationalist, if not of radical labourist views. To the great consternation of the Anglicans, Stuart Rendel and W. E. Gladstone, in June 1890 Lloyd George and D. A. Thomas, in tandem, made a rebellious stance in the Commons against the Tory government's Tithe Bill. Both refused to support F. T. Stevenson's amendment that the tithe charge should be revalued and decreased. Both voted with the Tories, Lloyd George arguing that the total sum of the tithe charge collected should remain the same, until the Church was disestablished, so that a large pot of money would be available for distribution to the poor and needy by a Welsh elected council – the embryonic Welsh parliament he hoped to see established. The two were also aware that the tithe, under the proposed bill, would be paid in future by the landlord, not the tenant, and the higher the charge on the Tory landowners the better, as far as they were concerned.

The two rebels were criticized widely in the Welsh Liberal press, however, for voting against the Liberal policy and apparently with the Tory government. It was an 'inexplicable act' (*gweithred anesboniadwy*) according to the Baptist *Seren Cymru*;[11] *Y Cymro* (The Welshman) insisted that 'the sooner the better Lloyd George is made accountable for his actions'.[12] The *South Wales Daily News* was particularly hostile, claiming correctly in a prophetic manner about Lloyd George: 'This was the first outward and visible sign of the Welsh Radical Vote against Gladstonianism.'[13]

Lloyd George was not ready to be a party hack and he enjoyed this first taste of parliamentary disobedience against his own party, as was portrayed in the Anglican weekly, *Y Llan* (The Parish), which dubbed him '*Yr Ebol Radicalaidd*' – The Radical Colt.[14] But he had the support of some Welsh papers such as *Y Genedl Gymreig* and the labourist-nationalist *Y Celt* for his 'rebellion', and from Thomas Gee, Alun Lloyd and John Parry Llanarmon-yn-Iâl, leaders of the anti-tithe movement, in *Baner ac Amserau Cymru*.[14]

He also wrote to his wife on 15 July, as he and Thomas still took an independent line on the Tithe Bill, that his supporters in the Caernarfon Boroughs supported his seemingly anti-Liberal stance. Referring to a meeting at Bangor to justify the rebellion, he told Margaret that his constituents there 'appeared highly delighted with my success. I explained my tithe vote but it was hardly necessary . . . they were all satisfied on the point.'[15] Then, in July, at a meeting at Aberdare, Glamorgan, on a visit there with his co-rebel MP, D. A. Thomas, he justified his rebellion, according to the *Western Mail*, when he claimed the tithe in Wales was the property of the Welsh people. He claimed that it should be nationalized, together with the endowments of a disestablished Church, to finance the care of the poor and the needy, with the money distributed by an elected council for Wales. At this meeting, though never an out-and-out republican, even during his early career, he nevertheless resorted to pouring scorn on the head of the Church, Queen Victoria. His colourful tirade was captured by one comment: 'The Church is English in its head, its origins, its liturgy and its bailiffs' – an anti-royalist and anti-English swipe by 'the Parnell of Wales'.[16]

Before his first parliamentary session ended in the summer of 1890, he also undertook another rebellious action with an anti-English, anti-royalist slant to it. In conjunction with Sam Evans, MP, he attacked the Church as an establishment and the queen personally, by insisting in a highly publicized, stage-managed motion that a reduction should be made in the monies given to the Crown and its entourage from the public purse. When the Royal List of payments was being discussed, he pounced on a grant being paid to a minor member of the royal family to criticize the maldistribution of wealth in society; he informed his wife in a letter before putting the amendment:

> S.T. Evans and I intend objecting to the making of some Princeling of Royal Lineage a Knight of the Garter at an expense of £400 to the country. People are starving or, what is worse, dragging a miserable existence through penury, poverty and toil, while these idle, aristocratic and Royalist vagabonds are spending the nation's money in idle frippery of this sort. Don't you think, old Maggie, I ought to have a fling at them, even if the Tories howl me down and brand me a wild, revolutionary fanatic?[17]

Considerable parliamentary uproar, not only from the Tory benches, ensued as a consequence of the intervention of Evans and Lloyd George on the Royal Estimates, which led to the queen objecting personally, according to press reports, to W. E. Gladstone, the Liberal leader, with whom she was not on the best of terms. She insisted that Gladstone should get the two Welsh rebels to apologize publicly to the Crown. Only the radical press supported their action, which was condemned in Tory papers and in a large section of the Liberal press.

At the end of his first parliamentary session, Lloyd George had secured much publicity as a Welsh radical and nationalist champion in a short space of time. However, his extreme actions and controversial ruses had antagonized moderate Liberals in his marginal constituency, according to the leading Tory weekly in the Caernarfon Boroughs, the *North Wales Chronicle*. It summed up in detail his parliamentary record with the arresting headline: 'The Parliamentary Raver'.[18]

The Tory Party in the constituency, detesting his strident anti-Toryism and anti-English statements, was also determined to portray him as an extremist and in the summer of 1890 made determined efforts to get a parliamentary candidate selected for the constituency who was a notable Welsh-speaking Welshman and a forceful political figure. To that end, in June 1890, they selected an eminent Nonconformist, Welsh-speaking parliamentarian from a distinguished Welsh family to depose 'The Parliamentary Raver'. He was Sir John Puleston, MP for Devonport. He was descended from a notable Vale of Clwyd family and was a well-known specialist in medicine, besides being a prominent Eisteddfodwr and an experienced politician. He was also the uncle of one of Welsh Nonconformity's most eminent preachers, 'The Blind Minister' (*Y Gweinidog Dall*), as he was known throughout Wales and a prominent Liberal, the Revd John Puleston Jones. Sir John Puleston, the Tories claimed, had allegedly given up the 'safe' seat of Devonport in order to fight Lloyd George. His sensational selection caused immediate panic in the Liberal ranks, even in the highest echelons of Welsh Nonconformity and Liberal circles, with Thomas Gee, in a leading article in his paper, calling for all Liberals in the Caernarfon Boroughs to unite to forestall Puleston's challenge for the seat. In the *Baner ac Amserau Cymru* Gee called on all Liberals in Wales's most marginal Liberal seat to defend Lloyd George, stressing that the Tories were pulling out all the stops to unseat him. The implication in Gee's call was that the seat could be lost, particularly in view of Lloyd George's controversial debut in politics: 'All Mr George's supporters must unite and do everything in their power to prepare for the battle ahead, because it is quite evident that the Tories are organising a concerted campaign to win once more this vital seat.'[19]

On 1 July, the panic in Liberal ranks escalated as the *Western Mail* highlighted in an editorial the tension and fear amongst Caernarfon Boroughs' Liberals, with the choice of Sir John Puleston threatening to regain the seat for Toryism. The Tory Welsh daily, lauding Sir John's Welsh Nonconformist credentials, claimed confidently: 'Sir John Puleston will win the Caernarfon Boroughs and the Radicals know it.'[20]

Further panic ensued later that summer, when Sir John Puleston secured a public coup over Lloyd George, followed by widespread publicity. He obtained a more prestigious role than Lloyd George on two public platforms within Wales and the Caernarfon Boroughs, causing distress in the Liberal camp. He was invited to take a leading role as a day president in the Bangor National Eisteddfod that year (Lloyd George was not asked) and was invited, too, to address that summer's Annual Arfon Calvinistic Methodist Session (*Sasiwn*) at Caernarfon, by the leading denomination in the Boroughs. Lloyd George again was not invited. To add insult to injury, through Tory machinations, he was also appointed by the

Conservative Home Secretary to the highly prestigious post of the constable of Caernarfon Castle – a post he could use to great effect to publicize his name in the royal borough and to secure vital support there for his election fight with Lloyd George. The *Western Mail* claimed the post was 'no sinecure' and that Sir John, through his own financial generosity, without any cost falling on Caernarfon citizens, would renew the castle and would attract thousands of visitors to boost the town's economy.[21]

Indeed, Puleston's appointment as the constable of the castle and his own personal reputation as a patron of Welsh culture (as well as the fact that he had a summer house at Pwllheli) must have been of great personal concern to Lloyd George who was well aware of the threat that Puleston posed in a forthcoming general election. However, he was not afraid of the challenge and had no respect for Puleston, as he wrote confidentially to his wife on 7 August: 'Puleston is a great hypocrite and fraud . . . Puleston trades on an appearance of good fellowship. But cunning as he is, I shall see that he does not win the seat with the ease he imagines . . .'[22] Confiding to his wife that he could well lose the seat, without taking a holiday in the late summer of 1890, he embarked on a speaking campaign in the constituency during August, culminating in a meeting at Pwllheli at the end of the month. There, according to *Y Genedl Gymreig*, he delivered a highly personal attack upon Sir John and his 'corrupt' appointment as constable of Caernarfon Castle.[23] He claimed, after Puleston had accused him publicly of being a wild Welsh nationalist and unfaithful to his Gladstonian Liberal Party in the constituency, that he was proud to prioritize the aspirations of Wales and the Welsh people rather than pay strict obedience to the official Liberal Party line, and in so doing, claimed he was fighting for the common people of his constituency and his nation.

In a similar speech at Caernarfon in November 1890, he again attacked Puleston and added that he would lead an independent Welsh Liberal nationalist movement if Wales was not promised priority in the next Liberal official manifesto for Welsh disestablishment of the Anglican Church and an elected Welsh national council to use church endowments and tithe funds for the welfare of the poor and underprivileged. Lloyd George, therefore, did not respond to Puleston's challenge by compromising his Welsh radical-nationalism, but pronounced that he would fight Puleston on that platform (in contrast to his posed Gladstonianism in the 1890 by-election).

Further evidence of his anti-Gladstonianism came immediately after the Caernarfon meeting at the National Liberal Convention at Sheffield in November, where he asserted publicly, according to a report from the meeting in *Y Genedl Gymreig*, that his one-time hero, Joseph Chamberlain, had been more in favour of Welsh disestablishment and 'Home Rule All

Round' (in 1886) than Gladstone had ever been.[24] He also asserted that if Gladstone's next government rejected disestablishment as a priority measure he and fellow Welsh members would form an independent Welsh party on Irish nationalist lines. The *Western Mail* in response to his statement dubbed him again 'the Welsh Parnell' – a label they were to use frequently in the years ahead.[25]

He preached the same message of rebellion at the end of November in the Merthyr constituency of D. A. Thomas, who had been involved with him in the tithe rebellion of early 1890. He claimed, according to the *South Wales Daily News*, that the tithe-charge money should be deployed for free, secular education in Wales and that the wealthy should be taxed to aid social welfare schemes; he also called for the establishment of a Welsh parliament, to legislate not only upon Nonconformist issues, but also on social reform.[26] He was using the disestablishment issue, popular with moderate Liberals, to call, in addition, for a national elected Welsh council, which would form the basis of a Welsh parliament, not only to deploy the Church's endowments for social reform, but also to embark on taxation policies to bring about a new society. To press ahead with this quasi-nationalist agenda, he started writing a series of weekly articles, 'O'r Senedd' (From Parliament) in November in *Y Genedl Gymreig*, a paper which had influence not only in north but in south Wales. This weekly column was a valuable propaganda medium for him, but also a means to add to his fragile weekly income, which was further boosted in the following years up to 1896 by penning columns in the *Manchester Guardian* and the *London Star*.

In his first parliamentary column in the *Genedl*, he wrote an article from a Liberal meeting at Sheffield, where earlier in the year he had castigated Gladstone publicly.[27] On this occasion, he repeated his earlier remarks that he would press for an independent Welsh party on the Irish model to be set up if the next Gladstonian government failed to deliver on Welsh issues. A week later, in his second column in *Y Genedl*, he devoted his remarks entirely to the Parnell scandal and the Irish leader's adulterous relationship with Kitty O'Shea, remarking, ironically and perhaps with his own sex drive in mind, that such adventures had ruined many politicians.[28] In order to please many of his Nonconformist readers, he condemned Parnell's behaviour, although he confessed that he was an inspirational leader of the Irish nationalists. He also ruthlessly exploited the rift which the scandal had caused in the Irish ranks (and the disgust felt by many Welsh Liberals) to insist that the time was now ripe to use the emotions raised in Irish nationalist and English Liberal quarters to demand that Wales's aspirations should be given precedence over Irish Home Rule. In this column, too, he significantly called for the Irish socialist and his early hero, Michael Davitt, to lead the Irish party – knowing that

Davitt was a supporter of Welsh Home Rule and far more radical measures that the aristocratic Parnell. But the main emphasis in this second *Genedl* article was to press for Welsh disestablishment and a national Welsh council. He claimed priority for Wales over Irish matters by stating: 'Wales will not be ready to sacrifice her demand for religious freedom before the altar of Mrs O'Shea.'[29]

This was a revealing statement of Lloyd George's dual attitude as a Welsh protestant towards Catholic Ireland, for, though he wanted Welsh Liberals to adopt Irish tactics, he wanted Nonconformist Wales to have precedence over Catholic Ireland. The article revealed, too, his own hidden fear, expressed even in his early teens, that his own sexual desires had to be restrained if he was to avoid public, political and personal scandal, which could destroy his career. Soon, however, he too was to face the first of several accusations that he had had extramarital adventures.

It was not only political columns and parliamentary and public meetings which he was to use in 1890 to promote his militant views; in December, he resorted to the methods of civil disobedience he had used in the 1880s in Llŷn and Eifionydd in the Anti-Tithe War. During the pre-Christmas week, he attended a protest by anti-tithe farmers at Llannor, near Pwllheli, who were seeking to prevent a distraint auction of their goods, because they had refused to pay the tithe charge. He was invited to address the protestors and disrupt the auction. According to *Baner ac Amserau Cymru*, he supported the farmers' act of civil disobedience but urged them not to riot, while also using the opportunity to claim that Wales required priority for Welsh disestablishment and tithe reform, with the monies used by a Welsh national council for social and economic reform, and that this aim should be given priority over Home Rule for Ireland. He also predicted that if this did not happen by the time of the formation of the next Liberal government, there could be considerable violence in rural Wales.[30]

There was an immediate uproar in Anglican and Tory papers. The Anglican journal, *Yr Haul* (The Sun), in its January 1891 edition, called his actions 'Welsh Barbarism', while the *Western Mail* condemned him for intervening in a 'terrorist' demonstration and called for his immediate resignation from Parliament for partaking in Irish-style lawbreaking methods. The paper claimed: 'A grave responsibility rests on men like Lloyd George who are inciting the ignorant peasantry to terrorism.'[31] However, Lloyd George, as in his pre-parliamentary career, was prepared to use not only parliamentary methods but activities bordering upon the unconstitutional and illegal in order to bring about his radical-nationalist goals.

Over the Christmas period, Lloyd George rested from political activities after a tempestuous first seven months as an MP, during which he had been prepared to use all manner of methods to secure publicity for his activities as 'The Parnell of Wales'. Soon, however, he was back in the political harness, resuming his column in *Y Genedl Gymreig*, in which he reported a visit he had made to the Hartlepool by-election, where he supported an independent Liberal, of labourist views, rather than the official Liberal candidate.[32] He (like Lloyd George) supported an eight-hour day for all workers, and supported the then controversial railway strike. The columnist from the Caernarfon Boroughs also supported the Hartlepool independent candidate's call for railway nationalization. Lloyd George was never a socialist in any didactic sense, but he was far to the left of Gladstonianism and early in his parliamentary career he was interested in new Liberal-radical-labourist ideas, a decade and more before historians claim he became a 'New Liberal' after 1905. He was not in 1890 merely a Welsh radical seeking to promote the old Liberal Nonconformist demands, but he had a vision that a Welsh government could more readily bring about social welfare and labourist changes than any Westminster government could or would secure. Indeed, in his *Genedl* column, a week after the Hartlepool by-election remarks, he wrote again that he was fully in support of the current railway strike and a similar railway strike in Scotland, claiming that a Scottish parliament could also deal more sensitively with the needs of the working class there, than could any imperial, London Parliament or government.[33]

In this column, too, he criticized fiercely the North Wales Liberal Federation because they had just refused to press the Liberal Party in London to give priority to Welsh disestablishment in the manifesto for the next general election. He also stated in the same column, despite the objection of the majority of Welsh Liberal MPs, that he intended to approach the leaders of the Irish Nationalist Party to obtain from them a promise that if they would agree that Welsh disestablishment would be given priority after the next general election the Welsh members would also support the policy of Irish Home Rule. This, he claimed, could be achieved on a side-by-side basis if the next Liberal government depended on Welsh and Irish support for its survival in office. This was an audacious attempt to make Welsh Liberalism an independent force in Parliament and was another blow aimed against Gladstone's policy of Irish Home Rule as the priority issue, because the Liberal leader's Anglican sympathies meant that he was reluctant to disestablish the Anglican Church in Wales. The *Western Mail* pounced on Lloyd George's proposed controversial initiative, claiming that his remarks were 'a direct insult to Gladstone', underlining that Lloyd George had no faith that his Anglican leader would ever countenance Welsh disestablishment. The Cardiff paper also reiterated its criticism that Lloyd George was in a secret compact with 'Irish terrorists'.[34]

Another opportunity came in February and March to promote Welsh disestablishment, allied to a Welsh national council. During these two months, alongside S. T. Evans, Lloyd George conducted a fierce and orchestrated campaign to obstruct the Tory government's protracted progress of the Tithe Bill through the Commons. The two Welsh rebels introduced amendment after amendment to the bill to prevent its progress and to highlight the need for it to be changed so that all tithe revenue should be distributed in Wales by an embryonic Welsh parliament – an elected national council. While the controversy over the bill raged in the Commons, caused by Evans and Lloyd George's obstructionist tactics, Lloyd George reported the proceedings in highly egotistical terms in his weekly 'O'r Senedd' columns in *Y Genedl Gymreig*.

From Egypt, where he was continuing to recuperate from a major illness, Tom Ellis wrote the two a letter lauding their activities and emphasizing that their efforts were preparing the ground for a national awakening in Wales and making the case for Welsh devolution at the same time. Ellis wrote: 'Your attacks were able, skilful and daring and apart from the satisfaction I feel that the younger members have so distinguished themselves individually, I am delighted to think what an impetus and strengthening the fight will give to the national movement.'[35] Ellis's remarks came only months after he had been deeply disappointed at the lukewarm response he had received in a seminal nationalist speech at Bala in September 1890, when he had called upon Welsh Liberals to unite to secure Home Rule for Wales. He had said:

We desire to see the Church endowments being liberated and used to finance Welsh National demands . . . secure better agreements so that those who cultivate the land receive their deserved earnings and secure homes: we demand the greatest welfare being accorded our coalminers: we call for the full development of our fisheries and rivers: to use Crown lands and wasteland and common land to plant forests and beautify the hillsides: to reduce the number of taverns and control them more effectively: to unite our railways and organise them for the benefit of Welsh people, to develop our village crafts and establish a network of local libraries and establish village halls everywhere. We need a Welsh University to promote Science and The Arts and a National Library . . . Above all else we must have a Parliament elected by all Welsh men and women . . . a symbol of our unity and a medium to fulfil our social ideals and industrial social welfare.[36]

Tom Ellis's vision of a parliament for Wales dedicated to industrial and rural social welfare – the welfare of small farmers, agricultural labourers and coalminers, together with cultural and educational objectives – was no doubt shared by his friend Lloyd George. But both were aware how fragile Home Rule was as an issue, in the minds of many Welsh people, and even in their own party ranks in Wales. However, neither, at this stage, were ready to give up the fight for national devolution, despite Ellis's plea at Bala falling on stony ground and Lloyd George having had to compromise on Home Rule in his by-election in 1890. Tom Ellis and Lloyd George, in particular, were determined to reach that objective of a measure of self-rule for Wales through an issue such as disestablishment, which would have a measure of devolution attached to it in the form of an elected council for Wales.

The Welsh press were also aware of how Lloyd George and his small band of followers were using Welsh issues to awaken 'Welsh National Consciousness' through rebelling at Westminster against their party line. During long protracted debates on the tithe measure in the Commons, the Welsh press lauded them – *Seren Gomer*, for example, declaiming that S. T. Evans and Lloyd George were 'The Princes of the Welsh Army', in Parliament, 'who had pressed 95 amendments against the Tithe Measure.'[37] During these tithe debates, too, a motion on Welsh disestablishment was proposed in Parliament and in his *O'r Senedd* in *Y Genedl Gymreig* in mid-February Lloyd George raised the hackles of official British-Welsh Liberals like Stuart Rendel MP, when he attacked Gladstone personally 'for keeping clear of the debate in parliament because Anglican clerical influences had preyed on his mind'.[38]

In April, in the same column in *Y Genedl Gymreig*, he again attacked the North Wales Liberal Federation for continuing to refrain from pressing the London Liberal Party to support disestablishment and obeying Gladstonianism slavishly.[39] At the same time, in the Commons, he proposed a motion calling for a £500 reduction in the Army Estimates, because soldiers had been used a few weeks earlier at Llannefydd in Denbighshire, in a violent manner, he alleged, to prevent tenant farms there from disturbing a tithe distraint auction on their goods. He had boasted in a letter to Thomas Gee on that occasion that his motion might be defeated, but it would, nevertheless, raise the political temperature in Wales: 'Of course, we shall be defeated but by these discussions we manage to keep the pot boiling and the Liberal Party is awakening to the fact that Welsh Questions are very useful – quite as useful as Irish ones to throw at the government.'[40]

He proceeded after this action to keep the nationalist pot boiling when in April, after the publication of the 1891 census, he condemned the fact that in many Welsh-speaking areas in Wales the census officials had failed to register how many monoglot Welsh speakers there were in those areas – a ruse, he claimed, so as not to provide public services in Welsh as well as in the English language.[41] This was another indication, as in his county council days, that he had a revolutionary vision of official bilingualism in Wales – not, as has been often claimed by historians, merely a sentimental attachment to the language.

He continued his crusade for labourite social reform emanating from a Welsh parliament in a remarkable speech, alongside Tom Ellis, at Bangor in May. There, at the Penrhyn Hall, which had been donated to Bangor by north Wales's richest industrialist/landowner, Lord Penrhyn, he delivered a vitriolic speech showing that his agenda was to use disestablishment as a platform to secure home rule and Welsh labourite policies. With reference to the two industrialist/landowners of the Faenol and Penrhyn estates, he condemned capitalist monopolists and landowners and called not only for a radical system of taxing their land profits, especially from the increasing value of land owing to industrial development, but called for a huge increase in taxes on their earnings and profits from their industrial undertakings and to redistribute tithes and endowments after the Church was disendowed and disestablished. *Y Genedl Gymreig* welcomed his proposals and also welcomed Tom Ellis's speech, which called in its peroration for Welsh Home Rule, despite the fact that his great Home Rule speech in Bala had fallen on stony ground.[42]

Disestablishment was Lloyd George's hidden agenda for secular radical change in Wales and his secularism was much in evidence a month after the Bangor speech, when he participated in the debate on the Free Education Bill, then proceeding through the Commons. He called for the new free system of elementary education to be completely secular, without denominational or Church control. He was prepared to congratulate the Tory government on initiating the bill as a means of securing further educational opportunity for the under-privileged, so long as the Church had no special control of a sector of the proposed new system. He failed in his amendment, but was to continue the fight for secular education in the Welsh Education Revolt of the early 1900s.

At the end of the parliamentary summer session of 1891, in July, he again sought to stimulate Welsh national consciousness on the linguistic plane, coupling the issue to labourite demands. He joined forces with the Colliers Union leader from south Wales, William Abraham MP (Mabon), to condemn in Parliament the appointment of a monoglot Englishman to inquire into coal accidents in Wales; *Y Genedl Gymreig* called them champions of the coalminers and of the language in public and industrial life. Once more, Lloyd George was raising the profile of the Welsh language in Welsh public life, when there was so much apathy and, indeed, opposition to its extension into the whole realm of Welsh life, even from leading Liberals and Nonconformists. Equality for the language in Wales was for him a matter of social justice and his promotion of its use for modern, contemporary and secular purposes underlined how his nationalism was far seeing, comprehensive and tailored towards the goal of a dynamic, modern, bilingual Wales.

When Parliament closed for the summer recess of 1891, Lloyd George did not rest from political activity in Wales. He returned to an early project he had started in 1889 as 'The Boy Alderman' on Caernarfonshire Council when he had urged all county councils in Wales to form an all-Wales body, which would evolve into a Welsh parliament. *Baner ac Amserau Cymru* gave him much support and urged all Welsh councils to heed his call.[43] Then he took a break from politics so as to help his brother with the family business and earn money to keep his growing family, no doubt feeling that he had already, since 1890, depended heavily on the money he drew from the family firm, with almost all the work carried out by William George. In September, he began again to take up his political crusade in Wales, resurrecting his call for Welsh Liberals to take an anti-Gladstonian line on disestablishment, when he launched an appeal to raise £2,500 to finance the cause and give it priority over Irish Home Rule.

Nevertheless, he was not hypercritical of Gladstone, but was prepared to take the view that some time could elapse before the general election and that before then Gladstone might give disestablishment its proper prominent place in the next Liberal manifesto. Lloyd George hinted at this in a speech he delivered in September at Pontypridd, but also at the same time, according to the *South Wales Daily News*, he threatened that if such priority to Church reform in Wales was not given by the next Liberal government, he would establish an Independent Welsh Nationalist Party with Home Rule as its top priority.[44] Then, at Maesteg, according to the same paper, he delivered an oration which was the clearest commitment he had made towards Home Rule for Wales.[45] In his speech, he referred to Switzerland as a prosperous nation with its government devoted to social welfare – a model that a new Wales should adopt – adding that a Welsh federal government would legislate on progressive labour and social welfare issues in a mode far more radical than any London government of whatever political hue would do. The accusation that has been made by historians such as John Grigg that Lloyd George's militant Welsh policy was merely 'playacting', and only tactics to try to exert pressure on official British Liberalism to give Wales concessions, is far from being an accurate interpretation of his views in this period. True, he was a superb tactician, but he had a commitment to Home Rule for Wales and a vision of how it would have highly beneficial consequences for her people, and believed that a small country like Switzerland was an European model, which Wales should follow. He was not afraid to use disestablishment as a back-door tactic to secure Welsh devolution, which would evolve into a parliament, but at times, as at Maesteg, he was ready to call for Welsh

Home Rule directly. He took such a position when such a controversial standpoint could prove fatally damaging for him, such was the hostility towards the issue in his marginal constituency and in Wales's official Liberal circles.

He continued to pursue his anti-Gladstonianism and to call for disestablishment as a priority for Wales and a precursor to devolution, in November 1891, at the British National Liberal Federation meeting at Newcastle. There he spoke strongly for the matter to be given the ultimate priority in the soon-to-be held general election. The executive decided, however, that it should take second place to Welsh disestablishment in the manifesto, when the election took place. According to his report in his column, 'From Parliament' in *Y Genedl*, the following week, Lloyd George was pleased that disestablishment had now been given real prominence in the Liberal programme, although privately he doubted greatly Gladstone's commitment to anything that might prejudice the integrity of the Anglican Church. Later that month, he showed his doubts about Gladstone and antagonized Welsh Gladstonians and Tories when he made a vitriolic attack on the Church in the press. He claimed that the Church Congress gathered at Rhyl, with the archbishop of Wales present, was held amidst much drinking of intoxicating liquor by the delegates. He alleged that the archbishop and his clerics 'were floating on a lake of beer barrels'. *Y Llan*, the Church's Welsh-language monthly, countered by stating that his attack was 'tasteless and redolent with untruths',[46] while the *Western Mail* called him a slanderer. However, the Baptist *Seren Gomer* retorted 'that every Baptist was proud of this thorough nationalist and Liberal'.[47]

By the end of 1891, with a general election looming sometime in 1892, (the end of the seven-year maximum period for a government was approaching), Lloyd George had created a name for himself throughout north and south Wales, with his frequent speeches in the south, as a representative of the 'New Wales' and 'The Parnell of Wales'.

Since the 1880s he had realized the power of the press as a political propaganda tool and had already launched his own paper, *Yr Udgorn Rhyddid*, as early as 1888, and had written a weekly column for *Y Genedl Gymreig* since 1891. With an election approaching in a difficult constituency, he now realized that he would have to have the most powerful press company in his constituency under his control and at his beck and call. Not surprisingly, therefore, in December he had secretly detailed negotiations to bring under his control the *Genedl* company's three newspapers, *Y Werin* (The People), *Y Genedl Gymreig* (The Welsh Nation) and the *North Wales Observer and Express*, even if it was difficult for him publicly to be its owner or a major shareholder in the company, showing blatantly that it was his own personal propaganda machine.

Consequently, he engineered the whole takeover secretly, as the company's solicitor, and was one of several who signed the company's articles of association, side by side with other nationalist Liberals such as Tom Ellis and Alfred Thomas, the Pontypridd MP who was soon to be involved in formulating a National Institutions (Wales) Bill in 1892. W. J. Parry, 'The Quarrymen's Champion', was also deeply involved in the takeover, and both he and Lloyd George had, at the same time, been involved in seeking to acquire secretly the *Herald* company papers at Caernarfon – papers which had opposed Lloyd George so stridently in the 1890 by-election. That attempt failed, but the *Genedl* papers were now under his control, though not apparently publicly.

When the papers of the new company were launched in January 1892, the most interesting development was that *Y Genedl Gymreig* would have a weekly south Wales edition so that the national message could be spread throughout Wales, at a time when the greatest influx of non-Welsh speakers had yet to take place in the south-eastern mining valleys of the country. The newly launched *Genedl*, *Y Werin* and the *North Wales Observer and Express* carried a labourite nationalist message in their first editions: 'Our main aim is to make our papers truly Welsh national journals paying special attention to the needs of the sons of labour (*meibion Llafur*) while interpreting and promoting the national awakening of Wales.'[48]

Lloyd George also ensured that the quicksilver and quixotic journalist, author, dramatist and nationalist, Beriah Gwynfe Evans, was seduced and drawn to Caernarfon from the *South Wales Daily News* to act as managing editor of the new company's papers. However, as in the case of his first paper, *Yr Udgorn Rhyddid* in 1888, Lloyd George was the new *Genedl* company's creator and manipulator. The Anglican *Llan* monthly journal, like a host of other Tory papers, summed up sarcastically who was behind the venture, stating bluntly: 'The newspapers are Lloyd George's Trumpet, (*Udgorn*) to sing his praises and broadcast his superiorities.'[49]

Under the new regime, Lloyd George continued to contribute his parliamentary column, *O'r Senedd*, with Tom Ellis MP writing a column under the same heading each alternate week for *Y Genedl*. In their first two columns, both trumpeted Lloyd George's visit in January to Pontypridd, to speak at a huge gathering to launch the National Institutions Bill, which would soon be brought before the Commons by Alfred Thomas, the local MP. The bill sought the establishment of a Welsh elected council and a Secretary of State for Wales. It also proposed that other linguistic, cultural and socio-economic institutions for Wales should be established, such as a National Library, National Museum and National University.

The Pontypridd meeting aroused a fierce response in a leading article in the *Western Mail* which condemned Alfred Thomas's measure as a back-door attempt to establish a Welsh parliament.[50] The paper also condemned Lloyd George's call for support for the bill and after his Church Congress attack earlier in the year, at Rhyl, dubbed him 'The Barrel Boy'. It also attacked him as one 'who was more prodigal in his arrogance than anyone'. Such attacks, however, did not prevent him from calling at the meeting for a new devolved Welsh council, which would embark on land nationalization and the heavy taxation of landowners and industrialists. This nationalist message was further enhanced by Lloyd George, Alfred Thomas and David Randell, the tinplate union's Swansea radical-nationalist MP, when they published a booklet championing the National Institutions Bill.

When the House of Commons resumed in February, he continued to press the nationalist case, this time on a linguistic basis. He attacked in Parliament the appointment of a monoglot Englishman, Judge Beresford, as a circuit judge in Mid Wales. He lost his vote of censure, but Beresford was forced to renounce his post and move to an English circuit – another parliamentary feather in Lloyd George's cap and further evidence that to him status for the Welsh language in public life was at the core of his beliefs, when the language was reviled in so many circles. Then, in his parliamentary *Genedl* column, he boasted that he had just delivered another linguistic vote of censure against railway companies in south and north Wales for promoting Englishmen to managerial/foremen posts at the expense of Welsh-speaking Welshmen – a particularly characteristic linguistic-labourite action and one which would bring considerable kudos for him in the Caernarfon Boroughs, particularly at Bangor, where hundreds worked at the engineering headquarters of north Wales's largest railway company.[51] Then, in another labourite parliamentary missive, he announced in his column at the end of March that he would be seconding William Abraham MP (Mabon) in his motion calling for an eight-hour maximum day for coalminers.[52] In this issue of *Y Genedl*, he also stated that he was personally preparing a motion to put before the House that MPs should be paid a salary, to enable working-class members to be elected to the House of Commons and, indeed, for persons of his own impecunious background and fragile-income status to participate in politics on the radical-labourite front.

However, Lloyd George's most notorious and most highly publicized parliamentary crusade before the general election of 1892 was his second campaign of parliamentary obstruction with S. T. Evans on the Irish model, this time using the seemingly innocuous Clergy Discipline Bill to create mayhem and arouse nationalistic passions, while also calling for Welsh devolution. For months, in amendment after amendment, they delayed and changed the bill, though at the same time arousing the Anglican Liberal Gladstone's wrath and the ire of Gladstonians in their constituencies. Many Gladstonians were supporters of the Clergy Discipline Bill, including Gladstone personally. However, Lloyd George and S. T. Evans argued that no government should have the right to discipline wayward Anglican clergymen, but that it was a Church matter, while, at the same time, they used clauses in the bill and amendments to it to raise Welsh demands, not connected to the central aim of the measure. After the start of their campaign, in early April, the Tory *Western Mail* went so far as to claim that Lloyd George's obstructionalist tactics were not only disgraceful, but would lead to political suicide for him at the next general election:

> In regard to Lloyd George there is the reasonable and exceedingly pleasant prospect that he will be defeated (on his opposition to the Bill) and Welsh politics will be purged of one of the principal factors that have made them stink in the nostrils of decent men.[53]

As the Evans–Lloyd George campaign increased in intensity and public comment and criticism escalated, he and Evans did not relent, even in the teeth of Gladstone's parliamentary condemnation of them in a speech. He informed his wife, Margaret, in a letter written after a bitter night of parliamentary obstruction with Evans: 'We defied everybody all round and kept them dancing at least to closure us and even then we divided the House five times. We'll fight their confounded Bill in season and out of season, Gladstone or no Gladstone.'[54]

Although papers like the *Western Mail* and the *North Wales Chronicle* blackened him as 'The Welsh Parnell' and 'a professional agitator' after this, another rebellion, and claimed that he would certainly lose his seat to Sir John Puleston, he did not refrain from heightening the controversy further, with S. T. Evans, over the Clergy Discipline Bill. He had his own *Genedl* company papers to defend his and Evans's behaviour in a special edition of *Y Genedl Gymreig* with a pamphlet inserted and entitled 'Barn Y Wlad Amdanynt' (The Country's View of Them).[55] It claimed, exaggeratedly, that Welsh public opinion was in their favour. *Y Llan*, in its June edition, however, railed against them, stating that 'the two had succeeded in emulating the Irish in their idiocies', and further claiming that Lloyd George would lose his seat as he had alienated every moderate Gladstonian by his anti-Gladstone stand over the Clergy Discipline Bill: 'They have flouted Mr Gladstone and offended the more reasonable section of their party by their spiteful tactics.'[56]

Stuart Rendel MP, Gladstone's confidant and the unofficial leader of Welsh Liberals and Gladstonians, was also disgusted with the antics of Evans and Lloyd George, writing to his friend, and foe of Lloyd George, A. C. Humphreys-Owen: 'He and Evans have seriously disgusted not only the official Liberals but downright radicals . . . I fear our position as a party is gravely compromised.'[57]

To add to Rendel's woe and to the consternation of official Liberals, a storm of controversy erupted around the two rebels in June 1892, when both participated in a highly publicized anti-royalist demonstration. In a dinner at the Mansion House, London, Evans refused to stand when the royal toast was proposed and Lloyd George declined to raise his glass to the queen. London and north Wales papers highlighted the incident and in the election campaign of 1892 Lloyd George had to deny in public that he had sat down during the royal toast at the Mansion House incident.

After this controversy and the Clergy Discipline Bill fracas, and soon after the Mansion House incident, a general election was announced and the polling day set for 9 July. Lloyd George faced a formidable struggle to retain his seat after two years of controversy and the opposition of the redoubtable Tory, Sir John Puleston, who had been nursing the electorate diligently since his selection and appointment as constable of Caernarfon Castle, while Lloyd George was busy in Parliament and often away from his constituency on Wales-wide speaking tours. His radicalism and nationalism were still a handicap for him in the conservative marginal Caernarfon Boroughs, underlined by the fact that in Caernarfonshire County County elections, held prior to the general election, the results in each of the six boroughs were unfavourable to the Liberals, with the Tories winning more seats there than the Liberals. Many Liberals, like John Morley, a Liberal luminary and close confidant of Gladstone, privately wished he would lose his seat, while the first pre-election issue of *Y Genedl Gymreig* announced that, of all the Welsh contests, the Caernarfon Boroughs campaign would be 'Wales's Waterloo'.[58] His own paper was afraid of defeat and posed the contentious question in this edition – would Wales's and Welsh Liberalism's most advanced radical, after merely two years in Parliament, be cast into the political wilderness, an incalculable loss?[59]

Before an intense and dirty campaign really got into top gear, however, Lloyd George, during his last months in Parliament, had found time to raise many issues of direct concern to his electors in the constituency, which brought him considerable publicity. In May and June he asked several parliamentary questions – for financial aid for local seagoing fishermen; a financial reduction in the cost of fishing licences in local rivers; a reduction in royalties on local slate, to aid local quarries and the Port of Caernarfon while also pressing Caernarfonshire County Council to raise workmen's wages and use local slate and granite in their public works schemes.[60]

He also revealed his labourism and nationalism in Parliament on 3 July by challenging the postmaster-general to hold an inquiry into a dismissal scandal at Pwllheli Post Office. He alleged that three postmen in the town had been sacked for speaking Welsh at work and demanded their reinstatement not only for reasons of social justice, but also to counter official discrimination against the language, a theme he had highlighted since 1890 and even before then as the 'Boy Alderman'.[61]

However, despite this local work for his constituents, he was defending a small majority in his constituency and there was considerable discussion before his campaign began officially in private and in public circles, because of his militant reputation, that his seat would be lost. That, indeed, was the private view of Stuart Rendel in a letter to A. C. Humphreys-Owen (previously referred to in this chapter), stating quite categorically and with much hope – 'Puleston is in for a triumph'. When the election campaign started in mid-June 1892, *Y Genedl Gymreig*, referring to the coming of the 'Welsh Battle of Waterloo', also feared a triumph for Puleston, stating nervously in its opening salvo that: 'The Tories and the Church will use every trick in the book to ensure that he will never again enter parliament and that the Napoleon of the Tories [Puleston] is determined to defeat him.'[62]

The *Genedl* company's papers were to be of key value to him in the campaign, however. The editor, Beriah Gwynfe Evans, suffered from cramp after the campaign, according to a later *Genedl* editor, E. Morgan Humphreys, after endless writing of articles in the three papers he edited. Apart from these papers, throughout the campaign every Thursday Evans published a supplement in the two Welsh-language papers, under the heading *Gwerin yr Etholiad* (The Election and the People). They included a detailed account of Lloyd George's parliamentary record and the work he had done for his constituents, together with the allegedly poor attendance record of Puleston, as the MP for Devonport. They further alleged that Sir John had given up Devonport as it was a constituency he was bound to lose. The *Genedl* papers also published weekly in Welsh, 'The Songs of the Election', composed by local poets to be sung at Lloyd George's election meetings, one being 'Lloyd George Yw'r Dyn I Ni' (Lloyd George's the Man for Us), with its simple message enshrined in the last two sentences of each chorus (*Cytgan*):

Daw Cymru gaeth yn Gymru Rhydd
Dros ein hawliau, bois, Lloyd George 'yw'r dyn i ni'.

(Downtrodden Wales will be a free Wales
For our rights, boys, Lloyd George's 'the man for us'.)

Perhaps the songs lacked literary merit, but they were easily learnt and, accompanied by popular tunes, they were effective tools to be deployed in the age of great political meetings at venues like the Caernarfon Pavilion and the Bangor Penrhyn Hall and throughout the constituency at Liberal meetings. The *Genedl* press was Lloyd George's main weapon to counteract a hostile boroughs-based Tory press duo, the *North Wales Chronicle* and its sister paper *Y Gwalia* (Wales), which indulged, throughout the campaign, in vicious attacks on Lloyd George personally and politically. For example, a week before polling day the *North Wales Chronicle* issued a 'Ten Question Attack' on Lloyd George, including the four following jibes:

> Didn't people believe that there were more than enough avaricious solicitors in parliament already? Didn't people agree that giving a salary to M.P.s of a terrorist bent was a disgrace and would increase taxes? Wasn't Lloyd George completely unprincipled in attending every chapel in the constituency to win votes? Wasn't he really an extreme Home Rule for Wales advocate but gave it a secondary place in his election manifesto?[63]

That election manifesto was published, however, (though preceded by Welsh disestablishment) with a clear statement of support for a Welsh parliament (unlike the by-election manifesto of 1890):

> I am a confirmed adherent of local self-government for the nations of Britain . . . a measure conferring on Wales a large slice of it. I fail to understand why questions affecting our national system of education, our fisheries, or the mineral resources of the Crown in Wales, which are far better understood and apprehended on the spot, should be administered by government clerks in London.[64]

Though disestablishment was given the prime role in the manifesto, devolution was also urged in the form of a national council to distribute the tithes and endowments of a disestablished Church to the poor, again emphasizing Lloyd George's support for 'Home Rule' on two fronts. But, perhaps, the most significant social welfare/labourist element in his manifesto was his call for the provision of old age pensions, again an indication that his alleged 'New Liberalism' of the post-1906 era was already a part of his agenda as a radical-nationalist labourite in the early 1890s – as it would be financed by taxing rich landlords/ industrialists like the Faenol and Penrhyn families, on their industrial profits and land value capital gains and earnings. The manifesto was far more radical, anti-Gladstonian and nationalist than the compromising by-election address of the 1890s, although the *North Wales Chronicle* again claimed (similarly to 1890) that: 'He has shirked the Welsh Home Rule issue in the campaign.'[65]

The campaign was full of tension and muckraking, with both sides indulging in vitriolic and personal attacks. The *Genedl* press, for example, alleged that Tom Ellis MP had been injured physically by a riff-raff of drunken Tory louts at a Caernarfon meeting, while also alleging that similarly intoxicated Bangor Tories had thrown burning torches at Lloyd George and his wife at a Bangor meeting.[66] *Y Genedl* maintained that prostitutes were being paid for by the Tories at Caernarfon to lure men to vote for Puleston and that Tory bigwigs at Bangor were providing free coal and tea to voters throughout the constituency. *Y Genedl Gymreig* also said that Puleston was using his influence as constable of the castle to display his election posters and hoardings on its walls.[67] In its first post-election edition, the paper further alleged that one of Caernarfon's most noted Tories, the businessman Issard Davies, a former mayor of the town, had stood by the booth in one area of the town on polling day, threatening voters who were tenants of Tory landowners/landlords in the town that they would be evicted if they voted for Lloyd George.[68]

On the other hand, papers such as the *North Wales Chronicle* alleged, in successive editions, that a campaign of dirty tricks was being deployed by the 'Separatist' followers of Lloyd George, including a stone-throwing attack on Puleston at Pwllheli. The paper also alleged that students of the Independent Bala Bangor Theological College had participated in an unholy riot in the city, at a Puleston meeting at the Penrhyn Hall, while they asserted that the *Genedl* papers' supplements attacking Puleston's alleged poor parliamentary record were a pack of lies.

In only his second election, Lloyd George undoubtedly faced an uphill struggle to retain the seat on a far more radical programme and without the resources from all parts of Wales which he could command in a by-election. But he stood in 1892 on an advanced radical, nationalist platform, enshrined in his declaration opposite Tom Ellis MP at Caernarfon, reported in *Y Genedl Gymreig*, that both were nationalists. He stated: 'Wales and her national aspirations is our call to work. Here is Young Wales and it also stands for a Free Wales.'[69] He also added that Sir John Puleston, the prominent patron of the National Eisteddfod, was a hypocritical Welsh patriot: 'Wasting his patriotism on patronising eulogies on Eisteddfod platforms to squires and aristocrats who dominated the highly anglicised National Eisteddfod.'[70]

Lloyd George campaigned personally, with total commitment, throughout the contest, confessing to his wife, mid way, in a letter of 23 June from Conwy, that he was under tremendous strain and informing her, days before the poll in another letter on 5 July, that the contest was too close to call and urging her that at Criccieth she should 'visit every house, go at it, I implore you'.[71] He also confessed, in an undated letter during the height of the struggle to his Uncle Lloyd, that he feared defeat, stating: 'I must honestly admit that I am not all sanguine about the result.'[72] There was much trepidation amongst his closest followers, too, that, since he had fought the campaign on his militant parliamentary record of 1890–2 and had not shrunk from taking an anti-Gladstonian line in the election, he could face political oblivion in the 'Welsh Battle of Waterloo'.

However, with scenes reminiscent of the by-election count of 1890, where there had been several recounts, it was announced from the Guildhall on Monday, 11 July, that the 'Welsh Napoleon', Puleston, had lost the seat to the 'Welsh Parnell', by a majority of 196 votes, far more than the paper-thin majority of 18 in 1890. He had secured a record number of votes in the small constituency, 2,154. Lloyd George had won the seat, against a tremendous challenge by Puleston, while defending a radical labourist and nationalist reputation as the 'Parliamentary Raver'. He did not 'tend to reticence' over Home Rule for Wales in the campaign, as J. Graham Jones has suggested.[73]

After the result, Lloyd George undertook a tour of the constituency, with crowds of supporters everywhere carrying 'Young Wales' banners and messages on them such as 'The Triumph of Young Wales', according to a highly evocative account in his own *North Wales Observer and Express*.[74] On his way to London by train to resume his parliamentary career, he stopped at Conwy and there he claimed that he was ready to take his already militant nationalism a step further in a new parliament, with a new minority Gladstonian Liberal government again in office. He was ready to form an independent Welsh party unless Gladstone promised Welsh disestablishment and a national Welsh council and other Welsh measures as a priority in the forthcoming new session of Parliament. The *South Wales Daily News* gave considerable coverage to this speech, which, it claimed, bordered on blackmail against Gladstone in its peroration:

> The Welsh members want nothing for themselves, but they must get something for our little country and I do not think they will support a Liberal Ministry – I care not how illustrious the Minister (Gladstone) who leads it – unless it pledges itself to concede to Wales those great measures of reform upon which Wales has set its heart. Wales has lived long on promises. She has in hand a number of political I.O.U.s . . . and is in a splendid position, by the exigencies of the electoral results, to insist on prompt payment.[75]

The exigency of the electoral result was that Gladstone led a minority Liberal government, with 31 of the 34 Welsh seats in Liberal hands and thus Gladstone was particularly dependent on their support (together with that of the Irish Nationalist MPs). Lloyd George believed that Welsh MPs were in a favourable position to exploit the fluid political situation to fulfil Welsh national aspirations (although he knew that Gladstone was in even greater hock to the Irish nationalists and determined to proceed, firstly, with Irish Home Rule). Nevertheless, by 1892, as William George, his brother, maintained, Lloyd George was determined that he would secure Welsh national aspirations at the expense of his party: 'He roundly declared that, henceforth, Wales must be given its rightful place in the Liberal Party programme.'[76] The message was even clearer in the weekly journal, *Y Brython Cymreig*, which declared: 'Lloyd George will never again appear as one of the mute dogs of his party.'[77]

Indeed, since 1890 he had not muted his call for Welsh national aspirations and both directly and indirectly he had called for self-government for Wales. After 1892, increasingly, the 'Parnell of Wales' was to call for a complete restructuring of Welsh politics and, in 1894, he was to set up the first modern movement for Welsh Home Rule – the Young Wales League. He was also to be dubbed by his Tory and Liberal enemies 'Wales's Monkey Patriot', but he was much more than the merely 'playacting rebel' and 'pragmatic patriot' that John Grigg suggests. He had a deep and long commitment to Welsh Home Rule from 1885–6 and, in the following years, was to take Welsh politics on to a higher and even more extreme nationalist plane.

IX

'THE MONKEY PATRIOT' AND YOUNG WALES, 1892–1895

Ever since Lloyd George had nearly committed political suicide in 1886, when he supported Joseph Chamberlain's 'Home Rule All Round', he had not abandoned up his belief in self-government for Wales within a federal or quasi-federal British context. True he had compromised on the issue in the 1890 by-election, but, in Parliament between 1890 and 1892 and in Wales, he had not only declared war on Gladstonianism and for Welsh disestablishment with its hidden agenda of a Welsh national council, a step towards Home Rule, but he had also constantly referred directly to his belief in federal Welsh self-government.

However, despite threatening open rebellion against Gladstone in his Conwy speech after the 1892 election and threatening to form an independent Welsh party, he was well aware that he could not immediately rebel against the new Gladstone government until he had taken stock of the fragile position of the new government and bided his time before taking positive action to demand that Wales's IOUs were paid.

As he did between 1890 and 1892, after the election of 1892 he could thus play a dual role – on one hand pressing the Liberal government to give priority for disestablishment, with devolution attached to it, while, on the other hand, at times promoting the cause for outright Home Rule. There is no doubt that, from 1892 to 1895, if Gladstone and any other Liberal successor were to refuse to give Wales disestablishment and a devolved body, which would provide aid for the poor from the proceeds of disendowment, Lloyd George was ready to bring the cause of Welsh Home Rule and an independent nationalist party to the forefront of his agenda. These were tactics used in a committed cause, but not 'playacting' for, since 1885–6, he had had a long commitment to Home Rule.

In the summer of 1892, he faced the dilemma of whether he should immediately wage war against Gladstone's government or bide his time before striking, although he was well aware of Gladstone's primary obsession with Irish Home Rule and his apathy, if not opposition, to Welsh Church disestablishment. Another problem faced Lloyd George, too, as the new government was formed, after his friend and co-nationalist,

Tom Ellis, was invited into government as a whip; this severely curtailed Ellis's ability to act independently, although he had the ear of the Liberal hierarchy in government. Would Lloyd George accept Ellis's appointment – 'grasping the Saxon gold' as it was vividly described by J. Arthur Price, the notable nationalist – with Ellis directly tied to official Liberalism?[1] Or would Lloyd George view Tom Ellis's elevation to power as an instrumental lever to secure Welsh national aspirations in the corridors of power?

It is obvious that the whole issue was of considerable concern to Lloyd George and perhaps, finally, the evidence shows that he believed Ellis took the wrong route by accepting the post of junior whip. However, Lloyd George took a complex, paradoxical line on the issue. Initially, in a personal letter to Ellis on 16 August, he warned him against taking the post unless he received definite assurances that the new government made *carte blanche* promises to Wales. He told him that unless he had had a binding agreement to that effect, he should not accept: 'Unless it is an honourable one, I know you will not join [the government] at all.'[2] However, he seems to have given his blessing to Ellis's acceptance of office some days later, for Ellis wrote to him on 21 August, thanking Lloyd George for supporting him in accepting the post:

> I have received many congratulations – 30 came this morning – but yours was the most generous . . . this is an experiment I undertake relying upon the goodwill of my colleagues and their trustfulness that in this new sphere my ideals and loyalty shall be Welsh, and by being Welsh, democratic. Your letter deepens this conviction which our steadily growing partnership has planted in me that you will be my steadfast friend and outspoken counsellor.[3]

However, in the interval between these two letters, unknown to Ellis, Lloyd George, in a secret letter to his co-nationalist, S. T. Evans, the Mid Glamorgan MP, agreed with Evans that Ellis had made a fundamental error in accepting a lowly and tied government post, especially as he believed that Ellis had received no assurance from Gladstone that the government would legislate on Welsh disestablishment and that it was unlikely to honour its promise in the 1892 election manifesto to act on the matter immediately after an Irish Home Rule Bill. Evans obviously concurred that Ellis had made a fundamental mistake in taking part in a fragile minority government, as Lloyd George's letter shows:

> I quite agree with you that Ellis has made a great mistake in accepting office in such a broken-winded ministry. He could

have done much better work as an independent member without being involved in the discredit, which, I fear, must befall this Administration.[4]

Lloyd George would repeat this assertion several times and later during the administration he would oppose Ellis publicly, although they were to remain steadfast friends throughout the terms of government and even later when Lloyd George took an out-and-out independent stand with the Young Wales League in 1894–5. Indeed, up to March 1893, when Gladstone resigned from the premiership, Lloyd George did not revolt openly against the government and embarrass Ellis, but gave him and Gladstone a short-lived opportunity to legislate for Wales. Indeed, Ellis and Lloyd George spent a highly enjoyable holiday together at Cricieth and in the Vale of Clwyd in the summer of 1892. Then, in September 1892, when Gladstone came to Caernarfon and to Nant Gwynant, at the foot of Snowdon, to open the famous Watkin path, both Ellis and Lloyd George appeared together on public platforms and, indeed, Lloyd George spoke briefly at the ceremony at the foot of Snowdon, refraining from any attack upon the Grand Old Man and keeping his real feelings under control. Moreover, according to the *North Wales Observer and Express*, he declared of the Grand Old Man that: 'Welsh people had a special boast in him and his statesmanship.'[5]

Indeed, during Ellis's first session as junior whip, Lloyd George, uncharacteristically, for several months, took virtually no part in politics (indeed, there was a long parliamentary recess from late September until the New Year). But there was another reason for his political quietude and his absence from public platforms in Wales. Since the beginning of his parliamentary career, he had been financially stretched, with two homes to pay for and no parliamentary salary, and was almost dependent on the support of his brother, his partner in the family firm of solicitors. He was continually on the lookout for financial opportunities to boost his meagre income. In 1892, he started forth on a risky and dangerous venture, which proved ultimately abortive. It was to lead a syndicate which would explore for gold in Patagonia. He believed that it would be his financial salvation and throughout the winter of 1892 he expended most of his time and energy in setting up the venture, and on various occasions until 1896, when the venture folded in ignominy.

When Parliament resumed in January 1893, after a long recess, and after Lloyd George's lengthy financial diversion from politics, he returned to the political fold with panache in a public intervention following the Queen's Address, outlining Gladstone's policy proposals. The address gave priority to Irish Home Rule and only promised Wales, instead of disestablishment, a weak and subordinate Welsh Church Suspensory

Bill, which promised to place the Church's endowments in the hands of the Crown, without any promise of full disestablishment and disendowment (allied to devolution), which he had expected might happen. In a massive demonstration at Liverpool on 19 January 1893, after hearing of Gladstone's intentions, he voiced publicly his disgust at the news, in 'seditious language', according to the following day's *Liverpool Mercury*.[6] He threatened that Wales would cut her connection with Gladstonianism and that he would break the law in a campaign to secure disestablishment and Welsh devolution: 'Wales was prepared, if needs be, to sacrifice her political connections, her devotion to great statesmen and even her respect for the law, in order to ensure freedom and equality upon which her soul was bent.'[7]

His threat to act decisively was not carried out, however, as the Irish Home Rule Bill completely dominated parliamentary time and he returned to concentrate on the Patagonian gold venture. He was also anxious not to embarrass Tom Ellis. But, after a lengthy wait, he took the leading role in raising the stakes of disestablishment. In the summer of 1893, he wrote a letter to Gladstone personally, signed by the majority of Welsh Liberal MPs, demanding action on the disestablishment front – a letter which received no promise of priority for the issue. He did not press the matter further and, indeed, in August, he destroyed an attempt made by D. A. Thomas, the Merthyr MP, despite their joint rebellion in 1890 against the Church, to form an independent Welsh Party because of Gladstone's opposition to Welsh demands. He did this because he knew that Thomas wanted disestablishment of the Church so that most of its endowments would go to the populous south-east Wales region. He also knew that D. A. Thomas wanted to lead an independent Welsh party, which he himself wanted to control; he was aware, too, that such a party would not promote the labourite message he desired, such as the eight-hour day, as D. A. Thomas was a millionaire coal magnate. Lloyd George, in time, would find himself undermined by D. A. Thomas when he established the Young Wales League in 1894, in revenge for his action in 1893 in preventing Thomas from taking the initiative over a south-east Wales dominated independent Welsh party.

However, while preventing Thomas from establishing an independent party, he was determined, sooner rather than later, to take independent action against Gladstone or his successor, especially if disestablishment was further shelved by his party. That opportunity came in March 1894, when the long fight for Irish Home Rule came finally to grief, after inner tensions in Gladstone's Cabinet and the continuing opposition of the House of Lords. Gladstone resigned, with the Irish question having brought him to despair after his failure in 1886 and then in 1894 to bring about his 'mission to pacify Ireland' – an issue which had put him in a mental 'straitjacket'.

His successor as prime minister was the horse-racing fanatic, Lord Rosebery, who had no interest in the Irish question, although it was believed that he favoured Welsh disestablishment and promised to give it a high priority position in his government's programme. That hope did not materialize, however, and Lloyd George was now determined, after a year and a half of comparative silence and prevarication, to start on a campaign which led him to be accused in 1895 of bringing about the downfall of Rosebery's government. This was the beginning of a revolt, which ended in his formation of Wales's first modern nationalist movement – the Young Wales League – when he took unprecedented risks in his career, arousing the spleen of most orthodox Liberals and led an organization encompassing many of the labourite, radical, linguistic and nationalist aspirations he had held since 1886. The movement he was to lead was not posturing nor a personal power vehicle for himself, as so many historians have asserted, but the culmination of almost a decade of activity on the radical-nationalist front, which had started since the days he had called himself the Nationalist candidate for the Caernarfon Boroughs and as the newspaper owner of a nationalist and socialist regenerator, *Yr Udgorn Rhyddid* (The Trumpet of Freedom), as far back as 1888.

The first steps in this campaign of rebellion came soon after Rosebery had published his Queen's Speech, with no reference to Welsh disestablishment. After a private meeting with Tom Ellis, now promoted to chief whip, on 8 March 1894, he received from Ellis no clear assurance that Rosebery intended to legislate on Welsh disestablishment in the forthcoming session. Four days after the abortive meeting with Ellis, Lloyd George led a deputation of Welsh MPs to the leader of the Commons, Sir William Harcourt, to demand disestablishment, but they received only a vacuous promise of future action and Lloyd George, then, was certain that the government had no intention of passing through the Commons an act disestablishing the Anglican Church in Wales, knowing as well that it would be destroyed by a hostile House of Lords.

Revolt was inevitable. On 12 April, he, Frank Edwards, Brecknock and Radnor's MP, and D. A. Thomas (joined later by J. Herbert Lewis, MP for the Flintshire Boroughs), leaked a story to *The Times* lobby correspondent that they would refuse to obey the Liberal whip and that they would act as an independent party in Parliament. When the story broke, a storm of controversy erupted in both the Liberal Party and opposition ranks. This outburst of indignation forced Lloyd George to convene an emergency meeting at Caernarfon, the centre of his constituency, on 14 April, to justify 'The Revolt' and the formation of an independent party.

There, even according to his own paper, the *North Wales Observer and Express*, he faced a number of hostile interjections from the floor and much barracking, including allegations that his actions could precipitate the downfall of the government. In a challenging riposte, however, he justified the rebellion and, at least according to his own *Observer*, he was cheered by the overwhelming majority of the previously baying crowd of critics.[8] In his speech, he claimed that his government consisted of 'A Cabinet of Churchmen' and that he and his fellow rebels had to 'stand on independent grounds and tell the Liberal Cabinet that they could never again, break their promises to Wales'.[9] He prepared the way for an independent Welsh nationalist movement – The Young Wales League. Justifying their independent action, he said:

> Were they to go to the government in a humiliating spirit and say they had transgressed and that they only meant to frighten, like Sir Andrew Aguecheek, from Shakespeare, who after making a challenge, cowered when he found his opponent was ready to stand his ground? Had they, as a nation, not enough firmness? If not, they were not worth fighting for. They should rely upon their own strength. The English people who possessed reliance and self-respect were under the impression that the Welsh people were not in earnest. They regarded the Welsh people as parasites. He, however, would show them they were mistaken.[10]

The Tories in his constituency were baying for his blood, with the *North Wales Chronicle*, reflecting on the Caernarfon meeting, alleging that 'he was showing himself off' and castigating him for calling Welsh people 'parasites' in his speech.[11] However, with the 'Welsh Revolt of the Four' launched in a flurry of controversy, he was intent on establishing an independent Welsh party with self-government as his aim. On 2 May, he informed his wife that this was his aim, after telling her that he had received countless resolutions of support from all parts of the Welsh nation: 'I receive daily resolutions from different parts of Wales in support of my action . . . the game now is, an independent party at the next election.'[12]

A few days later, J. Herbert Lewis, a lifelong friend of Lloyd George and perhaps Cymru Fydd's most persistent and committed nationalist, tried, completely unrealistically, to get his and Lloyd George's friend, Tom Ellis, to renounce his government post and join 'The Four' in their rebellion, stating:

> Wales is being led on from step to step without any definite goal in actual view, that we have nothing to gain by subservience to the Liberal Party and we shall never get the English to do us justice until we show our independence of them.[13]

At the end of the same letter to Ellis, Lewis revealed that he and Lloyd George, by rebelling against the government, were putting their political careers in jeopardy. He told his friend, who had accepted a government post as chief whip, the disciplinarian of the party line, that he felt no option but to obey his conscience and appealed to Ellis, forlornly, to follow him: 'This is the critical hour. On the one hand is an official career, on the other the hardship of a nation. To go into the wilderness without you would be terribly disheartening, but go I must . . .'[14] Ellis declined, but the letter underlined that it was no small matter for Lewis (and Lloyd George) to risk their careers and rebel in the 'Revolt of the Four' (and subsequently to support the Young Wales League).

This is in stark contrast to John Grigg's claim that Lloyd George, in leading the revolt and subsequently the Young Wales League, had nothing to lose in putting his career on the line.[15] Indeed, Lloyd George's stand at this juncture resulted in fierce personal criticism of him, the threat of going into the wilderness and the potential loss of the friendship of one of his closest political allies, Tom Ellis, who was in an increasingly invidious position as the rebellion proceeded. Indeed, 'the Revolt of the Four' caused great personal sorrow and even anger to Tom Ellis, following the promise that Lloyd George had given him in 1892, that he supported his government promotion then, and given the fact that Ellis had regarded him as being a close and supportive counsellor. In a letter to their mutual friend, D. R. Daniel, on 30 April, Ellis confessed his disappointment: 'George is very threatening. He means to be on the warpath. His whole attitude is to upset the apple cart.'[16]

Attempts were made to mollify 'The Four' by Rosebery, early during the revolt, by promising that in the near future the government would present a Disestablishment Bill, but Lloyd George believed that no such measure would go through Parliament in that session, while it would also be obstructed by the Lords. He also knew that the minority government was extremely fragile and that it was unlikely to last long enough to carry the measure to its conclusion. (Indeed, an inadequate bill was presented before the House in the summer of 1894, but it reached only a preliminary stage before it was withdrawn and then again presented to Parliament in 1895 with no chance of becoming law.)

From April until the summer of 1894, Lloyd George was highly critical of his own government. For example, in an inflammatory speech at Bangor on 14 May, accompanied by his three fellow rebels, he justified their stand, according to the *North Wales Observer and Express*, by stating: 'Our support has fetched nothing in the political market and it is time in the interests of Wales to initiate a new policy.'[17] That policy, manifested publicly later that month, was the attempt to launch a new Cymru Fydd, Young Wales movement – this time the Cymru Fydd/Young Wales

League, rather than the former Cymru Fydd Society. Unlike its predecessor, that league was a militant, independent movement. However, earlier, at the Bangor meeting of 'The Revolt of the Four', Lloyd George had been given a taste of the opposition in his own Boroughs constituency, not only to the rebellion, but to any form of Welsh devolution.

The *North Wales Observer and Express*, his own paper, revealed that a prominent Bangor Gladstonian and anti-nationalist, Dr E. O. Price, had interrupted Lloyd George's speech there and had accused him of splitting the party locally and nationally by calling for an independent Welsh party.[18] The paper, naturally, attacked Price and claimed that a motion of support was proposed, supporting Lloyd George, and passed almost unanimously, after Price's intervention. However, that attack upon Lloyd George was indicative of future opposition in his own constituency to his independent action. He, however, was characteristically euphoric (and, to some extent, deluded into thinking that there was overwhelming support for him locally) after the meeting. Writing in his usual optimistic and egotistic vein to his wife, Margaret, after the Bangor meeting of 'The Four', and others, held at the same time in the constituency, he claimed: 'Magnificent meetings. Immense – swept all before us. Made many converts by my speech last night. I was in fine form and carried them, step by step, completely with me.'[19]

Another convert Lloyd George failed to make at the Bangor 'Gang of Four' meeting, in addition to Dr E. O. Price, was the redoubtable, sober Gladstonian MP for the neighbouring constituency of Eifion, J. Bryn Roberts. He was also present at the meeting and was no 'Radical Colt',[20] but in tune with many Gladstonian voters and the well-off middle class of Bangor, where he lived in some splendour at Bryn Adda, and could often be seen riding on horseback. When the Cymru Fydd League reached its zenith of rebellion, later in 1895, he was to be Lloyd George's most bitter critic, despite the fact that he was one of the barristers who gave him invaluable advice and got him off the alleged Cemaes Road sex scandal in 1896–7 – the first public sex scandal in which Lloyd George was involved, when he was alleged to have fathered the child of Kitty Edwards, the local doctor's wife in the Montgomeryshire village.

At the Bangor meeting, J. Bryn Roberts, seated silently on the stage, did not emulate his friend Dr E. O. Price's outburst against Lloyd George. However, it was remarked in the *North Wales Observer and Express* report that he was not best pleased at Lloyd George's nationalistic speech. The paper observed succinctly: 'Mr Bryn Roberts who was on the stage, did not say a word.'[21] But, as soon as Lloyd George's rebellion turned into a clearly nationalistic organization, he would be one of his most voluble critics.

Lloyd George did not only seek to justify the parliamentary 'Revolt of the Four' in his own constituency, but, in the early summer of 1894, he also tried to raise the political temperature throughout Wales, particularly in south Wales, conducting a widespread number of speaking engagements there in May. He wrote as overconfidently as ever to his brother William, on 30 May, after several meetings: 'We are carrying all before us now.'[22] Some days earlier, he had given an interview on a weekend return to north Wales, to the *Liverpool Daily Post*, stating that he was determined to set up an independent Welsh party. He told north Wales's widely read daily paper:

> There are many who deny our national existence and we can hardly be surprised at that, because our support has been so entirely given to one party, that our separate entity as a nation has become merged into one political party . . . the ultimate result of this independence will be to form a new Welsh National Party.[23]

By the summer of 1894, with the puny and ineffective Disestablishment Bill postponed by a hostile Commons amidst government apathy, Lloyd George had no lingering doubts that an independent Welsh party was the only solution for Wales, despite the fact that the four rebels had the whip restored to them that summer, if in his case in name only. Long before then, in May Lloyd George had set in motion the creation of the Cymru Fydd/Young Wales League, when he was responsible for formulating a draft constitution of the new organization, which was printed in the *North Wales Observer and Express*.[24] Then, in June, at a large meeting, at Chester of all places, of 400 North Wales Liberals, the League's constitution was discussed. It appears from the report of that meeting in *Baner ac Amserau Cymru* that there was agreement that a proposed league, having as its objective an independent party for Wales with its aim Home Rule, would be ratified, if agreement could be reached with South Wales Liberals.[25]

However, on the same day, the Tory *North Wales Chronicle*, condemned the meeting as 'The Monkey Patriots of Wales', with Lloyd George the main 'Monkey Patriot'.[26] Then, in August 1894, when north Wales and south Wales representatives met at Llandrindod to discuss Lloyd George's draft proposals for the league, the Tory press in the shape of the *North Wales Chronicle* again, dubbed the meeting 'The Big Goosebery of the Welsh Silly Season'.[27] Lloyd George, the main inspiration behind the meeting, was again labelled 'The Monkey Patriot'. Lloyd George believed, following both the Chester and Llandrindod meetings, that a nationwide Cymru Fydd League would soon be created, although there were damaging straws in the wind, even at Chester, where D. A. Thomas gave only a mixed blessing to the proposed league, on condition that it was not a centralized powerful body (under Lloyd

George's control), but a loose federation, where he and South Wales Liberals would have a preponderant voice. He reiterated this argument at Llandrindod in August but, nevertheless, Lloyd George was confident that the league would become an independent force in Welsh politics – a claim he had voiced before the Llandrindod meeting at Cricieth in July. There, according to the *North Wales Observer and Express*, he had called for an independent, nationalist movement to be established: 'The time has come for Wales to stand out for herself. The only nation worthy of support in its struggle was the nation which fights for itself . . . Wales must have a Welsh National Party.'[28] However, at Llandrindod, because of the opposition of D. A. Thomas and the South Wales Liberals, no firm consensus over the nature of the league had been reached to establish a powerful, central Welsh National League. Yet, Lloyd George was confident, perhaps overconfident, that such an organization would be formed, based on his draft constitution, printed in the *North Wales Observer and Express*, in May (see previous reference).

Lloyd George's aim in the draft constitution was to bring all the previously established Cymru Fydd societies into a nationwide Welsh movement and to establish new Young Wales branches throughout Wales, which would replace all existing Welsh Liberal branches. These would be local and democratic, but would be accountable to a newly established, centrally controlled executive council of the Welsh League, which would be the top body of the new movement. The central council would elect the main officials of the league, after names were sent in from the branches. It was obvious that Lloyd George was proposing a root-and-branch restructuring of Welsh politics, with the destruction of the moribund North and South Wales Liberal Federations and the emergence of a new, democratic movement of newly established Young Wales branches at its base and a strong, nationalist, central organization to coordinate and lead the movement.

The league also had revolutionary objectives, including disestablishment, land reform, local option; the extension of popular education; the vote for men and women over twenty-one; the securing of good working conditions in the coalmining and slate-quarrying industries and the promotion of the Welsh language as an official language of government and public and industrial life in Wales. But, underlying all these issues, was the establishment of Federal Home Rule for Wales, to secure a more just and egalitarian society.

According to the historian, Emyr Wyn Williams, in his article on Welsh Home Rule, the reference to the needs and aspirations of coalminers and slate quarrymen was vital to the league's objectives and a new departure in Welsh Liberal aims, confirming Lloyd George's labourism before 1894.[29] According to Williams, it differed completely in this respect from the

Cymru Fydd Society established since 1886, which had no labour aims. The historian K. O. Morgan has dismissed the view that the proposed league had a powerful labour message, stating that the league had but 'somewhat vaguely conceived Labour policies'.[30] The question of the labourist element in Lloyd George's new organization has been a moot one amongst historians, but there is no doubt that Lloyd George, from 1890 to 1894, had frequently proposed and supported labour and social welfare policies. Indeed, nothing was more pronounced in his labourism than his support for the lengthy struggle and the bitter strike at the Llechwedd Quarry at Blaenau Ffestiniog in 1893 which lasted from May to September – an involvement which shows how misinformed is K. O. Morgan's assertion that the first Penrhyn strike of 1897 was the first time that Lloyd George got involved with union matters.[31]

This notable strike has been described in detail in R. Merfyn Jones's seminal work on the Quarrymen's Union, but Jones failed to mention Lloyd George's involvement in the strike and in supporting the victimized workers. The strike ended in bitter failure, partly due to the inefficiency of the North Wales Quarrymen's Union and the existence of many non-unionized quarrymen in the Llechwedd works, managed by its major shareholder, J. E. Greaves. The majority returned to work, but the three martyr leaders of the strike – John Hughes, Ellis Hughes and D. G. Williams (Tanymarian), friends of Lloyd George since 1885 – were victimized by the employers when the workers returned in September 1893 and not allowed to return to the quarry. The quarrymen lost the largest ever strike in Blaenau Ffestiniog's history, but Lloyd George took two prominent roles in the workers' campaign. At a huge meeting of the North Wales Quarrymen's Union to support the victimized leaders, in August 1893 at Caernarfon, he spoke alongside Tom Ellis MP and called on all workers throughout north Wales to take strike action, to champion the quarrymen – stating, according to the *North Wales Observer and Express*:

> The whole mass of workmen in North Wales should support the men in their manly defence against the attempt made to crush them. This is a battle between the masses and the capitalists and it behoves every Welshmen and quarryman who cherished the principles of Unionism to stand by the men in their conflict.[33]

His call for such militant action fell on deaf ears, but he secured a partial victory for other victims of the strike in October 1893. These were eight ordinary quarrymen accused by the employers of violence against a blackleg, R. D. Hughes. After an initial hearing at Penrhyndeudraeth Magistrates' Court, where they were defended by William George, the matter was taken to the Merioneth Quarter Sessions at Bala. The *North*

Wales Observer and Express reported with glee that, after a protracted hearing lasting until 10 p.m., all charges against the workers were dismissed with 'the result received with considerable cheering'.[34] Lloyd George was the successful defence lawyer.

This incident, hitherto unmentioned in any of Lloyd George's biographies, underlines his unionism and labourist sympathies, as did his later involvement in the two major Penrhyn strikes. It also undoubtedly shows, as did his frequent involvement with the Quarrymen's Union, that he had powerful labourist objectives long before 1906 and that his Young Wales League had a labourist message. He believed that a Welsh parliament could legislate on widespread union, welfare and social reforms.

K. O. Morgan, in addition to criticizing Lloyd George's vaguely conceived labourism, has also suggested that his Young Wales League did not really prioritize Home Rule, but was merely a pressure group to influence Westminster Liberal politics. He claims: 'He saw it primarily as a political instrument for uniting Welsh constituency parties and thereby putting pressure on the Liberal Party leadership and the London based party machine.'[35] This view, that the movement was merely a pressure group, is shared by John Grigg: 'He had never intended to be the Parnell of Wales in any sense but one – that he wanted to control the Welsh M.P.s and to make use of their corporate powers.'[36]

However, these comments belittle Lloyd George's nationalist political views, which he had held since 1886, and his constant commitment to the cause of self-government for a lengthy period, when he had risked his political career on the altar of Home Rule and was to do so even more from 1894 to 1896. He has also been accused by historians of leading the Cymru Fydd League from 1894 to 1896 as an egotistical, self-centred venture – 'the temporary vessel for his ambitions', according to J. Graham Jones in his article on Cymru Fydd in 1895–6.[37] Jones argues that he was primarily motivated by personal, political ambition in leading the movement and he suggests, too, that it was only a pressure group. Of course, it cannot be denied that Lloyd George was egotistical and ambitious, nor that he wished to lead and control the movement, but in leading it he would sacrifice much, threaten his career and arouse intense criticism, particularly from his own party. There is no doubt, moreover, that he had a vision of a self-governing Wales, from his earliest steps in politics, within a British political context, and that a powerful Welsh parliament would embark on groundbreaking radical and socio-economic-linguistic matters – a programme of reform that a Westminster government seemed to him then, loath to implement.

Certainly, there was no stinting of energy in his determination to lead the Young Wales Movement and seek to build a nationwide organization after the Llandrindod meeting of August 1894, despite seethings of opposition there by South Wales Liberals. From the summer of 1894 to the autumn of that year, he travelled throughout Wales, seeking to found branches of his movement and to establish a strong, powerful movement for Home Rule, which would completely restructure Welsh Liberalism, through establishing an independent party. He travelled the length and breadth of Wales during the autumn of 1894, from Tredegar to Llangefni, from Caerphilly to Llandudno, to publicize the movement, which would counteract, indeed, replace, the official Liberal organization in Wales. For example, in September, even at the centrepoint of official Liberal power (at Bangor, in his own constituency base), he sought to establish a Young Wales branch as a counterpoint to the city's official Liberal branch, securing hundreds of new members for the branch, according, at least, to his own *Observer and Express*.[38] However, the *North Wales Chronicle*, a day later, said his recruitment meeting at Bangor for Young Wales had been a flop and that the meeting had been disrupted and damaged by searing criticism from a leading Bangor Liberal, Dr Rowland Jones.[39] Jones accused Lloyd George and his Young Wales League, of splitting the Liberal Party locally, by forming a Young Wales branch there, and of splintering the Liberal Party nationally and throughout Britain with his crusade for self-government. Jones claimed that Lloyd George's Home Rule views were not shared by the majority of Welsh Liberals, nor even his own constituents. He held that Welsh Liberalism was comprised of several factions but that self-government was not the primary aim of most of them and that they would not be coerced into a movement like Young Wales. Jones said: 'It is nothing, in effect, but a scheme for the coercion of the multi-coloured Liberalism of Wales into a single political organisation, animated by legislative autonomy for Wales, as its most vital principle.'[40] The *North Wales Observer and Express*, however, concluded that Dr Rowland Jones was a lone voice at the meeting, as it would, being Lloyd George's propaganda tool. But there is no doubt that Jones represented the unease, indeed, anger, of many moderate Welsh and Caernarfon Boroughs Liberals at his 'militant' policy.

A month later, there was further dissent towards Lloyd George and his new league in his own constituency, where he had organized a packed meeting at Llandudno to promote Young Wales, as part of his Wales-wide tour. Though hundreds were present, according to the *North Wales Chronicle*, several members rose and condemned his aims. The paper branded the meeting as promoting the cause of 'Wales for the Welsh' in Anglicized Llandudno. It further alleged that it excluded English-speaking Liberals in Wales. At the meeting, too, the fear was expressed by one speaker that Lloyd George's effort to set up a league branch at Llandudno would endanger the future of the local Liberal branch. Lloyd George countered that it was not just a movement for Welsh speakers, but that it

David Lloyd George's birthplace in Manchester.
(Gwynedd Archives Service)

Highgate – David Lloyd George's boyhood home.
(Gwynedd Archives Service)

David Lloyd George as a youth of 16.
(Gwynedd Archives Service)

David Lloyd George.
(Gwynedd Archives Service)

RESULT.

The result of the election was declared by the Mayor as follows:—

Lloyd-George	..	...	1963
Ellis-Nanney	...	...	1945
Majority	...	...	**18**

THE VICTORIOUS CANDIDATE.

Mr. Lloyd George was drawn in a carriage through the town by tremendous crowd, and he was accompanied by Mr. Acland, M.P., Mr. John Bryn Roberts, M.P., Dr. E. O. Price, Bangor, Mr. J. T. Roberts, and others. Arriving at Castle-square, Mr. Lloyd George, speaking in Welsh, but first of all greeted with " three cheers for the boy M.P.," which were lustily given, said:—My dear fellow-countrymen, the county of Carnarvon to-day is free (loud cheers). The banner of Wales is borne aloft and the boroughs have wiped away the stains (loud cheers). I hope that whoever will be contesting the next election (cries " It will be you ") will not fail to achieve a similar victory. The contest has been carried on by both sides in the best possible good humour. It has been a battle of principles (cries, "Coal," and laughter). I thank you from my heart, and all those who have worked so hard for the Liberal cause. I specially wish to thank the Ladies' Liberal League (three cheers were here given to the Ladies' League). Mr. George concluded by saying that he hoped the majority would be largely increased by the general election.

The carriage afterwards proceeded up Pool-street, followed by a great crowd.

After the declaration of the poll, Mr. Ellis Nanney was carried to the Conservative Club by his supporters with almost as much shouting as if he had been victorious. The large room of the club was at once filled with a large and excited crowd, who, for about five minutes, cheered Mr. Ellis Nanney in a remarkably lusty fashion. The cheers having subsided, Mr. Ellis Nanney rose and addressed his supporters. He said he was very happy to meet them all at the close of the contest which had been so gloriously fought, and which he regretted to any they had not won. ("Shame.") The

Report from the *North Wales Chronicle* re Home Rule for Wales 26 October, 1895.
(Gwynedd Archives Service)

The 1890 by-election result from the *Carnarvon and Denbigh Herald* (11 April 1890).
(Gwynedd Archives Service)

ly, the defendant himself in the sum of £10, and one surety in the sum of £20.

Home Rule all Round.

RADICAL LEADERS SNUB THE IDEA.

In the current issue of " Young Wales," the main feature is an article by Mr Lloyd George, M.P., on " National Self-Government for Wales," and a discussion under the heading, " Our Round Table Conference," in which, in reply to an invitation from the editor, a certain number of leading Radicals express their views on " Home Rule all Round " in preference to disestablishment as the foremost plank. Altogether there are no less than 22 who have a word to say on the question. Mr Gladstone comes first, but he refuses to say " yes " or " no," being afraid that any opinion from him would " be more likely to cause embarrassment than advantage." Mr Asquith declares that " the matter is not one in which he has any title to intervene." Sir H. H. Fowler " is not prepared to express an opinion." Sir Robert T. Reid, after a dig at the House of Lords and a snub to Welsh Disestablishers, pooh-poohs the Home Rule all round fad. Sir Frank Lockwood laughs at the idea, and closes with fine ridicule, " I have not read the Home Rule All Round Bill, nor have I met with anyone who has." Sir Walter Foster wisely asks, " How can Home Rule all round, or even disestablishment, be carried under the supremacy of the House of Lords ?" Mr Justin M'Carthy disclaims his ability to utter an opinion—a thing he evidently has not got on the question. Mr R. B. Haldane, Q.C., promises " to watch with interest the progress of the movement." Sir George Osborne Morgan prefers riding his old hack, Welsh Disestablishment, deeming it unwise to swap horses in crossing the stream. Mr T. P. O'Connor advises " Young Wales " to read some " lucid " speeches of his, and speaks of Home Rule for Ireland. Mr Timothy Healy is " not in a position to enter into the question." Sir Edward Grey does not think himself " competent, nor has he any desire to give any advice upon a question of tactics." Mr D. A. Thomas rides behind Sir George Osborne Morgan on the old Disestablishment hack. Mr R. W. Perks considers the Young Wales Party are " demented " destroyed, in fact, by the gods. Mr John Dillon thinks it is a question for Welsh Liberals, the while keeping his eye on Irish Home Rule. Mr John Redmond is " most strongly opposed " for substituting " Home Rule all round " for " Home Rule for Ireland.' Mr Henry Broadhurst agrees with the scheme, but regrets that Disestablishment " is not making great progress." Mr Joseph Arch swallows the pills, box and all, Mr R. M'Kenna, before replying, must feel the pulse of his " constituents." Mr Clifford Cory does not think Home Rule for Wales is " generally asked for." Mr Owen Philipps, Liberal candidate for the Montgomery Boroughs, jumps at the bait dangled before him. The Rev. Hugh Price Hughes, who comes in at the tail, puts one shoulder under Home Rule and the other under Welsh Disestablishment.

Thus " Young Wales " has received but little encouragement from the first meeting of its " Round Table Conference " to proceed with " Home Rule all Round."

David Lloyd George at a Disestablishment
meeting in the Caernarfon Pavilion, 1912.
(Gwynedd Archives Service)

David Lloyd George and Winston Churchill, Whitehall 1915.
(akg-images)

Mr and Mrs Lloyd George 1920.
(Gwynedd Archives Service)

THE STAMP
THAT WANTS
A LOT OF
LICKING

AND THE MAN

Picture Postcard celebrating
Lloyd George's National Insurance Act.
(Gwynedd Archives Service / Lloyd George Memorial Museum)

Two Interested Spectators of the Removal Operations at No. 10

The Table at which Mr. Lloyd George Presided
The famous Cabinet room at No. 10

Megan's last Public Appearance with her Father as Coalition Prime Minister

The Departure of Mr. Lloyd George, his Family, and Secretariat from No. 10

Mr. Lloyd George and his family left Downing Street last week for 86, Vincent Square, Westminster. The departure from office of a Prime Minister is always marked in this somewhat drastic manner, by an immediate vacating of No. 10. Furniture vans from various well-known firms rolled into the quiet little street, and into them went the personal belongings and furniture of the ex-Prime Minister. The family quietly took their departure for their new temporarily engaged home in Vincent Square. The Secretariat packed up their voluminous papers and left in their own way. The removal operations at one moment were watched by Sir Robert Horne and Sir L. Worthington-Evans, a little snapshot of whom appears on this page. Opposite appears a little group showing Miss. Lloyd George or "Megan," as she was popularly known during her father's brilliant "Conference" period at the opening of the new P.L.A. building. It was her last public appearance with her father during his term of office as Coalition Prime Minister. Dr. Macnamara also figures in the little group.

The quiet-looking portal, with its eighteenth-century fanlight above, has opened to many a strange and interesting gathering during Mr. Lloyd George's tenure of office. Stirring and even stormy scenes have been witnessed beneath the iron lamp with its little surmounting crown, and in the pillared chamber, designed by the architect, William Wilkins, who also did work in connection with Downing College, many an important meeting, conducted in the new manner, has taken place.

This famous house has been the residence of the First Lord of the Treasury, during his term of office, since 1735. The First Lord is, of course, nearly always the Prime Minister. The street was named after Sir George Downing, whose grandson founded Downing College. The first Prime Minister to reside in Downing Street was the famous Sir Robert Walpole. All his successors have followed this practice with the exception of Lord Melbourne, Sir Robert Peel, and Lord Salisbury. Next door to No. 10 lives the Chancellor of the Exchequer and at No. 12 is the office of the Government Whips. Nelson and Wellington once met at No. 14.

Mr. and Mrs. Lloyd George Leaving Downing Street Last Week

Mr. Lloyd George Superintending the Removal Operations at Downing Street

No. 18, Abingdon Street, which Mr. Lloyd George has Taken as Political Headquarters

David Lloyd George leaving Downing Street,
The Sphere, November 4, 1922.

Copy of the signatories to the Irish Free State Agreement,
December 1921.

Chairing of Gwenallt at the Swansea National Eisteddfod, 1926.

David Lloyd George with daughter Megan sitting under a tree.
(Gwynedd Archives Service)

Last portrait with Frances, 1945.
(Gwynedd Archives Service)

was a movement for all Welsh people; however, he did not reply to the question that the movement was a threat to official Liberal organizations and branches in Wales. Although a Cymru Fydd branch was formed at Llandudno, doubts were already being raised in 1894, even in his own constituency, about Young Wales.

Moreover, at this juncture, in the *North Wales Observer and Express*, J. Bryn Roberts, the MP for Eifion, publicly condemned the movement, after Lloyd George had established a Young Wales branch at Llanberis, in Roberts's constituency.[43] Roberts alleged that Young Wales was a crusade to form an independent Welsh nationalist party in Wales, with 'separation' as its final goal. In time, Bryn Roberts would help to undermine the league substantially. Undaunted by Roberts's criticism, however, Lloyd George continued on his Wales-wide tour. In October 1894, he addressed a huge gathering at Cardiff, to promote the movement, when he again had to deny, according to the *North Wales Observer and Express*, that Young Wales was a 'Wales for the Welsh' organization, but that it encompassed all the people of Wales, whatever their origins or language, be they Welsh, English, Scottish or any background by birth.[44] He also, once more, pressed for self-government and emphasized the failure of Westminster governments to give priority to Welsh aspirations. He stated, in an internationalist mode:

> The main factor in British legislation, therefore, is not so much which ministry is in office, but what is required by England at the hands of that Ministry. If anyone suffers from the obstruction of the reactionary forces represented in the House of Commons, it is the Celtic nationalities of this kingdom.[45]

After the Cardiff meeting and during his tour of Wales, he wrote a letter on 31 October to his friend, J. Herbert Lewis MP claiming that, because the tour was going so well, the appointment of a full-time organizer for the league would 'bring about a total membership of 10,000 or 15,000 in South Wales, before the winter is out'.[46] Indeed, by November 1894, he was arranging a further escalation of the campaign by the appointment of a full-time organizer. He was none other than the managing editor of his *Genedl* papers, Beriah Gwynfe Evans. The *North Wales Observer and Express* announced that he was leaving the company to take over the organization of the Young Wales League and, in a lengthy interview in the paper, Evans outlined his passion for the movement. In the interview, Lloyd George's own sentiments were expressed by Evans, when he declared: 'I am a Nationalist First and a Liberal Afterwards.'[47] Lloyd George's pre-parliamentary co-nationalist crusader, R. A. Griffith (Elphin), the Caernarfon solicitor and poet, had already been appointed secretary of the movement, having told the *North Wales Observer and Express* on his appointment, long before Beriah Gwynfe was made a full-time organizer, that his championing of the movement was due to the anti-nationalist Welsh Liberal official organization's attitude to Wales and that a Welsh independent party was required to fight for Home Rule. He stated: 'The Welsh Liberals have been firing blank cartridges for far too long. The time has come when if they wished their national character to be respected, they must be prepared for deeds as well as words.'[49]

The next propaganda move by the movement, after Elphin's and Gwynfe Evans's appointments, was to establish an official journal for the organization, the monthly, *Young Wales*, edited by J. Hugh Edwards, the historian, minister and journalist, and later biographer of Lloyd George. At its inception in January 1895, not for the first nor last time, it contained a portrait of Lloyd George, which verged on hero-worshipping, stating that he above all others was the embodiment of the ideals of the movement for self-government and the leader of the Cymru Fydd League:

> He is a man who believed with All Soul's passion in the sacredness of Welsh nationalism and in the future of the Welsh nation . . . it requires not the faculty of a seer to perceive that Mr. Lloyd George is leading in a new epoch in the history of Wales. The Youth of the Nation are rallying round his standard and he, in turn, is consolidating their enthusiasm and energies and stimulating their activities by inspiring them to make the glorious hope of ushering in for this grand old country of Wales that golden age whose light is of the dawn.[50]

Not all Welsh Liberals, by any stretch of the imagination, shared this glorification of Lloyd George in the *Young Wales* journal, nor its almost Messianic portrayal of him by the eulogist, J. Hugh Edwards. However, just before the launching of the *Young Wales* journal, a development in December 1894 had given Lloyd George grounds for optimism that the movement was making progress, when it was announced in his *Observer and Express* that the hitherto lukewarm North Wales Liberal Federation had allied itself officially to the league – a big boost.[51] However, at the meeting to formalize this arrangement, the Tory *North Wales Chronicle* reported that there were splits in the federation as to the move and amongst its local associates: 'The more moderate section of the Liberals opposed the formation of a Cymru Fydd League believing it to be antagonistic to the present Liberal Associations.'[52] The paper also added that a full, formal agreement to join the league had not been made by the North Wales Federation, but only an agreement on condition that the South Wales

Federation joined as well, and that overtures to it had been imprecise – a caustic comment, which was not far removed from the truth.

Indeed, that ambiguity between the two federations was to be revealed starkly on 4 January 1895 in a Cardiff at a meeting of both federations' delegates, with its highly ambivalent outcome. They agreed to join only if and when they could both agree, at a future meeting in Aberystwyth at Easter. The Cardiff meeting was inconclusive and chaotic. D. A. Thomas had opposed vigorously any highly centralized Cymru Fydd League, saying that he and the South Wales Federation preferred a more loosely structured 'federal' nationalist movement, where he and his federation would have a dominant voice. In January 1895, the Cymru Fydd League, therefore, did not have the support of the two major Welsh Liberal organizations and, from then on, culminating with the Aberystwyth meeting at Easter, chaos ensued. Indeed, D. A. Thomas announced in the *South Wales Daily News* prior to the meeting that he and his Southern Federation delegates would be boycotting the Aberystwyth meeting.[53] Then, on 17 April, in the same paper, he condemned the Cymru Fydd League's draft constitution and Young Wales's organizer Beriah Gwynfe Evans personally in a vitriolic attack on Gwynfe Evans's 'extreme nationalism' and, by implication, Lloyd George.[54]

D. A. Thomas had strong objections not only to the league's organization but also to its 'labourist message' – the millionaire coalowner having been shaken by that element in the league's objectives and by the fact that, at the Cardiff meeting in January, William Abraham MP (Mabon), the miners' leader, had agreed with Cymru Fydd's support for the miners, when he and Thomas were in heated exchanges over the proposed eight-hour day negotiations for colliers. D. A. Thomas opposed a labourist league and also an organization centrally dominated by Lloyd George. Indeed, he and Lloyd George had clashed previously in February 1895 when Lloyd George spoke in Parliament in a disestablishment debate and proposed an amendment that a powerful council of Wales, comprising elected local councillors, should be established to distribute Church endowments to the poor. Thomas feared that south-east Wales councillors would be in a minority on such a council, although the mass of the population lived there, and people in south-east Wales would receive an undue share of the endowments. Here was another D. A. Thomas–Lloyd George split on Welsh devolution. Then, with Thomas's boycott in April of the proposed joint federations meeting with the league at Easter at Aberystwyth, any notional unity between the groups was shattered.

However, at Aberystwyth, the North Wales Liberal Federation did join Young Wales, a development welcomed by the *North Wales Observer and Express*.[55] But there were obvious strains and huge obstacles to the efforts to create a unified Welsh movement, and the movement, was incomplete without the South Wales Liberal Federation. On 20 April, Lloyd George wrote angrily to his wife that he would seek revenge upon D. A. Thomas and 'smash up the remnants of his South Wales Federation'.[56]

However, that month, in two hostile moves, Thomas sought to undermine further the Cymru Fydd League, as led by Lloyd George. In a sarcastic letter to the *South Wales Daily News*, he called the Aberystwyth conference 'a farce' and implied that Young Wales was a paper-thin organization with no support in south Wales.[57] Then, to add to Lloyd George's misery, in an orchestrated move, D. A. Thomas's anti-nationalist partner in north Wales, J. Bryn Roberts, wrote a hostile anti-Cymru Fydd letter in the local Tory paper, the *North Wales Chronicle*, claiming that it was 'a lobscouse organisation' and that its alliance with the North Wales Liberal Federation was not constitutional. Indeed, he argued, it was illegal and it was only an incomplete movement written on paper.[58]

This friction between Lloyd George and D. A. Thomas and Roberts would continue for the remainder of Young Wales's existence, long after the Aberystwyth debacle in April 1895. However, Lloyd George continued on his tempestuous campaign in south Wales, including, in May, a huge meeting at Treorci in the Rhondda Valley. There, according to the *South Wales Daily News*, he called for a parliament for Wales, which would secure for Welsh workers an eight-hour day and other labour reforms and social welfare changes.[59] He was accompanied there by the Coalminers' Union south Wales leader, Mabon. Then, at Blaenau, another great coalmining centre, accompanied by the East Glamorgan MP, Alfred Thomas, who had piloted a mini-scheme for Home Rule in 1892 with his National Institutions Bill, Lloyd George said, according to the *South Wales Daily News*:

> The future of Wales must be placed in the hands of the sons and daughters of Wales. The day was past when the people of Wales would be content to be governed by a group of Englishmen 300 miles away who knew absolutely nothing whatever of their circumstances and needs.[60]

It was not only in Wales but at parliamentary level, too, that Lloyd George sought to promote his Cymru Fydd cause in the first six months of 1895. For example, on 30 March 1895, he had seconded a motion of 'Home Rule All Round' proposed by the newspaper owner, his close friend and 'nationalist' Liberal Scottish MP, Henry Dalziel, boasting as was usual in a letter to his wife that he had made a tremendous parliamentary impact: 'Biggest parliamentary stroke. I spoke tonight on Home Rule All Round, seconding Dalziel's motion. Never spoke better in the House of Commons in my life.'[61] Shortly afterwards, he created mayhem in a hostile,

English-dominated Commons, when he cut across the Speaker in a debate, claiming how oppressive the railway company, the London and North Western, had recently been in sacking several monoglot Welsh-speaking railwaymen from north Wales because they could not speak English at work. His interruption caused a great uproar in the House, 'a pertinacious protest', as he described it to his brother, William,[62] and it pleased him no end as he showed how his nationalism synthesized linguistic nationalism and social justice for working men.

On the parliamentary level, however, during the uneasy period of Young Wales's existence, especially between February and May 1895, he was to gain most publicity in his crusade to bring about a nationalist renaissance in Wales, ironically, in the lengthy debates on Welsh disestablishment and disendowment (the main concern of Welsh Liberals, not Home Rule). As he had done from 1890–2, he used the cause of disestablishment to demand that Wales needed a devolved body, elected democratically, to distribute the Church endowments towards social needs. Lloyd George knew, too, that the bill would never become law because of time restrictions in the Commons and the hostility of the Lords. But he was well aware of how he could use the debates to foment the 'national awakening' in Wales.

Surprisingly, before the debates began, he had attempted, paradoxically, to come to a secret agreement with leading clerics in the bishopric of Bangor, to compromise on disestablishment on condition that the clerics accepted a Welsh national body to distribute Church funds.

That initiative, an indication of Lloyd George's pragmatism at the height of the Cymru Fydd controversy, failed, but after this abortive attempt at Home Rule on a very minor scale for Wales, he participated in the disestablishment debates from February to May, in order to raise often the need for an elected Welsh mini-parliament to distribute Church endowments – again a back-door attempt to secure devolution, which would eventually lead to a Welsh parliament. His major intervention came in May, in the disestablishment debates, when the measure was being discussed at the committee stage. Contrary to his government's wishes, he called for an elected Welsh assembly of Welsh county councillors, which would prioritize social welfare spending from the Church's endowments.

Great consternation followed, when, at first, H. H. Asquith MP, who was piloting the measure through the Commons, refused adamantly to accept his amendment, but amid confusion, then seemed to relent, whereupon the Tories supported Lloyd George's motion, tactically, in order to defeat the minority government. Asquith had, in fact, told Lloyd George in the confused and noisy debate that he would reconsider his amendment at a later date. The Tories then insisted on seconding his amendment, whereupon (in view of Asquith's promise) Lloyd George (with his Cymru Fydd colleagues) had to vote against his own amendment or else the government could have fallen. It was, in effect, a *faux pas* at the end of debates where Lloyd George had raised the political temperature. Inevitably, he was criticized widely by the majority of his Welsh parliamentary colleagues for his seemingly reckless behaviour. The Tory press also blasted him for his controversial action in highly emotive articles, particularly, the *Western Mail* in an editorial headlined satirically, 'See the Conquering Hero':

> See the Conquering Hero – not since the days of Llywelyn and Glyndwr, Mr. Lloyd George's *beau ideals*, have we had such a man of thews and sinews. Like Parnell, in Ireland, he is now the uncrowned King of Wales . . . Though we have a wholesale hatred of Mr. Lloyd George's politics . . . yet we cannot fail to admire the man's pluck, his independence of spirit and to all appearances, his disinteresedness and self-sacrifice.[63]

The *North Wales Chronicle* was even more sarcastic, prophesying woe for Lloyd George in his own constituency because of his tactics in Parliament: 'There is not now a single Radical in either of the Caernarfon Boroughs who is not thoroughly ashamed of the contemptible part which Lloyd George played in parliament last week . . .'[64]

Lloyd George had stirred up a hornets' nest and had, according to several Liberal papers, brought shame on the government with its fragile majority and had threatened its downfall – a claim vigorously denied in May by his own papers at Caernarfon, even by the *Herald* company in the town and by Thomas Gee's *Baner ac Amserau Cymru*. The Liberal government, rocked by Lloyd George's controversial role in the disestablishment debate and already on its knees, was coming to the end of its tether after being a minority government under Gladstone and Rosebery since 1892.

On 21 June, after a controversial debate over the Cordite vote (and with the Disestablishment Bill yet to pass through the House), the government fell and a general election was announced. Lloyd George was going to be blamed for bringing about the fall of the government by weakening it terminally over his role as 'The Conquering Hero' in the earlier disestablishment amendment fracas, especially by sections of the Liberal press. He would reject these accusations in the forthcoming election, by claiming that Asquith had accepted his national council for Wales amendment in the disestablishment debate, on condition of postponing it for a short period. But the scandal was to be a central issue in his own election campaign, alongside his previous unstinting and highly controversial leadership of Young Wales and the call for an independent Welsh national party, with Home Rule as its underlying objective.

He faced an election challenge of intense difficulty with his own seat, marginal and conservative, in the balance, and that at a time when the Liberal Party was in a state of low morale, with many leading Gladstonians in the local Caernarfon Boroughs constituency party hostile to Lloyd George's nationalism. He could easily lose his seat and face oblivion as a Westminster MP.

Indeed, unsubstantiated rumours were immediately circulated by the Tory press that he was going to give up the Caernarfon Boroughs candidature (because he would lose), in favour of a safe Liberal south Wales constituency, held by a Cymru Fydd sympathizer. For example, the *Western Mail* claimed that he had been definitely offered a south Wales seat and was considering it seriously, because his party in the Caernarfon Boroughs constituency was split and leading Liberals there were opposed to his candidature. The paper stated: 'The feeling of dissatisfaction is so profound, many hitherto trustworthy Liberals will absolutely decline to vote for Lloyd George.'[65] During the same week, the *North Wales Observer and Express*, as expected, rebutted the *Western Mail*'s accusations and claimed he would keep the Caernarfon seat and win it for the third time. But, with the announcement that week that Ellis Nanney would fight him again, his own paper's editorial revealed grave concern over the outcome:

> The Conservatives have been fully prepared for the campaign and are confident of capturing the seat . . . The Tories in the Boroughs are leaving no stone unturned to bring about the overthrow of Lloyd George . . . already Ellis Nanney has made a thorough canvass of the Boroughs.[66]

That week, too, the *North Wales Chronicle* predicted he would lose his seat because of a split in his party locally and hostility towards his extreme nationalism:

> Mr. Lloyd George stands foremost as the spokesman of the wildest and most revolutionary proposals and his escapades in the House of Commons have filled his moderate supporters with alarm and disgrace. The electors of the Boroughs have the chance of substituting a dreamer and mere talker of the Lloyd George type, with a man of standing and a practical politician, Ellis Nanney. We have confidence in the electors they will choose wisely.[67]

Indisputably, he faced a considerable challenge and it was evident that his rebellion and his leadership of Young Wales was a handicap to him, although the historian John Grigg claims that his rebellion against the party line had enhanced, rather than hindered, his chances of retaining the seat in the 1895 election: 'The fact that he was branded a rebel against the Liberal leadership was a positive advantage to him. In the circumstances of the last year or so, rebelling had become the key to electoral success.'[68] This is surely an oversimplified view of his election prospects. In a constituency like his own, prospects of electoral success were far from rosy after he had made such a controversial stand on the Young Wales platform and during his rebellion in Parliament. Grigg's interpretation that 'electoral survival' was at the root of his rebellion in 1895 and his Cymru Fydd actions is nonsensical. Indeed, his actions during the rebellion and his Young Wales crusade were considerable risks for him to have taken, if his only motive was to retain his seat. Then, when his election manifesto was published, there was no doubt that he was standing as a labourite radical-nationalist.[69]

The manifesto was clearly bold and pioneering, compromising neither his radicalism nor his nationalism, and was extremely risky, considering that in his first by-election in 1890 he had had to trim his radical sails to win the seat. It is completely misleading to assert, as Grigg does, that his commitment to Home Rule in the 1895 election manifesto was 'pure rhetoric'.[70] Lloyd George emphasized at the centre of his manifesto that Wales would never secure social justice until it had its own parliament of a status 'second to none among civilised nations', adding:

> If we today love our country, our foremost desire is to see our country free from unjust laws, from ignorance, from drunkenness and immorality, from every oppression that falters the nation. In a word, I am a Nationalist because I am a Liberal and a Liberal because I am a Nationalist . . . I believe the future of Wales would be safer in the hands of her own sons and daughters who are attached to their country, than in the hands of those, who for the past 50 years have refused to listen to her appeals and redress her grievances. That is why I would give to Wales the right to manage such affairs as are distinctively her own, leaving the Imperial (London) parliament full control appertaining to the Empire at large . . .[71]

He also emphasized in the manifesto that such a powerful federal parliament would facilitate social, labourite and Nonconformist reforms, which Westminster parliaments had failed to deliver.

> In my opinion, this parliament is the easier and most effective
> way to secure Disestablishment for Wales, a measure of land
> reform to protect Welsh agriculturalists and labourers; a measure
> dealing with Leasehold Property, which would prevent the
> landlord depriving businesses and working men of houses they
> have built at the cost of their own hard won earnings; a measure
> which would put the control of the liquor traffic in the hands of
> the people: such adequate provisions for the old and disabled
> and amongst the honest and industrial workers as would place
> them beyond the fear of poverty or want when their physical
> powers fail either through age or sickness and a number of other
> measures calculated to elevate the people and for which Wales
> has long become ripe.[72]

Although his proposed Welsh parliament would legislate on old Liberal
measures like disestablishment and temperance, the manifesto emphasized
that a Welsh government would also legislate on the needs of rural and
industrial workers and, at a pioneering stage, effect old age pensions and
other welfare measures.

He closed his manifesto, seeking to rebut attacks upon him that the
Young Wales League wanted 'a Wales for the Welsh' and allegedly for
Welsh speakers, by declaring that incomers to Wales, the English, the
Scots, the Irish and others from wider backgrounds, were welcome to join
his Young Wales movement – 'the adopted sons of Cambria' as he termed
them.[73] He was referring particularly to those who had come to all parts of
Wales to find work in her docks, coal-pits, quarries and manufacturing
works.

Then, in the final flourish of his manifesto, he again referred to the
cause of Young Wales with an idealistic call to the Welsh 'cause of
freedom and justice':

> I earnestly appeal to you in the name of principle and conscience
> to put aside all personal and minor considerations and to record
> your votes in support of all those exalted ideas, which have
> always distinguished Wales as true to the cause of freedom and
> justice.[74]

The manifesto may have ended with a rhetorical flourish, but it referred
to specific labour and welfare measures, while also appealing to the
Non-conformist radical conscience. It is an exaggeration on the historian
B. B. Gilbert's part to assert (despite Lloyd George's great interest in old age
pension reform at this early stage) that his manifesto in 1895 was insubstantial
and non-labourite. Gilbert states: 'The only matter of substance in Lloyd

George's election speeches and, indeed, the only interest he showed in conventional social reform, until he became a minister, was a demand for old age pensions.'[75] On the contrary, his manifesto referred to several social welfare reforms apart from old age pensions and, during the campaign, he referred frequently in speeches to how a Welsh parliament could legislate on other labour/social welfare matters, although he did highlight the need to raise death duties to provide pensions for the aged in a speech at Caernarfon:

> Sir William Harcourt in his last budget which was one of the best if not the very best introduced to the House of Commons, imposed a death duty of 10 per cent on the property of millionaires . . . it was but right that such property should be taxed for the benefit of the state, than has enabled the millionaire to acquire their property. Suppose that death duties were increased towards the formation of old age pensions, what would Mr. Ellis Nanney say – or rather what would the Paymaster, the Duke of Westminster say, who had become possessed of about 10–20 millions – not through his own exertions but as a result of the labour and lives of miners? What would be wrong in charging that property for the benefit of the people and not to have it squandered on racehorses and hounds? My principle is: People First, Horses After.[76]

In the same speech, he linked the call for a Welsh parliament to serve the needs of 'the Welsh common people':

> Had Wales had a Welsh National Council, the land would have been freed from the tyranny of bloated game preservers and their puffed up agents and set free to be farmed by tenants and farm labourers . . . if Wales had had *Home Rule* we would have had a thorough system of education . . . it was also heartrending to notice how certain working class constituencies in England sent Tory blockheads to parliament to vote against *the dearest interests of the Welsh common people*. Wales would demand the right to manage her own affairs without reference to outside opinion.

Then, in an obviously labourite move during the election campaign, on the famous Castle Square, Caernarfon, according to the *North Wales Observer and Express*, at a meeting arranged specifically as a working-class gathering, he called for the taxation of the wealthy – raising taxes on profits from land and industrial development; increasing death duties and taxes on company royalties and upon quarrying and mining companies, in order to provide widespread welfare benefits to the less privileged in society – the sick, the old and the infirm and the unemployed. He claimed that a Welsh parliament was much more likely to achieve these aims than successive British governments which had failed to legislate in that direction.[77]

B. B. Gilbert's view that he not only fought the election on one social reform, old age pensions, but that he also fought centrally in 1895 on the 1890 by-election theme of merely attacking Anglicized landlords and the Anglican Church, is also wide of the mark. He certainly referred frequently in his 1895 election speeches to these issues, especially by casting aspersions on his landlord opponent Ellis Nanney, to personalize the election contest. But in the campaign, too, his central theme was Home Rule for Wales and a programme of radical and labourite reforms he had championed with the formation of the Young Wales in 1894, and ever since his first parliamentary election in 1890. The manifesto and his campaign activities were primarily geared to a high-risk strategy of putting Home Rule for Wales and social reform at the forefront of his programme.

Undoubtedly, using such a strategy meant that he had an enormous mountain to climb if he was to retain the seat, with an issue such as Home Rule hardly amenable to many of his own party. Another hurdle for him to face was the constant attack upon him (up to and during the election) from Liberal newspapers, which detested his Home Rule stance and the disestablishment rebellion, which they alleged had helped him to bring down Rosebery's Liberal government. He also had to contend with the venomous pre-election campaign of the Tory press (which continued during the election). Not only did the *North Wales Chronicle* and its Welsh-language counterpart, *Y Gwalia*, orchestrate a full-blown attack upon him, but, day by day during the hustings, the *Western Mail* continued to repeat its earlier malicious 'Conquering Hero' propaganda exercise against him, when it had labelled him a Liberal traitor after the disestablishment rebellion, earlier in 1895. He had also to face the election with a bare election chest, rifts in the Liberal camp, an anti-Liberal swing in Wales and Britain and a pro-Tory tide running in favour of the opposition, and allegations that he was bent on smashing the traditional orthodox Liberal machine in Wales to smithereens. In effect, he was depicted as 'a parliamentary raver' and a dangerous loose cannon. These were the disadvantages facing him in his third and most risky election challenge.

However, he had many advantages over his rival, Ellis Nanney. He had already beaten him in 1890 and could resurrect as part of his strategy the 'cottage bred boy versus local magnate' theme which he had deployed then. In addition, Nanney was not a charismatic figure and was a poor and ineffectual campaigner. Also, despite their well-tuned election machinery, the Tories suffered a desperate blow in mid campaign, when their talented agent, George H. Owen, the secretary of the North Wales Property Defence League, committed suicide; the scandal caused mayhem in Tory ranks and complete disorganization.

Conversely, despite weak party finances, Lloyd George had the backing of his own *Genedl* press machine to rebut all Tory allegations and he was even able to persuade leading and unlikely politicians, such as Tom Ellis, to address his meetings. Ellis, who was bitterly hurt by Lloyd George's rebellions in Parliament in 1894 and 1895, nevertheless came to Caernarfon to address an eve-of-poll meeting, where he defended Lloyd George's nationalist objectives. Lloyd George could also count on the support of the newly enfranchised voters and the Cymru Fydd activists in the constituency, who were ready to strive with might and main to secure his parliamentary base, from which he could further escalate the Young Wales campaign after a 'successful election'. Above all, his family, his wife and his nationalist brother, William George, were the instrumental backroom figures ready to sustain him privately during a highly stressful period for him. William George not only campaigned publicly for him (as did his wife and four young children), but William was his constant advisor and confidant during the hustings. For example, in the last week of the campaign, with early results declared and showing a Tory swing, Lloyd George was nervous and depressed, confessing in a letter to his brother on 14 July that he feared defeat and political oblivion:

> The first results came in last night. We have lost 5 and gained 1. Harcourt [the Liberal leader in the Commons] is out by 300. That, of course, is a staggering blow. It will have the effect of putting heart into the Tories and of depressing our people. I must apply myself next week to rousing then to a final effort. If I succeed, then we win. If not, I shall apply myself for the next six years to Criccieth and business.[78]

He was inferring to his brother before the campaign was finished that he could well lose the seat and that he faced life in the wilderness, without a parliamentary seat, and that the potential loss of his parliamentary base would be a mighty blow to his Cymru Fydd League aspirations, as he would no longer be able to use that stage to propagandize for the movement. On the day of the count, 21 July, his brother, as a secret diary entry shows, also believed that he would lose. Writing as he accompanied David and Margaret on the train journey from Criccieth to the count at Caernarfon, he concluded: 'The journey was the most anxious time of all. D., was agitated, poor chap. The Tory reaction throughout the country and the Tory confidence here, has made him feel depressed and anxious.'[79]

Lloyd George's secret worries stood in contrast to the highly optimistic expectations of the local Tory press. On the eve of the poll, the *North Wales Chronicle* and *Express* predicted that Nanney's return was on the cards, with the Tories already declared triumphant in the early constituency results: 'It is not impossible that the tide of Unionist success that has swept the country during these last few days will assist out local candidates in North Wales. In any case, the winning of the Caernarfon Boroughs is a dead certainty.'[80]

Indeed, on the day of the count, William George reflected in his diary how close the count was, with early boxes counted at Caernarfon showing majorities for Nanney, until the opening of a crucial, winning Bangor box (of all the six constituencies the most difficult for Lloyd George). Until then, according to his brother, Lloyd George feared a Tory win: 'I was convinced Nanney was preparing his triumphant speech, but then his heart went down with a thud and his attitude was that of a man inwardly cursing and swearing till his heart bled.'[81] His heart did bleed, for the count revealed that Lloyd George had secured a close 199 majority over Nanney, polling 2,265 votes. This happened in an election where the Liberals lost six seats in Wales and the Tories won a thumping majority throughout Britain. In particular, therefore, Lloyd George, prostrated by nervous debility after the campaign, was overjoyed. The *Manchester Guardian* heralded the victory the following day, stating: 'No candidate in this election has had to face a more bitter and desperate opposition than that which has been offered to Lloyd George's return.'[82]

Lloyd George's own papers, particularly, were even more effusive, claiming perhaps exaggeratedly, but with some justification, that his victory, based on a nationalist campaign, was a triumphal. The *North Wales Observer and Express* noted: 'In the return of Mr. Lloyd George, Welsh nationality has triumphed, despite the anti-Welsh element which exists in the constituency.'[83] Later, in a letter to his brother, he wrote egotistically about his own personal victory: 'Let me have news of how the victory has been received . . . They all say here [at Radnorshire where he was campaigning in a late contest for Frank Edwards, his Cymru Fydd friend], it is so far the biggest in Wales.'[84]

Lloyd George believed victory had been secured by his new politics of self-government allied to a radical-labourite agenda. The issue, he believed, had been vital as the campaign had proceeded, according to a post-election speech he made at Nefyn, reported in his *Observer and Express*. He claimed that: 'My argument in placing self-government for Wales in the forefront of the programme was strengthened from day to day.'[85] At the end of a tempestuous campaign which had been exhausting for him personally, he believed that he had been justified in fighting with Home Rule at the forefront of his campaign. However exaggerated that claim may have been, in the flush of victory, there is no doubt that it impelled him, after the election, to campaign even more militantly and zealously for the Young Wales League and prove that he was a real 'Conquering Hero' for the cause of establishing a powerful, independent nationalist movement in Wales, with self-government as its ultimate objective.

However, in that regard, he had a mountain to climb if he was going to fulfil that objective, in view of the hornets' nest he had already disturbed since forming in 1894 the still fragile organization that the Young Wales League represented in 1895 after a bitter election. In the summer of 1895, after immense strain, he collapsed dramatically while addressing a post-election meeting at Amlwch to promote the relaunch of the Cymru Fydd programme, and had to take a lengthy holiday in Scotland. Thereafter, however, rejuvenated by his victory and his holiday, he once more led a tempestuous and energetic campaign for the remainder of 1895 to seek to revolutionize Welsh politics and form an independent Welsh party with the objective of Welsh Home Rule.

From 1892 to 1895, the 'Monkey Patriot' had striven to bring that cause, by degrees, to the top of the Welsh political agenda, though if he was frank with himself, many disruptive Liberal forces had been arraigned against him in his crusade. These forces of opposition were to be even more in evidence in the autumn and winter of 1895 as he led the Cymru Fydd League into an even more militant phase.

X

THE FAILURE OF YOUNG WALES AND ITS DYING EMBERS, 1895–1899

After the 1895 election, before he proceeded to escalate the campaign to make the Young Wales League the most powerful political organization in Wales, Lloyd George endured a strange and worrying summer. After collapsing from nervous prostration at a post-election meeting on Anglesey, he took a brief holiday in Scotland before embarking on a short, three-week parliamentary stint at Westminster. But he was given no peace on his holiday nor on his return to Cricieth before leaving for London. Indeed, during this period, he was subjected to ceaseless criticism from within his own party for his militant leadership of Young Wales before and during the election and the alleged rift his actions had caused in Liberal ranks.

J. Bryn Roberts, the Gladstonian MP for Eifion, already a fierce critic of Young Wales, was the man who led the public accusations of treachery against Lloyd George, only a matter of days after the election. In May 1895, during Lloyd George's disestablishment 'rebellion', he had already taken his criticism of Lloyd George's behaviour to the highest echelons of the Liberal leadership at Westminster. He claimed then that, with his amendment, Lloyd George had been seeking to effect Welsh Home Rule via an elected Welsh council to distribute the revenues of a disestablished and disendowed Church and, in so doing, had split the party. During the 1895 election, although he had no opponent in his own constituency, Roberts had refused to support Lloyd George because of his rebellion and his militant Cymru Fydd campaign. Then, immediately after the election, after weeks of pent-up frustration, came his explosive press statement condemning Lloyd George's nationalism and justifying his silence during the election campaign. A letter from him was given surprising prominence in Gee's *Baner ac Amserau Cymru*. In it, he alleged that Lloyd George 'had conspired with the Parnellites and the Tories' in his disestablishment rebellion of May 1895, adding that this was 'the prime factor which had brought down Rosebery's government'.[1] He also alleged that he had asked Lloyd George personally during the 1895 election campaign to promise to be loyal to the Liberal Party, but that he had refused this request.

Lloyd George answered the accusation in a letter to the *Carnarvon and Denbigh Herald* at the beginning of August, defending himself and attacking Roberts's tepid and conservative Liberalism:

> The best reply to Mr. Bryn Roberts's attack on me is what a leading Conservative in Caernarvonshire said about him. The Conservative was asked: 'Why did you people not oppose the return of Bryn Roberts in the election?' The reply was: 'Why should we? He is doing our work.' I very much regret this attack by him because he and I have always been the best of friends, apart from politics.[2]

Lloyd George's barbed reply was only a partial answer to Roberts's accusation, but the local Tory press made hay of the summer madness in the Liberal camp. The *North Wales Chronicle* reproduced most of Roberts's article in *Y Faner* and concluded it with the most vitriolic quote in the whole piece, accusing Lloyd George of treachery: 'He joined the Tories and Parnellites to upset the Liberal ministry . . . and I and others believe the fall of the Liberal Government was due to his conduct.'[3]

This was the first shot delivered by Roberts in a relentless campaign via the Methodist weekly, *Y Goleuad*, from this point until November 1895 – a war waged against Lloyd George personally on grounds of alleged treachery against his own party and in an effort to stop the rejuvenation of his Young Wales League campaign. Preparations for the relaunching and rejuvenation of the Young Wales movement were put on hold while Lloyd George completed a three-week stint in Parliament in August, where he stoked the national 'revival' with a series of parliamentary questions on Welsh-language matters, fired at government ministers. He asked why there were no Welsh-speaking agricultural inspectors in Wales. He then asked why the Board of Trade in north Wales had no labour representatives. He inquired why the Public Record Office in London had no Welsh-speaking staff and why the new Ordnance Survey maps of Wales (then being compiled) had no Welsh-speaking officers on the surveying staff to enable Welsh names to be recorded correctly.

These questions were aimed deliberately at raising the political temperature in Wales as Lloyd George was preparing to relaunch the Young Wales League at a Llandrindod Wells conference on 5 September. There, he agreed once more to approach the South Wales Liberal Federation (SWLF) and its leader, D. A. Thomas, to seek again to put together, once and for all, a strong, united, fully fledged Young Wales League, which, up to that stage, had not included the SWLF, because Thomas wanted only a loose federal Welsh organization, dominated by himself and south-east

Wales Liberal delegates. In his speech at Llandrindod, Lloyd George stated that he did not mind approaching Thomas and the SWLF, but, in the meantime, his Young Wales League was ready to embark on a Wales-wide campaign to rejuvenate the movement without D. A. Thomas and his followers, if necessary:

> Let us proceed this day to arrange an elaborate campaign for the Winter . . . I am convinced Wales is with us. We have six years in front of us . . . Let us fight if we must. It will breed backbone. I move that we meet the South Wales Federation, but that in the meantime we fight.[4]

There was a fierce reaction in the Tory press to Lloyd George's relaunching of the Young Wales movement. The *North Wales Chronicle* sought to deflate the recommencement of the campaign and poured scorn on his redoubled efforts to create an independent Welsh party. The editorial claimed that it represented a new threat to the unity of the kingdom, although it was, in effect, a relaunch of a movement which had begun in 1894. The *Chronicle* warned its readers and official Liberals:

> Mr. Lloyd George has a new organisation he wishes to thrust down the throats of the people and like a good quack doctor, he has a programme, which will be a complete panacea for all the ills of Wales . . . a Welsh Independent Party is to be formed to thrust self-government down the throats of the people.[5]

The launch of the 'rejuvenated' movement did not get off to a promising start for, after the Llandrindod meeting, another conference was convened to meet at Shrewsbury on 25 September, to seek to close the breach between the league and the SWLF delegates. However, no agreement was forthcoming to form a powerful, all-Wales movement at Shrewsbury. Indeed, there was violent disagreement at the meeting, according to *Y Faner*, between the two factions as to the purpose and organization of the league.[6] Once more, D. A. Thomas was not enthusiastic about Lloyd George's domination of the league and its strident nationalism. The SWLF delegates refused the appeal for another meeting at Shrewsbury to form an united organization proposed for 7 November. Disunity still reigned supreme in Welsh Liberal ranks. Lloyd George was highly displeased at the outcome of the Shrewsbury meeting. Indeed, his own newspaper, the *North Wales Observer and Express*, highlighted this friction in a leading article, stating: 'Lloyd George was fed up with the S.W.L.F., for dilly-dallying so long before joining the Cymru Fydd League.'[7]

As he had already threatened, Lloyd George was ready to embark on a Wales-wide tour to seek to create a unified Welsh movement without the cooperation of D. A. Thomas and his federation, appealing over their heads to the Welsh people, in particular, in south-east Wales. Before embarking on that campaign, however, he wrote a lengthy article in the October edition of the *Young Wales* journal, emphasizing that the only way ahead for Wales was federal Home Rule for all the nations of the UK, including Ireland. Under the heading, 'National self government for Wales', he reiterated the aims of the Young Wales League and the objectives of his forthcoming campaign.

At the beginning of his article, he once more denied the accusations of Bryn Roberts, repeated in *Y Goleuad* that month, that he had brought down the previous Liberal government. Indeed, he asserted that the administration had been on its last legs when he had proposed the devolutionary disestablishment amendment in May 1895 – an amendment, he claimed, that Asquith had accepted.[8] However, the thrust of his article was devoted to calling for a regalvanized and powerful Cymru Fydd League to be formed to demand equality and Home Rule for the Celtic nationalities of the British Isles:

> The Celt and the Englishman are at cross-purposes. This diversity of opinion on political, social and religious questions, instead of disappearing, widens as the years go by, while it has at last produced a state of things intolerable to the Celt and inimical to the goodwill which ought to exist between the various nationalities constituting the United Kingdom.
>
> When the Imperial parliament is Conservative, the demands of the Celt are voted down. When it is Liberal, England must be attended to and the Celt who has so many arrears to dispose of, finds that England is not ripe on those questions, or before their treatment arrives, she has changed her mind and either rendered impotent or dismissed the Liberal Ministry before a tithe of the poor Celts' wrongs have been even so much as looked at . . .[9]

After he had referred to Wales's failure over decades to secure social legislation to improve the people's welfare, he then suggested that only powerful federal, domestic parliaments for Wales, Scotland and Ireland could solve the problem, leaving foreign and imperial matters to the Westminster government:

> The only practical remedy left is . . . a system of Federation which confers upon each nationality the right to manage its own affairs . . . neither foreign policy, nor the hostility of other

nationalities, nor the necessity of dealing with the affairs of colonial empire, can possibly interfere with the work of a local legislature engaged only with domestic concerns.[10]

Lloyd George was determined that his new campaign had Welsh Home Rule as its priority but, in the same edition of *Young Wales*, D. A. Thomas poured scorn on his views, writing: 'I am in favour of Home Rule All Round but I see no immediate prospect of securing this and I regard Welsh Disestablishment as the more practicable aim at this moment.'[11] However, Lloyd George was determined to secure Home Rule and was ready to lead a nationwide onslaught to recruit support for his league. He confirmed his aims in a letter to Thomas Gee on 9 October. He called for 'one great agitation for national self-government', adding with frustration, 'for heaven's sake, let something be done this winter . . . we need something to show for all this controversy'.[12]

He was feeling anxious and frustrated, because while he was organizing his campaign, which would be centred on south Wales, J. Bryn Roberts, in October, was still seeking to discredit his parliamentary record and his leadership of Young Wales. Roberts's criticism, voiced anonymously through an intermediary, the editor of *Y Goleuad*, E. W. Evans, was reported week by week in the Methodist journal, perpetuating the allegations of treachery by Lloyd George against the Rosebery government and his traitorous, breakaway Home Rule movement.

Not surprisingly, Lloyd George's own newspaper, the *North Wales Observer and Express*, came to his aid, defending him resolutely and attacking *Y Goleuad* and Bryn Roberts for his cowardly, anonymous attacks:

> The *Goleuad* has deigned to hold Lloyd George up as an upstart who has betrayed his friends, wrecked his party and blighted the hopes of his country for a generation. The whole business is a scheme to drive Lloyd George out of political life – but the attempt will fail miserably.[13]

There was, no doubt, an element of truth in the accusation that Roberts was seeking to undermine the rejuvenation of Lloyd George's Home Rule campaign and attempting to destroy his political career. The controversy continued into November, when Lloyd George, in a letter to Tom Ellis at the beginning of that month, sought to clear himself of the charges in *Y Goleuad*, made by a writer who, he claimed, 'is simply a poor tool in the hands of one Welsh Member' (J. Bryn Roberts).[14] As the historian J. Graham Jones has shown in his analysis of the fracas, Ellis then responded to Lloyd George's letter by writing articles in *The Times,* the *Manchester Guardian* and Welsh papers, incriminating both J. Bryn Roberts and D. A. Thomas in launching the anonymous *Goleuad* attacks on Lloyd George, and defending Lloyd George's role in the alleged 'misunderstanding' over the disestablishment rebellion in May 1895.[15] Indeed, Ellis implied further that Asquith had accepted Lloyd George's amendment on a postponed basis.

However, *Y Goleuad*'s editor, E. W. Evans, responded to these Ellis articles and repeated the charge that Lloyd George had used 'Irish methods of politicking' in order to undermine his own government.[16] Asquith did not desire to keep the controversy boiling publicly, but, in private, he castigated Ellis for involving himself in it. In a letter on 2 November, he told Ellis that he believed Lloyd George had been disloyal to him personally and to the Liberal government:

> It is not strictly accurate to say we 'accepted' Lloyd George's amendment and I think you showed rather too great a tendency to whitewash him, after the underhand and disloyal fashion in which he undoubtedly acted. So far as I can remember, he had no associate or apologist among the Welsh members except H[erbert] Lewis. But, it is a squalid controversy, which ought to be brought to a close.[17]

Tom Ellis had come to Lloyd George's aid in defending him against Roberts, D. A. Thomas's henchman, in their efforts to destroy his career and stop the Cymru Fydd League in its tracks, but Lloyd George was bitterly hurt by the attacks on him. He told his wife, at the end of the whole fracas, that '*Y Goleuad* is a scurrilous, lying Methodist rag' and that he had been 'tarred and feathered as a traitor to Liberalism'.[18]

Despite these attacks, however, in the autumn of 1895 Lloyd George had commenced his great campaign of 'nationalist agitation' when, in late October, he organized a blitzkrieg of meetings in south Wales, to undermine the SWLF and make the Young Wales League a powerful, united, Welsh political organization. He began by focusing particularly on the Rhondda valley, where he was invited by the Liberal association to speak, but only on condition that he concentrated on the importance of a united Liberal organization and confined himself to official Liberal policy. Characteristically, he replied to this invitation contemptuously, telling the local secretary that he would do no such thing and that he would press the Home Rule case in his speeches, retorting that 'any self-respecting Welshman would be ashamed to accept any invitation to any society where the hopes and ideals of his nationality are treated as a proscribed subject.'[19] Indeed, he followed his own independent line with a series of supposed 'lectures' in the Rhondda and other mining areas, under the dual guise of speaking about Llywelyn the Great and also giving supposedly academic talks about the work of the House of Commons! He conducted one of his many lectures on this tour at Abertillery, on 5 November, informing his wife that he had used the speech to promote Young Wales. He told her: 'Tonight I lectured there on the House of Commons, taking jolly good care to point the moral of the whole business – Home Rule All Round.'[20] He claimed, too, in a further letter to Margaret, that 'this lecture tour is a decided success'.[21] Then, on 7 November, he arranged a convention at Shrewsbury to finalize details of the climax of his tour in south Wales, informing his wife: 'We had a most successful conference yesterday and arranged for our South Wales campaign.'[22]

Without sparing a moment, that same evening, he travelled southwards to Brynmawr, Breconshire, from where he informed his wife that he had 'spoken for an hour and a half',[23] again resorting to the Llywelyn the Great theme, stressing at the meeting that 'the national spirit is as alive today as it has ever been'.[24] On 8 November, he visited Ferndale in the Rhondda, informing his wife that he had shared a platform there with the eminent Independent preacher and hymn-writer, the Revd Elvet Lewis (Elfed) – 'a heart and soul advocate of the Cymru Fydd League'. He told her further, however, that, despite Elfed's invaluable contribution to the meeting, 'I made the best speech ever in my life'.[25] At Ferndale, he alleged that he had been warned to steer clear of controversial policies by the local Liberal association, a warning which was denied by the local secretary in the *South Wales Daily News*, who added a sarcastic remark about Lloyd George: 'Is it not strange that such an apostle of Welsh Unity should use his power to create dissent and schism in the localities that he visits?'[26]

However, despite this criticism, indicative of official Liberalism's hostility towards him and his league, he proceeded with his tour. *Y Faner* that week claimed, over-optimistically, that he had established numerous branches of the Young Wales League on his tour of south Wales.[27] Also, that week, according to a letter to Margaret, he made 'a hot and strong attack' on the *South Wales Daily News* at a meeting at Briton Ferry, incensed by their constant criticism of his tour at the prompting of D. A. Thomas and his followers.[28]

A week later, he was back on the campaign trail, again in a confident mood, despite further criticism of him from official Liberal circles and, in particular, barbed criticism in the *South Wales Daily News*. He addressed exuberant crowds at Tonypandy in the Rhondda, on 20 November, at two meetings of colliers, on both the day-time and night-time shifts. In a letter to his wife, in a characteristic sweeping statement, he informed her 'the Rhondda had been captured'.[29] At the same time, in a similar letter to his brother, William, he informed him in over-optimistic vein, that at these Tonypandy meetings: 'I talked Home Rule and freedom generally. Gydag arddeliad mawr [with great conviction].'[30] He also claimed, in the letter to his wife that day, that the meetings had had an immense effect:

> Nothing like it in the Rhondda – not in the memory of the oldest inhabitant – has anything to equal it been seen. Crowds from all parts of the Rhondda came down. Mabon looked blue. I talked Home Rule for Wales and all the nationalist stuff, which the Mabon crew so detest – but the people cheered me to the echo.[31]

His optimism was profound, if excessive; he believed that he had captured the Rhondda and other areas by the power of his oratory, for the cause of Home Rule. Underlying this was his weakness: a belief that words alone could move people to his crusade. This letter to his wife, revealing his enmity by this period towards the miners' leader, Mabon, also reflected a disturbing element to his campaign. A few months earlier, at Cardiff in January 1895, Mabon had supported the Young Wales movement, but by the winter of 1895 he was having cold feet about Lloyd George's labourism and intense nationalism and was, no doubt, afraid that he was challenging his own Liberal association in his Rhondda stronghold. Certainly, Mabon was no intense political nationalist and neither was he any more than a tepid labourite. The movement's failure to capture the leaders of the Liberal association in south Wales and its winning only token support from ordinary miners, were also worrying factors for Lloyd George as his tour progressed. Despite his constant letters home to his wife and brother, extolling the impact he believed he was making, he sometimes had to confess to them that in some areas, particularly the easternmost, Anglicized mining areas, he was doubtful of the effect he was having on the audiences there. For example, in the middle of the tour, he wrote from Tredegar in Monmouthshire, to his wife, on 19 November, that he was encountering apathy there, as compared with more predominantly Welsh-speaking areas: 'Got a capital meeting here last night, although the audiences in these semi-English districts are not comparable to those I get in the Welsh districts. Here, the people have sunk into a morbid "footballism".'[32]

He believed that rugby was the opium of the south-east Wales coalfield and that the increasing influx of non-Welsh speakers and the English and Irish into the easternmost valleys by the 1890s had weakened feelings of nationality there, despite his frequent claims that Young Wales was not 'A Wales for the Welsh movement', but was inclusive and bilingual. Here was another indication that everything was not running in his favour during the campaign, with the 'Welsh language' factor creating a problem for him – an issue which was to be seized upon by his enemies to portray the league as a movement for 'Wales and the Welsh'.

However, his campaign was somewhat boosted in early December, when he was joined in his crusade by two Welsh Liberal MPs – his closest colleague, J. Herbert Lewis, MP for the Flintshire Boroughs, and William Jones, MP for the Arfon division, who had been elected in the 1895 on a radical-nationalist ticket, at the expense of Lloyd George's former Gladstonian enemy, D. P. Williams, the Llanberis businessman. The loquacious William Jones, with his 'silvery tones', addressed a huge Ferndale meeting on 3 December, where he preached a labourist and nationalist message, but where, according to the following day's *South Wales Daily News*, he created 'an altercation between the two sectors of the Liberal Party'.[33] J. Herbert Lewis also addressed similar meetings in the Valleys, but was mortified by the cauldron of politics there and, according to a letter from Lloyd George to Margaret, he had to be 'stiffened' before embarking on the tour; Lloyd George added: 'He is alright, but as you know, mortally afraid of anything in the nature of a row.'[34] The fact that Lloyd George had to rely on these two Welsh MPs alone, to fight the Cymru Fydd League campaign, revealed the hostility in Welsh parliamentary ranks towards his movement. All the other Welsh Liberal MPs refused to put their heads above the parapet – a distinct blow to Lloyd George personally, to the success of the campaign, and to J. Herbert Lewis, who was to admit before the end of the campaign in early 1896 that he was bitterly disappointed by the apathy and, in many cases, clear hostility of his fellow members towards Young Wales. He told Lloyd George: 'Heavens! That out of 25 men for whose return electors have toiled and made sacrifices, it should be so hard to secure 6 or even 4 or 5 who will work together, steadily and purposefully for Wales.'[35]

Without many parliamentary followers, Lloyd George had to depend on the support of extra-parliamentary public figures and orators such as journalists, intellectuals, writers and preachers to sustain his campaign. For example, two eminent south Wales preachers, Elvet Lewis, already mentioned, and J. Towyn Jones, a noted orator and future Liberal MP, lent him much aid, as did the eminent Welsh-language scholar and poet, John Morris-Jones, and especially the author and journalist, W. Llywelyn Williams, another future Liberal MP. At this time, he was editor of the *South Wales Post* and was to play a crucial role, in an Anglicized area, in securing press support for the Cymru Fydd League. However, this over-reliance on preachers and intellectuals underlines how precarious and fragile was the Cymru Fydd movement; the impression was conveyed that the movement was handicapped by appearing to be the preserve of a limited clique of the intelligentsia, despite Lloyd George's own radical views.

Indeed, Lloyd George had other handicaps to face as he conducted his campaign. The Young Wales League organizer, Beriah Gwynfe Evans, an able journalist, was, nevertheless, an inept and inefficient organizer and Lloyd George blamed him frequently for his incompetent and quixotic organization of the public meetings in south-east Wales. He informed Herbert Lewis in December that Evans was 'abominably defective'.[36] Lloyd George, however, made tremendous efforts to win the press over to his cause, with only partial success. Of course, in north-west Wales, he had his own *Genedl* press machine at his disposal and in north-east Wales, Gee's *Baner ac Amserau Cymru*. Llywelyn Williams's *South Wales Post* supported him in the Swansea area as did other papers there, such as the Baptist *Seren Cymru* but, denominationally, the Calvinistic Methodist *Y Goleuad* was a pungent and aggressive opponent, in both the north and south. But he was primarily concerned about winning support for Cymru Fydd in the Cardiff and south-east valleys region. He made a successful attempt to win over John Owen Thomas, the socialist and nationalist editor of the *Merthyr Times*, whose farm labourers' union movement in Anglesey he had supported in 1890. He also won the support of the *Glamorgan Free Press* and papers in the Aman Valley, but his most ambitious attempt was to effect a takeover of the most influential of all the Welsh papers, the *South Wales Daily News*, so supportive of D. A. Thomas and a constant anti-Cymru Fydd mouthpiece. From August until December 1895, he was involved in a conspiratorial plot with the wealthy newspaper owner and former Sunderland Liberal MP, Samuel Storey, to secure the paper. However, after protracted discussions, the unreliable Storey failed to produce the finances necessary for such a venture. Without a powerful English-language daily in south Wales to win support for him, despite the other press connections he had secured, great difficulties faced him in his campaign, not least the 'abominably defective' Beriah Gwynfe Evans.

The first stage of that tour came to an end in December 1895 with Lloyd George expressing increasing acrimony towards Beriah for failing to organize enough meetings during that month. He informed J. Herbert Lewis on 28 December that he had written to Evans, castigating him for his incompetence and commenting, 'he is getting quite accustomed to my scoldings'.[37] Three days later, in another letter to Lewis, Lloyd George reflected on the highs and lows of the campaign in 1895, before once more taking up the full thrust of the crusade in January 1896. He informed Lewis, in a paradoxical assessment: 'I do not think that the tide is running strongly against us in any quarter. What we have to contend against is not active opposition but apathy. When the people are roused, to the point of interest, they are with us.'[38]

Lloyd George, as yet, on the eve of 1896, was not prepared to suffer a humiliating rebuff to a movement he had led since 1894 and to those nationalist-labourist ideas that he had evolved and championed since 1885. He would revisit the south in the New Year, knowing that in January the SWLF would be meeting at Newport, where he would have to convince them, once and for all, to support a Welsh independent party, along Young Wales lines, with Welsh Home Rule as its priority. He was well aware, however, that since he had first launched his league in 1894 D. A. Thomas and the SWLF had consistently refused to join such a movement. However, before the Newport meeting, he addressed a huge meeting at Bangor, in his own constituency, at the start of the New Year, where he delivered a speech which underlined the labourist-nationalist message of his Young Welsh League. Here, where he had already met fierce opposition from official Liberals to his league, he made a passionate plea for Home Rule and emphasized that Young Wales was a working-class movement, seeking to establish a Welsh parliament, which would give priority to labour and social welfare reforms.[39] This was the centrepiece of his oration, as reported in the *North Wales Observer and Express*:

> You may depend upon it that the working class will not tolerate the system much longer. Every hour of delay means suffering and increasing destitution for thousands of them. They have on one hand, the Tory scheme for transferring the power of parliament to the Cabinet. On the other hand, they have Mr. Keir Hardie's proposals for social revolution. They have oligarchy on one hand and anarchy at the other extreme offered to them. The progressive part of the country offers, the more moderate, but I venture to think the more rational alternative of all round devolution, which will enable all their grievances to be dealt with in reasonable time.[40]

This quotation encapsulates how Lloyd George foresaw a Welsh parliament as being a powerhouse to effect labourite and social welfare policies, such as the eight-hour day, the provision of old age pensions and social welfare measures for the sick and infirm and legislation to provide trade union rights, in addition to measures of graduated and progressive taxation. He was pioneering the advent of a new, self-governing social democracy in Wales, with even a socialistic element to it, particularly where land nationalism and municipal ownership were concerned. He was convinced, perhaps over-optimistically and unrealistically, that his proposals for radical change were more immediately practicable and attainable than Keir Hardie's revolutionary socialist proposals. He was also probably aware that Hardie's Labour movement represented a threat to his own alternative route of reform and the promotion of Welshness, culturally and linguistically. This Bangor speech certainly echoed many of his views since 1890 and even earlier, in its criticism of unfettered capitalism and landlordism, and underlined his belief that powerful devolution with taxation and legislative authority could effect social and welfare legislation more quickly, more effectively and in a more careful and progressive way than dogmatic, revolutionary socialism. He claimed in the peroration to his Bangor speech:

> I would make these local parliaments so many searchlights to flash into all the dark places of our land, so as to shame oppression, wretchedness and wrong out of their lurking places. I repeat the present system of things cannot long endure. The contrast is too acute between the wealth and luxury of one class and the destitution and degradation of others . . . that system which macadamises the road to luxury for a few out of the hearts of the many, is doomed *and I for one, advocate so strongly the scheme of devolution, because I believe it is the surest method of expecting that happy day.*[41]

The final episode in that crusading scheme of devolution came a week after the Bangor meeting, when Lloyd George returned to south-east Wales in a last-ditch effort to win more support in the valleys before the crucial SWLF meeting at Newport on 16 January, upon which the whole future of the movement depended. In a series of letters before that meeting, to his confidant and co-nationalist, J. Herbert Lewis, and to his wife, he confided how the campaign was reaching its climax. On 4 January, he informed Lewis that he feared 'that we shall be beaten' at the forthcoming Newport meeting.[42] However, on 12 January, he was in a more confident mood, informing his wife, Margaret, how many meetings he had addressed in the Rhondda and how busy he was contacting Cymru Fydd supporters, who would accompany him as delegates to the Newport meeting to seek to undermine D. A. Thomas and swing the SWLF behind the Cymru Fydd League. He told his wife that success would ensue at Newport, after his machinations against D. A. Thomas in the Rhondda valley:

> We have decided to swamp the Rhondda with letters for the meeting of delegates, which is coming off there tomorrow. A good deal will depend on it. I wrote two letters yesterday on this point. If we carry the Rhondda, it will mean the turning of the scales at Newport on Thursday. *Dyma fi eto yng nghanol y rhyfel.* [Here I am, again, in the midst of war.][43]

Then, in the following days, he was full of optimism, after another Rhondda meeting, when he heard that the Rhondda delegates were ready to support him at Newport, after strong objections from the Rhondda MP, William Abraham (Mabon). Lloyd George buoyantly reported Mabon's defeat to his wife: 'Heard from Rhondda that the Cymru Fyddites scored a grand victory there last night and that all the delegates to vote for us tomorrow at Newport. That cripples Mabon's mischievousness!'[44]

The meeting at Newport proved to be even more momentous than Lloyd George had envisioned. It was to be more tempestuous and anarchic than any other meeting held during the friction-filled history of the Young Wales movement, since May 1894, and was also one of the most controversial conventions in modern Welsh political history. The Tory *Western Mail*, on the day after the meeting, delighted in the fracas and friction, which occurred there between Lloyd George's and D. A. Thomas's followers, and gloried in the searing hostility between the two factions as they traded insults. The *Western Mail*'s 17 January edition exulted in their main headline, highlighting the split in the Liberal fold: 'The Radical Bear Garden – Outbreak of Anti-Welsh Feeling at Newport'.[45] Lloyd George's own newspaper, the *North Wales Observer and Express*, was, conversely, profoundly disappointed by the seemingly mortal blow the SWLF had delivered to the hopes of Young Wales of securing a united league and Home Rule for Wales. It informed its readers that Young Wales had been roundly defeated by the plotting and machinations of the SWLF alleged vote rigging and a political fix. It stated: 'The meeting of the South Wales Liberal Federation at Newport has made all Welshmen who are jealous of the good name of their country hang down their heads in shame.'[46]

The long and passionate history of friction between Lloyd George and D. A. Thomas and their respective followers over the issue of Home Rule for Wales and an independent party for Wales had plumbed the depths of animosity and despair at Newport's 'Bear Garden'. The *South Wales Daily News* reported in detail the scenes of disorder and enmity at the meeting, which was chaired by the English-born, anti-nationalist MP for Monmouth Boroughs, Albert Spicer.[47] Accusations were levied at the meeting, by Young Wales speakers, that D. A. Thomas and the SWLF secretary, Morgan Thomas, had packed the hall with delegates inimical to Cymru Fydd. It was also alleged that Cymru Fydd sympathizers had been prevented from entering the hall by D. A. Thomas's henchmen and that the SWLF secretary had not sent invitations to his members from Pembrokeshire, Carmarthenshire and the Valleys of Glamorgan, who he believed were favourable to Young Wales's aspirations. Then anarchy and disorder ensued at the meeting on the central issue of whether the hoped-for 'new' Cymru Fydd League would have as its dynamic leader a full-time, professional, fully paid-up executive secretary. Lloyd George spoke in favour of such an appointment and for Home Rule for Wales, but was howled down and the issue was discarded. Then, a contentious debate followed, on old familiar lines, over whether any 'new' movement should be a loose, federated one, with power centred in the hands of the SWLF and D. A. Thomas or a powerful, all-Wales democratic independent party, with Home Rule at its forefront, as Lloyd George had advocated. The latter proposal, in favour of Lloyd George's Cymru Fydd, was made by the Revd Elvet Lewis, the 'star' preacher of the Independent denomination in Wales, but his pleas were opposed stridently by the businessman and Liberal alderman of English descent from Cardiff, Robert Bird.[48] He alleged that Lloyd George was leading a nationalist, extreme movement of 'Wales for the Welsh', which sought to undermine official Liberalism. He asserted in strident tones:

> We will not submit to the domination of Welsh ideas . . . Throughout South Wales, from Swansea to Newport, there were thousands of Englishmen, as true Liberals as yourselves, who would object to the ideas and the principles which Lloyd George has enunciated.[49]

Robert Bird's denunciation of Lloyd George's movement reflected the anti-Welsh prejudices of the English and cosmopolitan business class in the Newport–Cardiff–Swansea region who feared the domination of Wales by the mass of the people of Wales and their representatives from outside their class and their distinctive geographical area and the spread of labourism implicit in Lloyd George's movement. Bird's views also mirrored their fear that the Young Wales movement was one of 'Wales for the Welsh' and underlined their opposition to Lloyd George's advocacy of a bilingual Wales. Lloyd George had also encountered this prejudice in his own constituency at Llandudno and at Bangor, despite his pleas that his movement represented all the citizens of Wales, whatever their linguistic or ethnic background, so long as they sympathized with Welsh aspirations.

At the meeting, Lloyd George sought to intervene to answer Bird's allegations but, amidst scenes of rancour, was not allowed to speak a second time – in his own words in a letter that night to Herbert Lewis, his opponents had done everything possible 'to shut me up'.[50] Another speaker for Young Wales, was, however, allowed to second the resolution by Elvet Lewis, to establish an all-powerful Welsh National League, but their joint motion was defeated by 133 votes to 77. Then, a further motion to convene a further Welsh National Convention at Swansea to discuss the matter further was dismissed in a frenzy of recrimination. Thereupon, the SWLF's delegates, as one man, left the meeting to celebrate their victory over Lloyd George and Young Wales – repairing to a nearby hotel, for a sumptuous dinner, paid for by D. A. Thomas.[51]

Meanwhile, the Young Wales delegates remained behind in the hall, to express feelings of the deepest rancour towards Bird, Thomas and their followers, according to the *South Wales Daily News*. Lloyd George himself was livid at the action of the SWLF, calling them, significantly, in a socialistic vein, 'a small coterie of English capitalists, who have come to Wales and made their fortunes here'. He added: 'Wales belongs to the Welsh people and the Welsh people have a right to have their policy directed in accordance with Welsh views, as the English people have to have England governed according to English principles.'[52]

The editorial of his own paper, the *North Wales Observer and Express*, under the heading 'Strife and contrition at Newport', thundered against the South Wales Federation, reflecting Lloyd George's bitter, personal feelings. In its summary of the Newport 'Bear Garden', it stated: 'It was fairly hoped and believed that it could settle all questions in dispute as to the machinery of Welsh politics and unite Wales in one strong and solid organisation. This hope has been bitterly disappointed.'[53] Lloyd George's own deep disappointment was reflected in a letter to his wife, Margaret, but he also told her that he was still able and ready to continue the fight for Young Wales: 'The majority present were Englishmen from the Newport district. The next step is that we mean to summon a Conference of South Wales and to fight it out . . . I am in bellicose form.'[54] In a letter in the same vein to J. Herbert Lewis, his closest associate in the Young Wales Movement, he expressed similar feelings of disappointment, but also a readiness to carry on:

> *Yr ydym wedi ein trechu heddiw* [we have been defeated today].
> The meeting was disgracefully packed with Englishmen . . . we
> have decided to summon the annual meeting of the W.N.F. [the
> Welsh National Federation] at Swansea, at once. Wales is with
> us – the Rhondda proved that.[55]

He believed characteristically that he could rescue the movement after the disastrous Newport meeting and, according to copious notes he made, to prepare for the subsequent Swansea meeting; he was determined that the Cymru Fydd League would continue to flourish. These notes also reflect how he was determined to reject the view that the movement had been 'a vessel for his own personal and political ambitions', as his opponents, especially D. A. Thomas, had alleged: 'I am neither President, Vice President, nor any kind of officer in this new organisation, so I am fighting for no personal end.' His notes also included the sentiment that he could not understand why D. A. Thomas and his followers had rejected a movement that had 'the enthusiastic support of the official organs of the press, of the two largest denominations in South Wales, of labour and other leaders of undoubted influence'.[56]

Lloyd George's own assessment of the real level of support was grossly exaggerated, but, only two days after the Newport fiasco, he still convened a secret meeting of his followers, at Swansea, to make an attempt to revivify his Cymru Fydd League. Nothing concrete emerged from this meeting and hopes of reviving the movement appeared to be doomed, although he believed that the Swansea meeting had been a partial success and represented a regrouping of his forces to fight another day. However, in a revealing letter to his wife from Swansea, he wrote about the divisions and jealousies which seemed to characterize Welsh life, despite stating at the outset that Young Wales was still alive:

> Welsh Wales is with us to the fore. We have got to simply stir it up. I went to Swansea today and saw a number of friends. They are delighted we should have chosen Swansea. I told them that we had asked the South Wales Federation to do so but the Cardiff chaps were jealous of Swansea – there is a deadly rivalry as you know between the two towns. *Just fel Bangor a Chaernarfon*. [Just like Bangor and Caernarfon.][57]

This ironic and erratic letter, written after the Newport 'Bear Garden' and the abortive Swansea follow-up meeting, marked the end, the death knell, of the Young Wales League, to all intents and purposes, and Lloyd George's long-cherished hopes of establishing a powerful, all-Wales movement for Home Rule and establishing an independent Welsh party. However, as his letter to Margaret indicates, after the Newport and Swansea debacle he was not entirely without hope that he could still secure Home Rule for Wales. Indeed, he continued, in a spasmodic and highly erratic fashion, until 1899, to seek to bring Welsh Home Rule and the ideals of Young Wales to the forefront of the political agenda, although during this period only the flickering embers of the movement continued to glow. In the immediate aftermath of the Newport and Swansea meetings, he persisted in his efforts to promote at home and at parliamentary level the issue of 'Home Rule All Round', especially through the Radical Committee in the House of Commons. He informed his brother in a letter on 3 March 1896 that he was preparing a Home Rule motion in Parliament:

> At Radical Committee today decided to summon full meeting next Tuesday to consider my motion of Home Rule All Round. Must lobby in the meantime and buttonhole and argue with members lest thing be a failure. If we carry it that will at once lift the question to a quite different level.[58]

Nothing came of this initiative and Lloyd George had to admit defeat, the debate being adjourned to a future unspecified date. Yet he informed his wife that evening, with much self-delusion: 'The general sense of the meeting was in favour of Home Rule All Round. Some excellent speeches were delivered in favour of it.'[59]

Nevertheless, despite this setback, at Bangor in December 1896, he once more flew the kite of Home Rule in a speech featured in *The Times,* where he reverted to the argument that he had used in the heyday of the Young Wales movement, that an English-dominated parliament could never legislate for Welsh working-class reforms:

> The House of Commons had done nothing for the working classes. They have no right to obtrude their claims until their betters have been saved. The Unionist machine is a series of breakdowns. If they refuse the powers of discussing Bills to the Commons they transfer the power to the Cabinet, which means setting up an oligarchy. The only remedy is Home Rule, for the block in Parliament is attributable to the greater demand of legislation.[60]

At this meeting, too, he re-echoed the labourite message of his Cymru Fydd League movement in a hostile indictment of the landed-capitalist system:

> One man labours and yet starves: another lounges and still feasts. One set of men strive all the days of their lives in the vineyard, amid the plenty and profusion which they themselves have helped to produce and sink un-honoured into a pauper's grave. Another set of men enters into the precincts of the vineyard only to partake of its most luscious fruits and they live and die amongst the pomp and the prodigality of millionaires. They can't go on for ever.[61]

However, since the debacle of Newport 1896, Lloyd George had been gradually becoming more and more aware that Home Rule was not the panacea for social reform that he had promoted so vigorously before 1896 and that he was flogging a dead horse by striving to sustain it. Increasingly, between 1896 and 1899, he concentrated in Parliament on issues such as trade union rights during the first Penrhyn Strike of 1896–7, agricultural rights for tenants, free education; and by 1899 he sat on the Select Committee inquiring into the provision of old age pensions. However, he did not entirely dispense with the cause of establishing a more democratic structure for Welsh Liberalism and continued to press the case for devolution. In 1898, he made a vigorous attempt to propose the establishment of a democratic, all-Wales National Liberal Council, firstly at a fractious meeting at Cardiff – an attempt to set up a body to organize a radical agenda for Wales. But, according to K. O. Morgan's analysis of the proceedings, the fragile organization formed at Cardiff – the Wales National Liberal Federation – was 'no more than a body for co-ordinating propaganda, the mouthpiece of English Liberalism in Wales and a quite different body from Cymru Fydd'.[62] Once more, significantly, at this meeting it was D. A. Thomas and J. Bryn Roberts who defied Lloyd George's aim to resurrect, albeit in a moderate way, the Cymru Fydd League. Then, at a second convention, again at Cardiff in 1899, Lloyd George sought unavailingly to increase the federation's powers and roundly condemned the existing organization as one 'which had been in existence for eighteen months and the sum total of their work, was the apparent appointment of a Secretary'.[63] The Cymru Fydd movement was finally dead and buried.

The years 1896–9 marked the slow, lingering death of the remnants of the Young Wales League, despite occasional attempts by Lloyd George to revivify the movement. But, to all intents and purposes, it had been mortally wounded in 1896, after a brief, if explosive, commitment to it since 1894 by its dynamic, sometimes deluded, but visionary architect and leader, 'The Parnell of Wales'. In 1899, with the advent of the Boer War, Lloyd George increasingly became a British politician as he realized that he could serve Wales and secure radical changes in society only through the Westminster Parliament he had criticized so bitterly. He came to this conclusion, however, only after his long pioneering efforts for Welsh Home Rule and an independent party had been rejected by his own people and, particularly, by his own party.

Why did this movement, which he led with so much conviction, fail? And why did Lloyd George abandon it relatively quickly, despite his unstinting efforts for its ideals, not only since the creation of the Young Wales League in 1894, but, indeed, during his lengthy if at times wavering obsession with the nationalist cause from the beginning of his political career in 1885–6?

It would be an oversimplification to ascribe the failure of his league entirely to the long and bitter personal acrimony and political hostility between Lloyd George and D. A. Thomas. However, both were ambitious, powerful and aggressive politicians with varied backgrounds and conflicting views, particularly in the nature of their nationalism and on social and economic issues. Indeed, Thomas contributed considerably to the undermining of the league on frequent occasions as he became increasingly hostile to Lloyd George's linguistic and socio-economic objectives and his call for federal Welsh self-government. Also, he believed that the league, in its structure and objectives, was inimical not only to Wales's most populous region, the south-east; Thomas also felt he was the guardian of the cosmopolitan capitalists of that region and viewed Lloyd George's aims as seeking to undermine the hegemony of his class. Throughout the league's short, tempestuous existence, D. A. Thomas, assisted in north Wales by J. Bryn Roberts, ensured that Lloyd George's baby, if not strangled at birth, did not survive beyond its early infancy. D. A. Thomas, the capitalist entrepreneur, was determined that Lloyd George's movement would create neither a free Wales nor a movement which would lead Wales in a radical collectivist direction.

As part of this personal and political antagonism between Lloyd George and D. A. Thomas, there also existed, to some extent, a north south divide which contributed to the movement's downfall, although historians have tended to exaggerate this geographical division. Certainly, there was friction between the south-east Wales cosmopolitanism of the leadership of the SWLF and the leaders of the Cymru Fydd League, which they felt was dominated by Lloyd George's north Walian supporters. There certainly existed in the SWLF ranks a number of leading south Walian, Anglicized and English-born bourgeois, Cardiff and Newport based, who had a neurotic obsession that Young Wales was 'a Wales for the Welsh' organization, which also wished to foist the Welsh language on to those who were either hostile or apathetic towards it. However, the league, at least judging from anecdotal evidence, did secure much support, especially in the western coalfield valleys of south-east Wales and in the south-west, while it must also be remembered that there was no all-encompassing support for Lloyd George even in north Wales and certainly not in parts of his constituency. While Lloyd George secured support and recruitment for his league in coalfield, tinplate and rural areas of south Wales, he also met fervent opposition to his league not only from his own constituency, but also from other parts of north Wales. Undoubtedly, J. Bryn Roberts and his cohorts, Dr E. O. Price and Rowland Jones, at Bangor, were indicative of not only Gladstonian official Liberal opposition to his movement in his own patch, but also evidence that the movement was not torpedoed by south-east Wales alone. Indeed, south-east Wales and the Cardiff area was not the only region inimical to his movement, although the 'small coterie of English-born capitalists' there certainly helped to undermine Young Wales. However, it was not a simplistic north–south divide which broke the movement, but rather the disunity of Wales, where communal jealousies were prevalent and where communities were riven, too, by linguistic factors. Lloyd George was well aware of the growing linguistic divide in Wales and there is no doubt that the 'Language Bugbear' was played to the full by his opponents, in order to undermine his pioneering aims for a truly bilingual Wales.

Another factor which contributed to the demise of the league was its own incompetent organization, with the quixotic and 'abominably defective' Beriah Gwynfe Evans at its helm. At the height of the campaign in December 1895, Lloyd George had wanted him replaced, writing to J. Herbert Lewis after one of Evans's many organizational blunders: 'I fear you have been a victim of Beriahism . . . he really must go.'[64]

Upon close examination of its membership, despite its claims of high recruitment figures from 1894–6, the Cymru Fydd League never succeeded in taking over Welsh Liberal constituencies in any part of Wales and there was much evidence that J. Bryn Roberts was right in his accusation that it was 'a paper organisation'. Moreover, the league, despite getting the nominal support of the NWLF, never really established itself as a complete all-Wales organization and never had a Wales-wide organization nor competent, all-embracing, elected leaders and professional officers. Also, despite Lloyd George's heroic efforts, the league, with its own journal and sympathetic press in some quarters of Wales, did not have a comprehensive, bilingual well-oiled press machine. The *Liverpool Daily Post* and particularly the two south Wales dailies, the *South Wales Daily News* and the Tory *Western Mail*, were highly effective media, which poured scorn upon Lloyd George and Wales's first modern nationalist movement and helped to undermine it.

Lloyd George's movement also had minimal support from the Welsh Liberal MPs, with the exception of the talented, but hapless, William Jones and the nervous, if well-meaning, J. Herbert Lewis; it had the occasional grudging help of Alfred Thomas and the Anglesey Liberal, Ellis Jones Ellis Griffith, and quiescent support from the sidelines in its latter months from Tom Ellis. Indeed, most Welsh Liberal MPs were either apathetic to the movement, if not distinctly hostile towards it, on the grounds that it was opposed to official Liberalism and that it endangered their careers and their political clout within the great British Liberal Party. The Welsh Liberal parliamentarians, fearful of incurring the wrath of their local executive associations, were distinctly antagonistic towards the movement. Lloyd George also had to rely on intellectuals and ministers of religion to speak on behalf of the movement and, though trade unionists from the North Wales Quarrymen's Union and trade unionists like John Owen Thomas, the editor of the *Merthyr Times*, supported him the movement had no powerful union base. William Abraham MP (Mabon) for a while supported the movement, as leader of the South Wales miners, but he withdrew from it at a crucial stage, when Lloyd George appeared to be a threat to him personally in the Rhondda and beyond, and when the movement became intensely nationalistic.

The absence of leading Liberal figures from the Cymru Fydd ranks underlined one of the most salient factors in its demise – the opposition of the Liberal establishment, in Britain, Wales and in the constituencies, to its proposals, partly because Cymru Fydd had sought, with only partial success, to replace the Liberal apparatus in Wales and in the constituencies with Cymru Fydd branches and, particularly, because Lloyd George was seeking to establish an independent Welsh party. Dr E. O. Price of Bangor had exemplified such dissent in Lloyd George's own constituency in 1894, while J. Bryn Roberts's opposition to the league had also demonstrated the same enmity. Equally dissenting voices had also been heard from other constituencies from the Rhondda to Mold. The sober, respectable middle-class Liberal hierarchies throughout Welsh constituencies were afraid that Young Wales was a dangerous, nationalistic, labourite movement, which would split official Liberalism asunder and destroy the intimate and delicate partnership which Stuart Rendel and others had forged with the Liberal hierarchy in London. The Welsh Liberal 'establishment' had also been satisfied with the moderate progress that they had achieved in securing Welsh legislation, such as the Welsh Sunday Closing Act of 1881, the Welsh Intermediate Education Act of 1889 and measures such as the Land Commission of 1893 and the Welsh University Charter of the same year. They were not prepared to see the bond with the official party in Britain being broken nor were they dissatisfied with the influence they had gained on the new county and district local authorities after 1888.

Certainly, this was the thrust of an article written by Jenkyn Thomas in the *Young Wales* journal at the height of the Cymru Fydd controversy, in March 1895. In this article, Thomas entered Lloyd George's lions' den and claimed that it was a mistake for Young Wales to seek to form an independent Welsh party, since it had gained so much from partnership with British Liberalism:

> The question of a separate Welsh party, independent of the Liberal Party and all other political combinations, is being more and more discussed in the Principality . . . In this article, therefore, I propose to point out that I consider grave objections to the proposal to sever the historic connection between Wales and the Liberal Party . . . the best way to promote Welsh interests in parliament is to leaven the Liberal Party from within and not to form a Welsh party distinct from and independent of that organisation.[65]

Jenkyn Thomas's Liberal opposition to Young Wales summarized official Liberalism's deep-rooted opposition to and constant undermining of Cymru Fydd. They believed that Wales had received many benefits from being *in British politics*, rather than *without*, while Lloyd George, conversely, was of the opinion that Wales had received only crumbs off the British table and needed an independent party and a considerable measure of self-government to change society. Liberal opposition and the apathy of the Welsh people, rather than their opposition to Young Wales, undoubtedly, were major factors in its downfall.

There is no doubt also that the vision Lloyd George had of a self-governing, federal Wales, enacting labourist legislation, incurred the wrath of middle-class, laissez-faire businessmen like Robert Bird and D. A. Thomas and the coterie of English capitalists in the Cardiff–Newport region, and that they were determined to stop Young Wales in its tracks, despite the fact that historians such as K. O. Morgan impute that Lloyd George had but 'vaguely conceived labour policies', while J. Graham Jones insists that 'the movement was light years removed from labour, industrial and social questions'.[66] B. B. Gilbert is equally critical of Lloyd George's labourist commitment, when he states: 'The common mistake is the assumption that there was, in his make up, a species of left wing reformism, associated with South Wales and that somehow he was, or should have been, an ordinary labour-oriented social-reforming, anti-capitalist radical.'[67]

Although there is an element of truth in these interpretations, it cannot be denied that Lloyd George did obtain some support in south Wales amongst rank-and-file workers and miners and, indeed, on frequent occasions, expressed both left-wing reformist views and social reforming, anti-capitalist views, providing Young Wales with a labourist message. He was a champion of old age pensions, measures for the sick and infirm, leasehold enfranchisement, taxation on a graduated scale to redistribute wealth from both landed and industrial interests to the underprivileged, and combined these with the view that such measures could be more effectively facilitated through a Welsh government than via Westminster. He viewed powerful devolution as a more practicable and more progressive and effective way of changing society than Keir Hardie's revolutionary proposals. Certainly, D. A. Thomas, the millionaire coalowner, feared his call for an eight-hour day and his left-wing views as he attacked 'English capitalists' in his Newport speech. Of course, much has been made of the fact that Mabon and his union turned against the Cymru Fydd League, after initially supporting it and, despite Lloyd George's union sympathies (particularly in the Llechwedd strike) and his attempt to win ordinary colliers to his movement, there is no doubt that he lacked comprehensive union support. In a sense, Lloyd George's failure to get widespread working-class support was an example of his falling between two stools. He may have not been enough of a militant labourist to obtain support and, yet, Mabon turned against him because he had dangerous labourist and nationalist ideas, while many official

Liberals thought his social and economic interventionist views were far too radical. His movement was certainly not confined to the traditional, rural-based, Welsh, Nonconformist issues of rights for tenant farmers, disestablishment and temperance reform. But failure to win widespread working-class support, despite Lloyd George's fervent attempts to champion their cause, was an important factor in the inability of the league to become a powerful force in Welsh life.

Moreover, another factor in its failure was not only that it was propounding a new labourist slant, but that its nationalist message was bold and challenging and inevitably, therefore, in 'Imperial Wales' aroused fierce resistance and much controversy, even amongst Liberal supporters. Wales before 1868 had seen centuries of political quiescence and the almost complete absence of nationalist thinking and Lloyd George, in pioneering an aggressive, linguistic and political nationalism, met not only apathy, but fear and opposition. In launching his nationalist cause, he was cultivating virgin territory, the surface of which only a few nationalist predecessors had dared to scratch – 'eccentrics' such as his mentor, the nationalist and radical, Michael D. Jones, the socialist and nationalist pioneer from Llandderfel, R. J. Derfel, and the land socialist and admirer of Michael Davitt, E. Pan Jones. Not unnaturally, with the Anglicized educational system rendering most Welsh people ignorant of their history, literature and the reasons for their economic plight, they were apathetic and indifferent to their nationality; as Lloyd George had informed J. Herbert Lewis in 1895: 'What we have to contend with is not active opposition but apathy.'[68] Moreover, Lloyd George had to contend with that central fact which Jenkyn Thomas had stated in his *Young Wales* article in 1895. Official Liberals were satisfied with a semblance of national equality within Britain, through legalization concessions and local government power, rather than seeking a substantial measure of self-government for Wales.

All these separate, interweaving factors contributed to the downfall of the Young Wales League. But what was Lloyd George's real commitment to Welsh Home Rule and why did he turn away from it relatively quickly by 1899? Indeed, was the movement, as many historians have asserted, but a short-term machine and pressure group for his own personal political ambitions? It has been described as: 'a bid for power . . . to redirect Welsh Liberalism now that the Liberal Leadership had been swept away' (K. O. Morgan),[69] and 'a temporary vessel for his political ambitions' (J. Graham Jones);[70] John Grigg has written that Lloyd George 'had never, of course, intended to be the Parnell of Wales in any sense but one – he wanted to control the Welsh MPs, and to make use of their corporate power'.[71] Even B. B. Gilbert has viewed it as primarily a pressure group, but he does confess that the Young Wales League 'was an Irish style political machine' and, further, admits that Lloyd George 'had views on every topic but commitments to none save land nationalisation and Welsh nationalism'.[72]

Indeed, the Young Wales League was much more than a pressure group. It was a nationalist movement. Lloyd George, of course, was never an out-and-out dogmatic, unbending nationalist, yet Home Rule for Wales had been a commitment he had consistently championed during his pre-parliamentary career and during the first six years of his parliamentary career. He had, in particular, fought for a measure of Welsh autonomy between 1890 and 1892 and had championed the cause of Home Rule with a pioneering, socio-economic, linguistic, cultural and, indeed, feminist programme during his daring and controversial leadership of his innovative Young Wales Movement. Although, at times, during this period, he had used pragmatic and tactical methods to seek his objectives, and although he was often deluded by the power of his own oratory into believing that he was leading a successful nationalist movement, there is no doubt that he was seeking to effect a radical and permanent change in Welsh politics. He was to be personally and bitterly disappointed by his failure to establish a movement which would lead, he believed, to a system of government as radical and progressive as that of Switzerland and he had refused to capitulate to the humiliation he had suffered at Newport in 1896.

However, once he had realized that he had been deeply let down by a conservative Welsh Liberal hierarchy and a largely apathetic majority of the Welsh people, he moved away gradually from his overtly nationalist stance and, from 1899 onwards, he became convinced that he could only achieve social reform and enhance his own people's welfare through securing political power at Westminster. Inevitably, the only route ahead for him was a London-based career as a primarily British politician. Wales and, particularly, his own party had rejected the alternative route of Welsh Home Rule, which he had advocated since his first entry into politics. He did not reject Wales, in dropping the Home Rule issue, but rather Wales and Welsh Liberals rejected his pioneering overtures.

For the remainder of his political career, while rising up the Westminster ladder and exercising political power at the highest levels from 1906–22 and even as the 'wizard in the wings' in the 1920s and 1930s, he never dropped entirely his belief in Welsh devolution, nor did he fail to champion certain Welsh causes, while his Welshness certainly impinged on his policies in power, in both positive and negative directions. Moreover, his Young Wales League – the first modern, nationalist movement – had a continuing effect on Welsh politics in both the short and long term. It was to prove to be, especially after Lloyd George's death, a beacon of inspiration for politicians, like his daughter Megan, to resurrect the cry for Home Rule for

Wales and the movement was to inspire politicians both within and without the British political parties in Wales, to secure a measure of Welsh political autonomy, resulting in the formation of a National Assembly for Wales, almost a century after the demise of Young Wales.

THE BRITISH-WELSH POLITICIAN, 1899–1945, AND THE LEGACY OF YOUNG WALES

The Boer War, 1899–1902, was a real watershed in Lloyd George's political career. His militant anti-war, anti-imperialist stance in that tempestuous conflict – unpopular at first, in his own constituency, in much of Wales and especially in Britain – led him to be verbally and physically attacked, in his own patch at Cricieth and at Bangor and most revealingly in the lion's den of Joseph Chamberlain's imperialistic Birmingham, from where he had to escape a baying mob, disguised as a policeman. However, he emerged from the war unscathed, indeed, with his reputation in the highest circles enhanced, with a Cabinet post in any future Liberal government beckoning. The Boer War transformed 'The Welsh Parnell' into a British-Welsh politician of prominence for the first time. Henceforth, though he was to continue to highlight Welsh issues at times, he was primarily concerned about widespread social reform on a Westminster scale. Moreover, he certainly never again reverted to the extreme cause of Welsh Home Rule which he had championed so relentlessly in the mid-1890s. Indeed, he was to pay only lip-service, infrequently, to the issue of Welsh self-government after 1899. He did that on only three occasions during his subsequent glittering rise up the greasy pole of British politics to its top as prime minister from 1916–22, when he became increasingly a 'Big Brit' politician with a subsidiary and declining interest in Welsh Home Rule.

The first occasion was in 1905, as he was being touted as a potential Cabinet minister. On the brink of his first Cabinet post as president of the Board of Trade, he informed his wife, in an undated letter, that he would accept office in a new Liberal government, only if, in return, he was promised Welsh Home Rule. He reported to Margaret that he had informed John Morley, a leading Liberal, of his intention: 'Told him, I must see Wales right. That I would stand by my people whatever happened – self government including power to deal with temperance.'[1] It was more bluster than a threat to be executed and Home Rule did not materialize during Campbell-Bannerman's subsequent ministry. Then, in

1910, displaying his ever-readiness to stray from the party line, in the midst of the Peers versus People controversy over the House of Lords' refusal of his 'People's Budget', he conducted secret negotiations with top Tories to discuss a comprehensive programme of social and constitutional reform, including Home Rule All Round.[2] Again, however, nothing concrete emerged from this initiative, although Home Rule All Round was again broached on the eve of the First World War in 1914. Finally and thirdly, in 1919–20, as prime minister of a coalition government composed of Liberals and Tories, he told Welsh members of the Speaker's Conference, then inquiring into the question of devolution for Scotland and Wales, not to go for a moderate solution but 'Go for the Big Thing' – Welsh Home Rule.[3] However, he did nothing to facilitate the issue and there is little doubt that by then he was not in earnest about the matter as he had been in the days of the 'Welsh Parnell'. Nevertheless, as he became a leading politician from 1905 onwards, the legacy of Young Wales did find expression in his efforts for more limited devolution for his country and the establishment of Welsh national, cultural institutions, especially up to 1912, while his social policies were, to a marked extent, influenced by his Welsh radical background. However, after the Boer War he was primarily the British-Welsh politician.

Historians are in general agreement that it was his courageous stand in the war which propelled him into the limelight as a British politician for the first time, although they are not in unison as to how far his anti-war stance was impelled by his Welshness and nationalist sympathy for the downtrodden Boers of the Transvaal and Orange Free State republics. Indeed, B. B. Gilbert rejects outright the traditional view that Lloyd George was principally, or at all, motivated to support the Boers on Welsh nationalist grounds. He states categorically: 'It is hard to see that he was a friend of the Boers because of a belief in the right of small nationalities, as is asserted in the Du Parcq biographies and has been studiously repeated ever since.'[4]

However, this assertion is surely an over-exaggeration because he was considerably motivated by his Uncle Lloyd's and his brother William's Nonconformist sympathy for the Boers; and, indeed, he himself used nationalist analogies in his speeches during the campaign in condemning the imperialistic and capitalistic motives of the Tories in conducting the war, especially the motives of his *bête noire*, Chamberlain, who had once been his Home Rule All Round idol. Of course, Gilbert is right in emphasizing that he was using the issue primarily to attack the corruption and waste of the war and to stake out a British reputation for himself, but nationalism was also a factor in his anti-war stance. Nevertheless, historians are agreed that the war propelled him to prominence on the British political stage for the first time, as public opinion by 1902 had moved substantially against the war and in its wake brought considerable kudos to Lloyd George in the highest Liberal circles.

Also, two Welsh issues prior to his attaining Cabinet office in 1905, had their British resonance and enhanced his status in the period as well. During the great Penrhyn slate quarrymen's lockout of 1900–3 – the longest dispute in British labour history – he received publicity throughout Britain, as he was in the forefront of opposition to the lockout of the thousands of quarrymen by the owners, whom he despised. He had, since 1890, crossed swords frequently with the Penrhyn family and led the workers' campaign against them. As Professor R. Merfyn Jones has shown in his authoritative work on the quarrymen's union Lloyd George not only defended the victimized quarrymen in court cases but also led the parliamentary onslaught against the owners and took a leading role in raising money for the workers during their lengthy strike.[5] Here again was a throwback to the Cymru Fydd era, for in 1897 he had supported strike action by the Penrhyn quarrymen as he had earlier supported similar action by Blaenau Ffestiniog slate-quarrying trade unionists. His actions in 1900–3 at Penrhyn were also impelled by his fear of the rise of Labour but they underlined his social reform priorities and enhanced his status on a British scale, as the dispute was covered in detail by the British press.

However, it was his militant and protracted leadership of the 'Welsh Education Revolt' of 1902–5 which really consolidated his reputation as a politician throughout Britain, as he led the opposition to the Tory government's Education Bill of 1902 and increasingly undermined the morale of the Conservative administration. Lloyd George actually agreed with the main thrust of the bill, that county councils should be responsible for education. However, he was much opposed to the sectarian element in the bill, whereby Church schools would be financed from the rates. Unlike English Liberals, he was prepared to make the bill unworkable, leading the Welsh county councils in an 'Onward Christian Soldiers' campaign of civil disobedience against it, which was captured vividly by the *Western Mail* cartoonist, JMS. Lloyd George partially succeeded in rendering the bill inoperable and it was to be several years before a more secular system of education emerged, under Asquith's Liberal administration, with some concessions made to the Church schools. Lloyd George gained great praise throughout Britain for his opposition to the bill of 1902–5, which helped to undermine the Tory administration and made a Cabinet place certain for him. Interestingly, too, during the controversy he sought perceptively, but unavailingly, to press amendments to the bill, to establish limited 'Home Rule' in education for Wales, through the proposed establishment of a National Elected Welsh Council of Education, another throwback to the Young Wales era and an initiative he was again to promote when he secured a Cabinet post.

That first Cabinet post came in Campbell-Bannerman's Liberal administration in 1905, an appointment he had prophesied secretly in a letter to his wife, as early as January 1904, when he informed her that he had been told in confidence by Edward Grey, the future Liberal foreign secretary, that he was in line for major office: 'He [Grey] says I am certain to have a seat in the Cabinet. Told him I must bargain for Wales.'[6] That prophesy did materialize in December 1905 when he was appointed president of the Board of Trade. He informed his brother, William, as he had earlier boasted to his wife, that he would insist on 'a guarantee of Welsh self government' – a threat he did not carry out. He had 'arrived' on the foremost political platform and had ensured for himself a seat at the top table of British politics. Henceforth, his priority was a Westminister career, leavened with a desire to seek concessions for Wales and a 'juggernaut' quest for more power to effect major social changes in society, particularly motivated by his Welsh upbringing. These early experiences were to be reflected in his first government post, at which he was to be a conspicuous success. Surprisingly, for one who was notoriously untidy with the practicalities of life (such as answering personal correspondence), with his civil servants always on tap but never on top, he showed considerable administrative acumen at the Board of Trade.

He also established close relationships with union leaders and businessmen, while introducing new bureaucratic initiatives, such as an annual census of industrial production. However, his main contribution, apart from settling large industrial strikes, was to introduce several pieces of enlightened legislation including a Patents Act, a new Companies Act and, especially, to set up a quasi-nationalized Port of London Authority, which contributed much towards improving conditions for dockers. But perhaps his most radical measure was a Merchant Shipping Act, prescribing decent working conditions for mariners aboard ships and ensuring better conditions for the poorer classes of passengers, while also ensuring that the Plimsoll line was used on foreign ships entering British ports, thereby further promoting the safety of mariners. The concern for the welfare of mariners was not surprising, as many of his constituents were seafarers as well as members of his family in law (through his sister's marriage), while during his period as a 'Boy Alderman' and young MP the welfare of sailors and fishermen had been uppermost in his mind. Thus, his Welsh radical background was much in evidence at the Board of Trade and as, a Cabinet member, he was also involved in the government's trade union legislation and new compensation legislation for workers.

As a member of the Cabinet, too, he resurrected his previous call for Welsh educational devolution. He failed to secure a Welsh National Council of Education but was instrumental in securing a compromise, namely, a Welsh department of the Board of Education.[7] A. T. Davies, a friend of his former legal partner, Rhys Roberts, was appointed the permanent secretary and Lloyd George took great care, too, that sympathetic Welsh officials were appointed to the department. This was especially the case with the key appointment of the chief inspector of schools. It was he who was ultimately responsible for the appointment of the Oxford don and the Welsh cultural nationalist, O. M. Edwards, to the post. Although Lloyd George did not like him personally because he believed him to be an Oxbridge academic snob, he was eventually persuaded by his early confidant, D. R. Daniel, and by J. Herbert Lewis MP, that Edwards was the man to de-Anglicize the Welsh educational system. Indeed, Lloyd George was much maligned for appointing Edwards, who was regarded by many Tories, Liberals and local councillors as a purveyor of nationalism in schools and as a champion of the Welsh language at the expense of English. It was an appointment which confirmed Lloyd George's Welshness and his championing of the Welsh language, but, despite heroic efforts, Edwards had only mixed success in creating a bilingual system of education.

Lloyd George had striven in his first government post to secure a major measure of devolution for Wales. However, he was not only ready to compromise over devolution, but was also prepared to go out on a limb to shelve Welsh aspirations when they endangered the priority of the government's programme of social reform. B. B. Gilbert has shown clearly how he supported Campbell-Bannerman's efforts during this period to postpone a Welsh Church Disestablishment Bill in 1907–8 – a measure he had not always supported for its own sake but rather as a medium to secure devolution for Wales. In Cabinet and in Wales, in 1907, he called for a postponement of the measure in favour of social reform, in the teeth of much opposition from nonconformist sources in Wales.[8] He preferred to put social reform in the van of public policy but he did receive assurances from Campbell-Bannerman that a measure of disestablishment would be forthcoming later in the administration's programme.

However, his main priority was social reform and that was to be underlined when he suffered the greatest tragedy of his life in 1907 – the sudden death of his beloved eldest child, Mair Eluned, from peritonitis at the age of seventeen. He was grief-stricken and only his work and the compensation he derived from the company of his infant daughter, Megan, kept him from the depths of despair. Mair Eluned's death might also have caused the beginning of the long estrangement with his wife, because he believed that Mair should have been operated upon earlier and because Margaret, to his mind, appeared to cope better with the bereavement than he did. Nevertheless, during the first days of their loss both comforted the other and in a highly revealing letter to his wife, he confessed to her that only the fact that they were not alone in suffering such a tragedy kept him going. He also added that, after such a bitter loss, he was more than ever determined to help the sick, the bereaved and the underprivileged, through fundamental social reform. A day after Mair's funeral he wrote to Margaret:

> It was the decree of fate which millions besides us are now enduring. What right have we to grumble? More than that I have a profound conviction that cruel as the blow may appear and purposeless as it may now seem, it will prove to be the greatest blessing that has befallen us and through us multitudes whom God has sent me to give a helping hand out of misery and worry a myriad worse than us.[9]

This was, perhaps, the most religious viewpoint Lloyd George ever expressed, at a time of great tragedy, although he was essentially a secularist and free thinker (even 'a pagan', according to his later private secretary, A. J. Sylvester).[10] The letter did reveal, however, the traumatic effect of Mair's death upon him; it also reflected his determination to 'change the world' in a more egalitarian direction and, in a sense, reinforced the social ethos and message of his Baptist upbringing. That was to be much in evidence in his next post as Chancellor of the Exchequer, in Asquith's new Liberal government, following the resignation and death of Campbell-Bannerman in 1908.

After his feats at the Board of Trade Asquith, in an inspired choice, elevated him to the Treasury where he was to become the star of a highly talented Cabinet. There, his first reform achieved considerable publicity; although the Old Age Pensions Bill had already been prepared by Asquith, the previous Chancellor, Lloyd George piloted the bill through Parliament with great finesse. The state provided a pension for the elderly for the first time, for those over seventy years of age, an issue which Lloyd George had championed since 1892. Although means tested, it was the first step towards the establishment of an embryonic welfare state. Indeed, the pension brought him great fame and was called in Wales 'Coron Lloyd George' (Lloyd George's Crown). Each single or widowed pensioner received 5s a week and married pensioners 7s 6d. It was, undoubtedly, a measure which helped to lift the shadow of the fear of the workhouse from the lives of countless elderly people, while the measure itself impelled him towards further more fundamental social welfare reform.

The pension needed to be financed and this led Lloyd George to embark on his famous and notorious 'People's Budget', partly to finance the pension but also to raise money for the building of the new

Dreadnought battleships, as German naval rearmament proceeded apace. The Budget was meticulously prepared and involved an ingenious amalgam of new progressive taxes, direct and indirect, together with taxation policies that Lloyd George had cherished since his youth, particularly taxes against the industrial plutocracy and large landowners. It also raised income taxes and death duties on the wealthiest sectors of society and supertaxes on those with incomes of over £5,000 per annum. At the same time, taxes on tobacco and alcoholic spirits as well as on luxury goods, such as cars and petrol, were raised. Also, allowances were introduced against tax for those with children and other allowances set against income, particularly for the lower-income groups. Many historians have interpreted the Budget as being mainly an attack by Lloyd George on his traditional enemy, the landed aristocracy, as he sought to tax unearned rents and profits on land and increased death duties, but the Budget also hit the industrialists and the middle classes. He dubbed it his 'war budget' not only for naval expenditure but, also, 'to wage implacable warfare against poverty and squalidness'.[11] Significantly, with the influence of his early Welsh radical views on the Budget, he devoted the bill to his Uncle Lloyd – 'the real author of the People's Budget'.

The Budget itself and the previous Old Age Pensions Act were remarkable developments, accompanied as they were by new government public finance initiatives to develop forestry and agriculture. But the Budget was even more remarkable in that it led to hostile opposition from the House of Lords which sought to wreck the measure. Lloyd George had not, it seems, deliberately framed the Budget to undermine the Lords but once they had rejected it so contemptuously, he pounced upon the opportunity to embark on further widespread social and constitutional reform. When he heard of the Lords' rebellion he was well aware of the opportunity it provided to undermine them, informing his wife that the Lords' obstructive power over generations against any radical legislation could now be terminated, once and for all. In Cromwellian terms he joyously told Margaret: 'Well, the Lords have made up their minds. The Lord hath delivered them unto our hands.'[12]

He was well aware that the House of Lords, which he had derided since his early days in his *Udgorn Rhyddid* newspaper, had continually torpedoed radical legislation and that it could now be permantly prevented by legislation from continuing to veto such changes. Once that was done he could then draft measures of widespread social reform. In countrywide pre- and post-election Budget speeches of 1910, called to give assent to the Budget and anti-Lords legislation, he poured scorn on the Lords in vituperative addresses. In his famous Limehouse speech on 30 July he claimed: 'A fully equipped duke costs as much to keep as two dreadnoughts and dukes are just as great a terror and last longer.' Then in other speeches, including a notable speech in his own constituency, during the first of two general elections in 1910, he drew analogies from his childhood to vent his spleen on the Lords' refusal of his Budget. In this speech he recalled his childhood experience at Llanystumdwy, when after a great storm he would be sent into the woods to gather fallen timber to warm his uncle's hearth at Highgate, adding that once the storm over the Lords had abated, the hearths of the poor throughout Britain would glow, ever more warmly. The Liberal victory in the general election of January 1910 and a thumping majority of 1,078 for him personally in the Caernarfon Boroughs did not signal the end of the Peers versus People conflict, however. Another election had to be fought in 1910 and pressure had to be exerted on the new King George V to threaten to create new Liberal life peers in the Lords, unless the Budget was passed, and then a Parliament Bill to curtail drastically the power of the Lords. Lloyd George, in a letter to his wife deliberately written mostly in Welsh so as to maintain secrecy, boasted that it would not be too difficult a task to threaten the monarch, as he was far from bright. Writing from Balmoral, he informed Margaret:

> The king is a very jolly chap, but *diolch i Dduw, does dim llawer yn ei ben o. Pobl gyffredin, syml iawn ydynt a hwyrach ar y cyfan bod hynny yn beth da.*

> [. . . thank God there's not much in his head. They're simple, very simple, very ordinary people and on the whole that's a good thing].[13]

Lloyd George knew full well that the king could be persuaded or forced into acquiescence over the Parliamentary Bill, especially after the Liberals were returned to power a second time in 1910. At the same time, he was also prepared to go out of his way, quite cynically, to please both the monarchy (and the royal burgesses of Caernarfon) and ensure their support for vetoing the power of the Lords by devising, organizing and even inventing a jamboree-like investiture of the prince of Wales at Caernarfon in 1911. Indeed, he remained on good terms with Edward even during the abdication crisis of the 1930s but his investiture was, primarily, a showpiece to persuade the king to diminish the power of the Lords.

This objective was fulfilled with the Parliament Act of 1911. Henceforth, the Upper House was no longer able to prevent the passage of fiscal bills, while it could veto other bills only for two years. Lloyd George had undermined the greatest obstacle to radical legislation and achieved one of his earliest aspirations. Ironically, in the midst of the Peers versus People controversy, in 1910, he had made secret overtures to leading Tories for a cross-party alliance to bring about a programme of social and constitutional reform, including a measure of Home Rule All Round.[14] That did not materialize, but Asquith's government established labour exchanges, strengthened trade union rights and fulfilled another of Lloyd George's earliest aspirations, namely the payment of MPs, in 1911, a great boon to democracy and, ironically, to the growth of the Labour Party. But with the power of the Lords now curtailed, his greatest social reform was yet to come – the National Insurance Act of 1911.

Historians have tended to interpret Lloyd George's reforms up to and including the Insurance Act as testimony to his 'New Liberalism' after 1906 and there is no doubt that he was influenced, especially with his Insurance Act, by new thinking in this period, particularly by the German model of social insurance. However, it is a mistake to erect an artificial divide between his pre- and post-1906 views, for some of the ideas which engendered his reforms after 1906 were grounded in his youth and in the Cymru Fydd era. He was also a dexterous and pragmatic master of changing and amending legislation as it proceeded through Parliament. This was very much in evidence as he piloted the highly ambitious Insurance Bill through the Commons, using both ruthlessness and conciliation to secure a new insurance system. The eventual act, although comprehensive and all embracing, in one sense, was also limited in scope, particularly the unemployment proposals. 'The Stamp That's Worth a Lot of Licking' brought considerable benefits to a substantial number of workers but many were excluded from the proposals. B. B. Gilbert in his work on Lloyd George has rightly commented on the restrictions of the act, but there is also much truth in K. O. Morgan's view that 'it was a decisive stride towards the welfare state',[15] despite the fact that Lloyd George was personally disappointed with the limited unemployment sections of the legislation. Nevertheless, it was his most considerable triumph as a social reformer and the act was further strengthened during his final post-war coalition administration.

The act of 1911, passed after tremendous opposition from the doctors and the rich, attacked poverty caused by illness and unemployment, with a system of national insurance – with contributions from workers, from employers and from the state to the national insurance fund. Workers paid a weekly stamp of 4d, employers 3d and the state 2d. From the fund workers (but not wives and children) were given free medical treatment by a doctor's panel, but it was not a universal health system, as introduced in 1948. The unemployment provisions were even more limited, confined to providing the 'dole' for those workers in a limited number of trades – such as building, engineering and shipbuilding. Nevertheless, it was a pioneering measure by the forty-nine-year-old Welshman and had its Welsh significance, too. The Campbellite Baptist had witnessed from a young age how his uncle's sect, every Sunday, devoted *y casgliad* (the collection) to help those of its members who were sick or unemployed – an early embryonic form of social insurance. Lloyd George also ensured that the act had another Welsh dimension with the appointment of special Welsh commissioners to administer it. He ensured that Welshmen were given these posts, including the gifted 'mover and shaker' from Rhymni, Thomas Jones, the Fabian socialist and future deputy secretary to the Cabinet, and R. T. Jones, the secretary of the North Wales Quarrymen's Union.[16] Acutely aware of the scourge of TB, *y dicau*, especially in rural Wales, he also ensured that funds would be forthcoming for medical research into the disease and that sanatoria would be raised throughout Wales to treat the victims of the white plague. Lloyd George, having lost a daughter in her teens, knew how much havoc TB had caused, killing thousands of Welsh youth.

During his chancellorship, too, Lloyd George used the public purse unashamedly to support Welsh national cultural institutions – the university, the national museum and the National Library. On one occasion, for example, in 1909, within twenty-four hours of listening to desperate pleas by J. Herbert Lewis MP for aid for these establishments, he had signed cheques of £1,500 for the Welsh National Museum; £2,500 for the library and £15,000 for the university, informing Lewis triumphantly: 'What's the use of being a Welsh Chancellor of the Exchequer, if you can do nothing for Wales?'.[17]

As Chancellor, too, he used his influence to get Welsh millionaires to support Welsh causes, persuading the London-Welsh draper, Pritchard Jones of Dickens and Jones, to establish the grand PJ Hall at the University College of North Wales, Bangor, and the Davies family of Llandinam not only to support the King's TB Fund but to give generously to Welsh colleges. As Chancellor, Lloyd George had blended his Welshness and radicalism as a pioneering social reformer, but, in the midst of his popularity and achievement, he seemed to be drifting away from Wales, while clouds of scandal, both financial and sexual, were gathering over his personal life. From 1912 up to the outbreak of war in 1914, his zeal for the old Nonconformist issues such as temperance and Church disestablishment (as in 1909) seemed to be diminishing. However, reluctantly, he did make a voluble appeal in Parliament in 1912 in favour of disestablishment and, by the eve of the war, he got the Cabinet to pass a Suspensory Bill allowing disestablishment to proceed at the end of hostilites, but he had really lost interest in the issue. He also mooted the possibility of Home Rule for Wales in 1914 and got the Cabinet to agree to a postponed measure of Irish Home Rule but significantly, with Ulster excluded.

However, in Wales he lent no support to E. T. John, the East Denbighshire Liberal-nationalist MP's spirited but abortive campaign for Welsh Home Rule in 1912–14.[18] He was moving away from Wales politically, physically and sexually in this period, symbolized by his taking a long-term, English mistress in 1913 and rarely visiting Cricieth in the years prior to the war. Frances Stevenson, the epitome of the sophisticated metropolitan woman, estranged him further from Wales, although, remarkably, until the end of his career there, he still held sway over a thoroughly Welsh-speaking household at Downing Street, presided over by the redoubtable housekeeper from Cricieth, Sarah.

His undoubted libido, which he knew from his early days could undermine his political career, also brought him into further public disrepute in this period. As early as 1908 rumours had been circulating in the highest aristocratic circles either that he was involved with a society hostess or that the previous scandal with Kitty Edwards, the doctor's wife from Cemaes Road (see chapter X), was continuing to haunt him, with allegations that he was being blackmailed as being the father of her child. In 1909 the populist Conservative paper, the *People*, without naming him or his lover directly, suggested he was involved in an extramarital affair. Lloyd George had to bring his wife to court to testify in a libel suit that he was guiltless, while his friend and political colleague, Rufus Isaacs, his advocate, strenuously denied any misbehaviour. The scandal did much harm to him but he won the case and secured £1,000 in damages, which he devoted to raising a village hall for Llanystumdwy. However, as in the case of the Edwards trial of 1897, he escaped relatively, but not entirely, unscathed from these scandals, although both cases could have destroyed his career.

He was also subject to even more scandal in 1912–13 and again he had to resort to the courts to clear his name. This was the Marconi Scandal, when he was alleged to have obtained insider knowledge, through Rufus Isaacs, that new shares in an American offshoot of the company would appreciate substantially on receipt of government contracts. Once again, he emerged scot-free from the scandal but the whole issue clouded further the last years of his peacetime chancellorship. The 'Welsh Wizard' may have again escaped the clutches of women and the law but his future was under a cloud on the eve of the First World War. Ironically, for one who had made his British reputation as an anti-war hero from 1899 to 1902, it was the outbreak of the Great War which resurrected his career and escalated him in time to the top of the British political pole. Though never an outright pacifist, the coming of war in the summer of 1914 filled him with dread, and there is no doubt that his pacifist, Nonconformist upbringing made him instinctively anti-war. Certainly, at the end of July, he was doing everything in Cabinet to avoid war and was even momentarily contemplating retiring from politics, should war be declared. However, when the Germans invaded Belgium – one of the 'five foot nations of Europe', like Wales – on 3 August 1914, after much soul-searching, he informed his wife in a highly emotional letter that he could no longer stand aside and had to remain in government:

> I am moving through a nightmare world these days. I have fought hard for peace and succeeded so far in keeping the cabinet out of it but I am drawn to the conclusion that if the small nationality of Belgium is attacked by Germany, all my traditions and even prejudices will be engaged on the side of war. I am filled with horror at the prospect. I am even more horrified that I should ever appear to have a share in it but I must bear my share of the ghastly burden though it scorches my heart to do so.[20]

That ghastly burden he took upon himself, though one can hardly surmise that he would have resigned himself to life at Cricieth and given up political power and the challenge that war presented. Indeed, his involvement in the war was to escalate him to unparalleled power for a British prime minister, as a quasi-presidential figure. He was already a god-like figure to many in Wales, after his reforming chancellorship. Now, as the leading figure in the war effort, he was to become, in the eyes of many Welshmen, even more deified. That acerbic Welsh critic, Professor W. J. Gruffydd, a serving seaman during the war, was to change his mind radically about Lloyd George as the war progressed and Lloyd George became more and more bellicose. In a highly ironic comment in his *Hen Atgofion*, he contrasted the heroic status Lloyd George had achieved in the eyes of his father's contemporaries, as he had acquired supreme power, with the more caustic view his own generation had of Lloyd George, the warmonger:

> *Pe clywsai fy nhad i sicrwydd fod Mr Lloyd George wedi lladd ei nain, buasai mwrdro neiniau ar unwaith yn llai o ysgelerder yn ei olwg. Canys Mr Lloyd George oedd Pab Rhyddfrydiaeth ac y mae popeth a wna'r Pab yn gyfreithlon ac yntau ei hunan yn Anffaeledig.*[21]

> [If my father had heard that Mr Lloyd George had indisputably murdered his grandmother, the murder of grandmothers would instantly have been less of a travesty in his view. Because Mr Lloyd George was the Pope Of Liberalism and everything that the Pope does is legally justifiable and he himself is Infallible.]

There is no doubt much truth in Gruffydd's allegation that amongst those who thought about the war, and were dismayed at Lloyd George's militant and increasingly imperialistic right-wing connections in wartime, he lost much of his credibility in Wales, particularly during the post-war coalition of 1919–22. But conversely for the majority, as Gruffydd also suggests, his wartime leadership brought him even greater status in Wales, while he undoubtedly used the Welsh people and his Welshness to glorify war and secure the support of the majority in Wales.

Wales was certainly, in the main, on his side during the war, although historians are not in unison about the extent of Welsh commitment towards the war. K. O. Morgan has asserted that the Welsh were more keen on fighting in the war than the nations of England and Scotland. He claims 13.82 per cent of the adult male population served in the forces as contrasted to a slightly lower percentage in England and Scotland,[22] although this is disputed in the *Llais Llafur* journal by Aled Eirug, who quotes figures from official sources showing that the proportion of young men who enlisted in the army was only 21.5 per cent in Wales compared with 24 per cent in England.[23] Moreover, John Davies has asserted that because there were far more young men in Wales than in England and Scotland because of industrial in-migration, the percentages quoted by Morgan are meaningless.[24] Nevertheless, what is indisputable is that Welsh youth flocked into the armed services and 40,000 were killed in the war, and much of this support, especially before conscription, was due to Lloyd George's orchestrated campaign of recruitment in Wales.

Before and after conscription was introduced in 1916, he made considerable use of his gift of oratory, his wife's personal prestige and every contact he could muster to lead and sustain the war effort in Wales. He caused xenophobic hysteria in 1914 with his notorious 'Road Hog of Europe' diatribe against the Germans at a massive London Welsh Rally, and used the National Eisteddfod platform to great effect during the war. At Bangor in 1915 he likened the Welsh boys at the front to the Welsh archers at the battle of Crécy and at Aberystwyth in 1916 he introduced the festival's first Gymanfa Ganu (singing festival), comparing the Welsh voices there to nightingales singing at their most perfect in the darkest of nights. Then in 1917, at Birkenhead, he stage-managed the highly charged empty-chair ceremony for the fallen Trawsfynydd bard, Hedd Wyn, who was unable to take his chair at the festival, having died on the battlefield in Flanders. He also used the eloquent talents of Welsh Nonconformist preachers to fan the flames of war – the most loquacious was his own personal chaplain, the Revd General John Williams, Brynsiencyn, who wore his uniform in the pulpit, and promoted a 'just war' against the alleged 'Anti-Christ', the German kaiser. Academics such as John Morris-Jones, translator of the German poet, Heine, also took up the war cudgels and the philosopher, Henry Jones wrote war tracts for Lloyd George, while the eminent hymn writer, Elfed, composed patriotic hymns to keep up morale. Lloyd George also ordered the authorities to issue huge propaganda posters in Welsh and was ruthless in his condemnation of many erstwhile friends who were conscientious objectors, being particularly condemnatory of the diehard absolutionists who refused to do any kind of state service. More positively but equally as ruthlessly, in the teeth of much English opposition, particularly from Kitchener, he set up a Welsh-speaking force, the 38th Division, under the leadership in north Wales of the quixotic Anglesey labourite and landowner, General Owen Thomas as the historian David Pretty has shown.[25] The division was massacred on the Somme in 1917 as were many of the Welsh Guards and the Royal Welch Fusiliers, although most Welshmen lost their lives in English regiments.

The Welsh dimension was also much in evidence in Lloyd George's choice of experts on the home front, particularly in his Garden Suburb Secretariat at 10 Downing Street, which included friends and colleagues such as Herbert Lewis, Evan R. Davies, Clement Jones and Ernest Evans, with John Rowlands acting as his personal secretary and Sir J. T. Davies as his personal private secretary. In addition, his erstwhile Cymru Fydd enemy, the industrialist, D. A. Thomas, was appointed the first food controller in one of five new high-powered government departments, streamlined to give him overall personal direction of the war effort. He also secured the services of Welsh trade union leaders such as Jimmy Thomas, leader of the NUR, but his most crucial appointment was the elevation of Tom Jones of Rhymni, to be his eyes and ears, as deputy secretary of the Cabinet. He and Lloyd George could exchange the highest state secrets in Welsh. Jones's appointment symbolized the elevation of the 'Welsh Taffia' to the uppermost reaches of government, which, in one sense, brought great prestige to Wales. Yet, a minority of Welshmen, such as David Davies of Llandinam, left their posts, disgruntled with Lloyd George's conduct of the war. Welsh Liberal MPs like Reginald McKenna, W. Llywelyn Williams, E. T. John and Ellis Davies, who were disgusted with his bellicose anti-Liberal actions, also aroused his spleen by becoming increasingly vocal in their criticism of his policies as he veered more and more to the right and offended Welsh pacifist and labour sensibilities.

However, on the military and home fronts he was determined to win the war, using methods of 'total war' to secure victory 'with a passion to win the war which none of the other members of the Cabinet seemed to understand'.[26] He was a brilliant military strategist and, as the 'Welsh Outsider', brought an external, visionary role to play in eventually winning the war, by using international contacts, such as the Welsh-born Australian prime minister, Billy Hughes, to exert a vital influence on the conduct of war and ensuring crucially that America entered the conflict in 1917. The 'Welsh Outsider' also ruthlessly sacked English incompetent public-school-educated, generals, such as Douglas Haig and Sir William Robertson, dubbing Haig 'as brilliant to the top of his army boots'.[27] He replaced them with efficient leaders such as the Frenchman, Marshal Foch, and the Ulsterman, Henry Wilson.

On the home front, too, the Welsh connection was vital as he brought his Welsh radicalism to bear on labour legislation, the employment of women, better wages in the munitions factories and better payments on the land and in the mines. He also presided over H. A. L. Fisher's groundbreaking Education Act of 1918 and he gave the vote to all adult males and women over thirty years of age. The Ministry of Reconstruction Act, together with his partial nationalization of the basic industries of Britain, underlined his strategy of 'total war'. He also exploited the agricultural resources of the country to the hilt, bringing much prosperity to farmers and their labourers, particularly in Wales. However, devolution for his native land had to wait until the post-war era and was then to prove disappointing.

He had brought much status to Wales and had used his Welshness and Welsh contacts to great effect in pursuing the war effort. However, it was brought at an immense cost to Wales and to his own split party, and it damaged the special bond that he had had with Wales. Amongst many labour leaders, academics, radicals, pacifists and intellectuals his reputation in Wales was gravely damaged as a result of his ruthless war policies and from 1917, in particular, as casualties mounted and with seething labour unrest at home, there was increasing opposition to his war premiership and his close connection with the Tories. Pacifists, in particular, became increasingly hostile towards him, led by Thomas Rees and his journal, *Y Deyrnas*, George Maitland Lloyd Davies and the poets, T. H. Parry-Williams and T. Gwynn Jones. In addition, labour pacifists and non-pacifists, such as the leaders of the miners' union, the Fed, criticized his bellicose ways, his treatment of strikers and his Tory cronies. The Fed even went so far as to demand federal Welsh self-government, based on Marxist lines, and one of their leaders, Arthur Horner, joined the Irish Citizen Army of James Connolly. Even more gentle socialists, in north Wales, such as Silyn Roberts of Blaenau Ffestiniog and the ILP north Wales pioneer and pacifist, David Thomas, were vehement critics of his wartime premiership.[28] Indeed, in Wales as the war progressed, the Labour Party was poised to effect a breakthrough and a new Wales was ready to emerge at the end of hostilities, ironically as a result of Lloyd George's premiership. The Great War had been a double-edged sword for him. On the one hand, he had whetted the appetite of the Welsh people for a more egalitarian, more modern, more socialist Wales, while, on the other hand, he had destroyed any hopes of the Liberals taking over as a radical united party. He had begun the destruction of the Liberal Party in wartime and was to complete that process in the post-war period as a coalition prime minister with the Tories.

In the coalition election of 1919, in order to retain power, he had to remain in partnership with the Tories. Having won the war, and having fixed most electorates with the Tories on 'the coupon', he emerged apparently triumphant from the war. In the poll, 520 supporters of the government were elected (437 with the coupon); 57 Labour members were returned and the Asquithian Liberals came bottom of the poll with only 30 seats. In Wales, 25 Lloyd George Coalitionists were returned but only one Asquithian. However, Labour won 10 seats, as the up-and-coming party. The Lloyd George triumph hid severe problems for him, however, for in a Tory coalition he was forced to distance himself much further from Wales and, indeed, by 1922, when he fell from power, his Tory-influenced policies cast him into the political wilderness and damaged forever his reputation in many parts of his native country. He did, nevertheless, in his final administration – much maligned though it was – bring to Welsh people some permanent benefits and limited concessions to Welsh devolution. Of course, Lloyd George never succeeded in fulfilling his promise 'to build a land fit for heroes' after the war, but it would be misleading to assert that the whole administration was an unmitigated disaster.

In Wales, as in Britain as a whole, there were some redeeming features to his government, especially in the early years. For example, a Ministry of Health was established in 1919, bringing concrete proposals to improve public health, nursing and hospital care. Christopher Addison, the health minister, also passed an enlightened Housing Act, which had a particularly beneficent effect on Wales, where local councils built homes for up to 15,000 Welsh families by 1921, although the programme was curtailed by the early 1920s with the Geddes 'Axe'. The National Insurance Act of 1911 was also extended in 1920 and saved many Welsh families from complete penury during the inter-war depression, because it extended unemployment benefit to many trades and occupations, particularly in mining. Also, another Education Act was passed in 1921 which improved teachers pay and the provision of school meals for poor pupils, which up to 1921, at least, guaranteed prices were paid to farmers and a minimum wage for farm labourers. The creation of the Forestry Commission in 1921 did much for employment in rural Wales, while pensions were raised until the Geddes 'Axe', and the Whitely Councils brought better conditions for health workers.

As far as Wales was directly concerned, there was no prospect any more of Home Rule for the nation from Lloyd George, but he did promote administrative devolution to some extent. As part of his health reforms, a Welsh Board of Health was set up, ensuring that in both health and education Wales now had a modicum of self-rule. He also was instrumental in securing the establishment of a Welsh Department of the Board of Agriculture, but in 1919 he stopped short of appointing a secretary of state for Wales, suggesting in a throwaway remark to Welsh MPs that they should go for 'the big thing', a Welsh parliament.

The overriding piece of Welsh legislation which he did secure, however, was finally the disestablishment and disendowment of the Anglican Church in Wales in 1920. In a much more secular era, it hardly aroused the passion it generated in Lloyd George's youth, but he ensured the passage of the act which, ironically, strengthened rather than diminished the Welsh Church at a time when Nonconformity was entering upon its long decline. Lloyd George was much criticized for taking communion with the archbishop of Wales – supping with the devil in the eyes of elderly chapelgoers – and he was castigated for allegedly settling on far too generous terms the disendowment aspects of the new set-up for the Church. However, the highly secularist politician by then had little interest in the controversy.[29]

Historians have been anxious in recent times not to exaggerate the failures of his last administration with regard to Wales but in this period there was a considerable decline in Lloyd George's popularity in Wales. He continued to widen divisions in the Liberal Party: He introduced swingeing cuts in public expenditure via the Geddes 'Axe' which brought particular pain to Wales. He had also promised to nationalize the mines as the Sankey Commission had suggested, but broke his promise to the miners, and his brutal handling of strikes towards the end of his premiership aroused the ire of the labour movement in industrial Wales. To add insult to injury, the notorious sale of honours in this period to enlarge his political fund brought much odium on his head and in Wales, in particular, there was much antagonism towards his anti-terrorist, repressive measures in Ireland through the notorious use of the Black and Tans, though many of them were Welshmen. Welsh-language newspapers, such as his once-faithful *Genedl* and the *Dinesydd Cymreig* (with David Thomas in the vanguard of criticism), fulminated against his anti-working-class policies and his use of violence in Ireland, where Lloyd George claimed, that he would see Sinn Fein 'in Hades first'.[30] E. Morgan Humphreys, the editor of the *Genedl*, was a particularly fierce critic of the way he had divided the Liberal Party and of his coercive Irish policy, and rejoiced as Lloyd George lost by-election after by-election in Wales from 1920–22, mainly to Labour.[31]

However, amazingly, before his time ran out in 1922, he succeeded in achieving a solution of sorts to the intractable Irish problem – *Potas y Diafol* (The Devil's Broth),[32] as he referred to Ireland in this period in a letter to his wife. Through a combination of threats, blandishments, diplomacy and the use of Welsh intermediaries, such as the saintly George Maitland Lloyd Davies, and the guile of Tom Jones, he finally managed after five months of negotiation to bring about a settlement in Ireland. He succeeded in providing Ireland, or at least twenty-six of its counties, with an Irish Free State, which paid only nominal allegiance to the English Crown, while getting the Irish Republicans, or at least a majority of its delegation led by Michael Collins and Arthur Griffith, to agree to the creation of a separate Home Rule parliament for the mainly Protestant six counties of the north, on condition that the situation could in future be reviewed by a Boundary Commission. When the Irish delegates seemed to baulk at the last moment, Lloyd George threatened them with the immediate restart of hostilities and refused them time to consult with colleagues at home, including De Valera, who wanted no link with the English Crown. His threat worked and the Irish Free State came into being. In one sense it was a remarkable achievement because it kept a fragile peace for Britain in Ireland for several generations, but only at the cost of violence and a bitter civil war breaking out in the Irish Free State between the De Valera anti-treatyists and Collins's pro-treaty faction.

The devil's broth had been temporarily pacified as far as Lloyd George was concerned and that, remarkably, while in a coalition with the Tories and Unionists. Welsh historians such as K. O. Morgan and John Davies have sought to praise elements of his solution to the problem – a 'solution' which lasted until the end of the 1960s, however fragile it was. Davies concludes that, though 'subsequent events were to prove that not even the Welsh Wizard could settle Ireland, for the Treaty created as many problems as it could solve', nevertheless, 'he extracted acquiescence in a settlement which gave to twenty six counties of Ireland far wider powers of self government than Gladstone had dreamed of'; Davies adds: 'The brutal truth is that the sovereignty and the unity of Ireland were incompatible.'[33] Morgan, too, praises the 1922 settlement (despite 'the immense harm' Lloyd George's earlier suppression of the Irish had done to his reputation) and concludes that it 'bequeathed a legacy of two generations of peace in Ango-Irish relations' and 'brought Southern, Catholic Ireland a far greater measure of self government than Parnell or Redmond had ever visualised'.[34] It has also been emphasized by those who defend him that he held out the prospect to the Irish delegation that the six counties would be so uneconomic that they would eventually be forced into a united Ireland, and that the Boundary Commission could effect such a change. Whether he really meant this is a moot point, but it certainly held sway with the Irish delegation and brought about a deal; however, this deal was condemned by the Irish republican hard liners as the grossest act of betrayal that Ireland had ever endured', particularly because of the continuing Irish 'allegiance' to the Crown. However, the 'deal' was a supreme piece of manouvering and diplomacy by Lloyd George and it rectified, to some extent, his coercive policy in Ireland, although his reputation in politics had been much tarnished by his earlier violent Irish policy.

It was an imperfect peace but a solution of sorts, reflecting the fact that since his early career Lloyd George had had an ambivalent attitude towards Ireland. Though using Irish nationalist analogies to press forward the case for Welsh Home Rule, he always felt that Irish national demands had denied priority to Welsh aspirations and his own Protestant upbringing also meant that he had an innate prejudice against popish Ireland and a measure of sympathy for northern Protestants. He did partition Ireland and was much criticized for it, but he also found a solution to the Irish problem in British terms. His earlier coercive Irish policy at the beginning of his final administration, however, was a contributory factor in his downfall in 1922 and it alienated many Welsh people. The 'solution' of the Irish problem also had its negative Welsh implication. In a period when Welsh Home Rule was a non-issue, it helped to bury the question. With Home Rule accorded to Northern Ireland and the Irish Free State established, the issue of Home Rule All Round for the four nations of Britain was dead and with it any hope of Home Rule for Wales on the back of Irish Home Rule. Moreover, to many Welsh people, the fact that a Welshman, like Lloyd George, could reach the top of the Westminster political tree was proof enough that Wales was a success in British politics and that the Welsh did not need self-government. In 1922 when he fell from power his one-time pioneering role as a Welsh nationalist was also, finally, well and truly spent.

When he left Downing Street in 1922, never to return, his reputation in Wales had been increasingly damaged during his last tenure of office and, symbolically, during that year he took up residence in Churt in Surrey on a small estate with his English mistress, Frances Stevenson. He returned infrequently to Wales during his years in the political wilderness – 'the Wizard in the Wings'. His links with Wales did not cease entirely but he became increasingly divorced from Welsh life. However, those links must not be underestimated, despite his estrangement from Wales. He was responsible for visionary initiatives in land reform and radical solutions to the Depression of the late 1920s and 1930s, particularly with his groundbreaking papers, *The Land and the Nation*, (1925), *We Can Conquer Unemployment* (1929), and his Council for Economic and Social Reconstruction of 1935 which could well have mitigated the harshness of Wales's 'Locust Years' but went unheeded by the political establishment. These plans impelled, especially land reform, by Keynesian ideas, were also driven by his Welsh radical background, but they came to nothing for the 'prophet in the wilderness'.

In linguistic and cultural terms, too, he kept an interest in various aspects of Welsh life, particularly the National Eisteddfod. He missed only two nationals during his long parliamentary career and prized the title of bard, *Sior o Ddwyfor*, more than any other honour he achieved.[35] After the war he still attracted thousands to listen to his presidential address on the Thursday of the Festival (*dydd Iau Lloyd George*) but, although the crowds enjoyed his oratory, the speeches were, in the main, by then, sentimental and vacuous. However, he made a major contribution to the formation of the modern entirely Welsh-speaking Eisteddfod in 1937 at the Machynlleth festival, alongside Cynan and W. J. Gruffydd, where in a controversial Eisteddfod he fulfilled his long-held dream, going back to the 1890s, of securing the Eisteddfod's 'All Welsh Rule' and establishing the Eisteddfod Council.[36] The Welsh Rule was only finally introduced in 1950 but Lloyd George underlined his passion for the language by fronting the movement to de-Anglicize the Eisteddfod, mirroring his early calls for official status to be given to Welsh as an official language in Wales in the Young Wales era and as the 'Boy Alderman'. Also, as John Davies has shown, he also played a crucial role, alongside Cynan and W. J. Gruffydd, in ensuring in the 1920s and 1930s that the language was heard on the BBC and in preparing the way, by 1937, for the establishment of the Welsh Home Service, although it was his daughter, Megan, a real chip off the old block, who played a seminal role in that achievement. Although disliking the Welsh Nationalist Party's founder, Saunders Lewis, for his Catholicism and his right-wing views, he praised his efforts in helping to secure the Welsh Home Service. In 1936, too, although not in favour of the arson attack by the three Welsh Nationalists, Saunders Lewis, Lewis Valentine and D. J. Williams, on the RAF bombing school at Penyberth, Llŷn, he was livid when they were tried and sentenced at the Old Bailey (rather than being tried in Wales). He wrote to his daughter, Megan, from Jamaica, urging her to raise the matter in Parliament:

> This is the first government that has tried Wales at the Old Bailey . . . They might at any rate have had a second trial, or removed it to some other part of Wales, but to take it out of Wales altogether and above all to the Old Bailey, is an outrage that makes my blood boil.[38]

However, he rejected completely the emergence of the Welsh Nationalist Party (Plaid Genedlaethol Cymru), led by Saunders Lewis, and dismissed the party as unrealistic, right wing and dominated by Lewis and his Catholic, reactionary social and economic ideas. He claimed, wrongly, that the party 'would wither in the wind in a night like Jonah's gourd'.[39] He never believed in complete separatism for Wales nor independence, though he did not eschew that elusive term entirely during his Young Wales days and was frequently attacked for being a 'separatist'. He was, of course, a Federal Home Ruler. He was criticized vehemently by Saunders Lewis in the 1930s for his attacks on Plaid, with Lewis in the *Welsh Nationalist* in January 1932 dismissing his Young Wales League as a farce and criticizing Welsh Liberalism of that period as being merely 'the hobby of corpulent and successful men'.[40] A later leader of Plaid Cymru, Gwynfor Evans, has been kinder to the Young Wales League and Lloyd George, claiming that he had made Wales a political entity then but that later, when he became the British politician, 'one can compare him to Henry VIII in his influence upon Wales'.[41] Such a view is misplaced for up to 1912, especially, and to some extent afterwards, he remained a strong advocate of Welsh devolution, but he certainly gave up the cause of Welsh Home Rule to all intents and purposes by the end of the nineteenth century. In the 1920s, he was also criticized bitterly by his former Cymru Fydd colleagues, such as W. Llywelyn Williams and Beriah Gwynfe Evans, for giving up on Home Rule; and in *Wales Drops the Pilots*, a great admirer of Lloyd George and of Young Wales, W. Hughes Jones, recalled in bitter-sweet terms and with much nostalgia, how Wales had lost a golden opportunity to bring about self-government with the demise of Cymru Fydd. Although blaming Welsh Liberals primarily for rejecting Lloyd George and leaving him no alternative but to serve Wales via Westminister, by implication Hughes Jones was also suggesting that Lloyd George had turned his back on the issue prematurely and peremptorily.[42]

There is an element of truth in this contention, but as this book has underlined, there is no disputing the fact that for a decade from 1886 to 1896 Lloyd George had been a nationalist of great drive and commitment and that during the leadership of the Young Wales movement, in the face of much opposition, even from his own party, he had led, at enormous risk and considerable personal cost, the first modern movement for Welsh Home Rule with a radical, labourist agenda and a vision of a new, more egalitarian, prosperous and modern, bilingual self-governing Wales within a federal Britain. It was not merely posturing or a pressure group or a vehicle for Lloyd George's personal ambition, nor did it lack a labourist agenda, as so many historians have contended. Despite many failings, Lloyd George was a committed nationalist during the Young Wales era, while some elements of his nationalism and of his labourism were enduring features of his career, particularly up to the First World War. Moreover, the influence of Young Wales had its long-term legacy for Welsh politics.

This was especially evident in the career of the apple of his eye, his daughter Megan, who took on the Cymru Fydd mantle of her father. As this author has shown, in *Megan Lloyd George*, she strove in the 1930s and 1940s to secure a Welsh secretary of state and federal Home Rule and then in the 1950s led the abortive cross-party Parliament for Wales campaign which, though it failed, set an agenda for the future, and paved the way for Labour under Jim Griffiths's leadership to establish the Welsh Office in 1964; by this time Megan, too, had moved to that party.[43] She was joined in the Parliament for Wales campaign by Young Liberals (if not the older generation). Most prominent of them was the future founder of an independent Welsh Liberal party in the 1960s, Emlyn Hooson MP, who remained a committed Home Rule advocate throughout his career,[44] and one who tried unsuccessfully in the 1960s to get the Welsh Liberals and Gwynfor Evans's Plaid Cymru to join together to secure federal Welsh Home Rule, only for his overtures to be rejected.[45]

The Cymru Fydd mantle was also inherited by another member of the cross-party campaign in the 1950s, the Labour MP Cledwyn Hughes. He and four other Welsh Labour MPs – Goronwy Roberts,[46] Tudor Watkins, S. O. Davies[47] and T. W. Jones – were threatened with losing the Labour whip for supporting the campaign for a Welsh parliament, while Cledwyn Hughes, inheriting the initiative of Jim Griffiths and his adviser, Gwilym Prys Davies, also played a vital role as Wales's second secretary of state for Wales (1966–8) in trying to establish an elected council for Wales – an embryonic parliament; Hughes was defeated in his own Cabinet by vicious Welsh Labour anti-nationalists, led by George Thomas, who then conspired to replace Cledwyn Hughes by elevating himself to the post.[48] Cledwyn Hughes kept the issue on the agenda into the 1970s, however, only for Wales and the 'cave' of five anti-nationalists in the Labour Party, led by Neil Kinnock, to destroy their own government's policy and secure a 'No' vote by 4:1 in the Welsh Assembly referendum in 1979. Cledwyn Hughes and other patriots in the Labour Party lived to see another referendum in 1997, however, when Wales secured a Welsh Assembly.[49] Cledwyn Hughes was instrumental in getting Labour and John Smith's Shadow Cabinet to secure that goal as official Labour policy after 1992; he was joined, in this, by John Morris MP, the Welsh secretary from 1974–9, another inheritor of the Cymru Fydd tradition, who had led the abortive devolution referendum campaign in 1979.[50]

However, the vital figure who carried a reluctant Labour Party to support a Welsh Assembly was Ron Davies, MP for Caerphilly, the shadow Welsh secretary under Smith and Tony Blair and then Welsh secretary for a tragically brief time in the 1990s. He masterminded the piloting of the bill giving devolution to Wales. Later in 1997, he secured a tense but masterly referendum victory after an inclusive campaign with the Welsh Liberal leader, Richard Livesey MP and the redoubtable Plaid Cymru leader, Dafydd Wigley MP. These three were the inheritors of the Lloyd George mantle of Young Wales, as were those Labour, Liberal and Plaid Cymru politicians who had fought so long since 1945 for a measure of Welsh self-government.[51] They had all been inspired by Lloyd George and his leadership of the first real, modern movement for self-rule in the 1890s.

Lloyd George was the pioneering advocate of a powerful parliament for the Welsh people and, whatever may have been the shortcomings of his passionately led movement, in the face of tremendous odds he set before the Welsh people an agenda and a fundamental question which still needs resolving: Can Wales reach its full economic, social, cultural and linguistic potential without a substantial measure of self-government?

Despite all his faults, Lloyd George was Wales's greatest modern politician, and part of his greatness was that early vision that a self-governing Wales would be an example for the world to emulate:

> Were self government conceded to Wales, she would be a model to the nationalities of the earth of a people who had driven oppression from their hillsides and initiated the glorious reign of freedom, justice and truth. (Cardiff, 1890)[52]

NOTES

Chapter I

[1] William George, *My Brother and I* (London, 1958), p. 127.

[2] Enumerator's census, 1871, Llanystumdwy Parish.

[3] John Grigg, *The Young Lloyd George* (London, 1974).

[4] Ibid., p. 31.

[5] Ibid.

[6] Ibid., p. 22.

[7] Emyr Price, 'Lloyd George's pre-parliamentary career', unpublished University of Wales MA dissertation, 1974, 33–6.

[8] Jack Eaton, *Judge Bryn Roberts: A Biography* (Cardiff, 1989).

[9] Enumerator's census, 1881, Criccieth Parish.

[10] K. O. Morgan, 'Lloyd George and Welsh Liberalism', in Judith Loades (ed.), *The Life and Times of David Lloyd George* (Bangor, 1991).

[11] Ibid.

[12] William George, *My Brother and I*, p. 73.

[13] Ibid., p. 127.

[14] Ibid.

[15] *NWE*, 5 November 1880.

[16] Ibid., 19 November 1880.

[17] Ibid., 26 November 1880.

[18] Emyr Price, *Y Port a Lloyd George, 1878–1890* (Porthmadog, 1995).

[19] *NWE*, 25 January 1882.

[20] J. L. Garvin, *The Life of Joseph Chamberlain* (London, 1933), ch. xv.

[21] *CDH*, 18 November 1882.

[22] Ibid.

[23] W. R. P. George, *The Making of Lloyd George* (Llandysul, 1976), p. 88.

[24] Garvin, *Joseph Chamberlain*, ch. xv.

[25] Price, p. 8.

[26] Diary, quoted in W. R. P. George, *The Making of Lloyd George*, p. 99.

[27] Ibid., p. 104.

[28] Ibid., p. 115.

[29] Ibid., pp. 115–16.

[30] Grigg, *The Young Lloyd George*, p. 43.

[31] Census, 1881, Carnarvonshire.

[32] Price, 'Lloyd George's Pre-Parliamentary Career' 1, 33–4.

[33] *CN*, 30 May 1884.

[34] For H. J. Williams (Plenydd), see J. Ll. Jones, *Plenydd (H. J. Williams): yr areithydd dirwestol enwog: hanes ei fywyd a detholiad o'i weithiau*, Caernarfon, (1929).

[35] For D. R. Daniel, see K. W. Jones Roberts, 'D. R. Daniel', *Journal of the Merioneth History Society*, 1965.

[36] For W. J. Parry, see J. Roose Williams, 'The life and activities of W. J. Parry of

Coetmor', *Transactions of the Caernarfonshire Historical Society*, 23, 24 (1962–3).

[37] K. O. Morgan, *Wales in British Politics, 1868–1922* (Cardiff, 1980), p. 62.

[38] Quoted in K. O. Morgan (ed.), *Lloyd George: Family Letters 1885–1936* (London, 1973), p. 14.

Chapter II

[1] Emyr Price, 'Lloyd George and Merioneth politics, 1885–6', *Journal of the Merioneth Historical Society*, 7 (1975), 294–6, delineates the sources used in analysing the socio-political make-up of the constituency of Merioneth.

[2] *Y Dydd*, 17 July 1885.

[3] Diary, 9 July 1885, quoted in H. du Parcq, *Life of D. Lloyd George* (London, 1912), p. 46.

[4] Ibid., p. 44.

[5] Ibid.

[6] *YGG*, 4 September 1885.

[7] *CDH*, 22 August 1885.

[8] Diary, 20 August 1885, quoted in du Parcq, *Life*, p. 46.

[9] *CDH*, 22 August 1885.

[10] Diary, 28 November 1885, quoted in du Parcq, *Life*, p. 48.

[11] Ibid., 18 November 1885, p. 47.

[12] NLW, 8823C, M. D. Jones to W. J. Parry, 7 January 1886: 'Mae Mr Gee wedi bod yn rhy lawdrwm ar was y Blaid Wyddelig ac yn rhy ofnus' (Mr Gee has been over critical of the Irish Nationalist Party and too frightened of supporting them).

[13] *YGG*, 17 February 1885.

[14] Ibid.

[15] Diary, 13 February 1885, quoted in du Parcq, *Life*.

[16] *BAC*, 21 April 1886.

[17] Ibid., 5 May 1886.

[18] *YGG*, 21 April 1886.

[19] *YHC*, 27 April 1886.

[20] NLW, Ellis MSS, 678, letter from Lloyd George to T. E. Ellis.

[21] *CN*, 25 June 1886.

[22] J. Hugh Edwards, *The Life of David Lloyd George*, vol. 1 (London, 1913), p. 138.

[23] Diary, 20 June 1886, quoted in du Parcq, *Life*.

Chapter III

[1] T. Gwynn Jones, *Cofiant Thomas Gee* (Denbigh, 1913), pp. 449–53.

[2] *BAC*, 3 November 1886.

[3] Ibid.

[4] Ibid., 24 November 1886.

[5] H. du Parcq, *Life of D. Lloyd George* (London, 1912), p. 745.

[6] *YGG*, 5 January 1887.

[7] Ibid., 12 January 1887.

[8] *Y Gwalia*, 12 January 1887.

[9] Ibid.

[10] *YGG*, 9 February 1887.

[11] *BAC*, 9 February 1887.

[12] *Y Gwalia*, 16 February 1887.

[13] *YGG*, 20 April 1887.

[14] *YHC*, 3 May 1887.

[15] J. Hugh Edwards, *The Life of David Lloyd George*, vol. 1 (London, 1913), p. 153.

[16] NLW, T. E. Ellis MS, 679, D. Ll. George to Tom Ellis, 19 May 1887.

[17] Ibid.

[18] *YGG*, 6 July 1887; *Y Werin*, 8 July 1887.

[19] Ibid.

[20] Diary, 27 June 1887, quoted in du Parcq, *Life*.

[21] *YGG*, 13 July 1887.

[22] *Y Tyst a'r Dydd*, 5 August 1887.

[23] *CN*, 23 December 1887.

[24] Ibid.

[25] *NWOE*, 14 October 1887.

[26] Diary, 4 September 1887, quoted in du Parcq, *Life*.

[27] NLW, Daniel MSS, 276, D. Ll. George to D. R. Daniel, 27 December 1887.

[28] Letter from D. Ll. George to Howell Gee, 7 November 1887, quoted in W. R. P. George, *The Making of Lloyd George* (Llandysul, 1976).

[29] Ibid.

[30] Ibid.

[31] *YGG*, 4 April 1888.

[32] *Y Llan a'r Dywosogaeth*, 13 April 1888.

[33] Jones, *Cofiant Thomas Gee*, p. 503.

[34] *Y Gwalia*, 30 May 1888.

[35] Confirmed beforehand to Lloyd George in a letter to D. R. Daniel, 5 July 1888, NLW, Daniel MSS, 2751.

Chapter IV

[1] NLW, Daniel MSS, 243, D. Ll. George to D. R. Daniel, 4 December 1887.

[2] Ibid., 12 December 1887.

[3] Ibid., 19 December 1887.

[4] Ibid., T. E. Ellis to D. R. Daniel, 21 December 1887.

[5] Ibid., D. Ll. George to D. R. Daniel, 6 February 1888.

[6] NLW, Daniel MSS, 2913 (Daniel's short unpublished biography of Lloyd George suggests he wrote the first two leading articles).

[7] *UR*, 4 January 1888.

[8] Ibid., 15 January 1888.

[9] Ibid., 15 February 1888.

[10] Ibid.

[11] Ibid., 22 February 1888.

[12] NLW, Daniel MSS, 2749, D. Ll. George to D. R. Daniel, 27 February 1888.

[13] *UR*, 29 February 1888.

[14] *Gwalia*, 21 March 1888.

[15] *UR*, 22 February 1888.

[16] Ibid., 18 February 1888.
[17] Ibid., 1 February 1888.
[18] Ibid., 18 January 1888.
[19] Ibid., 4 January 1888.

Chapter V

[1] Emyr Price, 'Lloyd George's pre-parliamentary career', unpublished University of Wales MA dissertation, 1974, 100.
[2] Y Gwalia, 2 November 1887.
[3] YGG, 2 May 1888.
[4] A full account of the first two stages of the case appeared in the journal Cymru Fydd, October 1888.
[5] Gwynedd Archives Services, MSS 766.
[6] CDH, 18 May 1888.
[7] CN, 18 May 1888.
[8] Including NWOE, 25 May 1888.
[9] NWOE, 8 June 1888.
[10] CDH, 6 July 1888.
[11] NLW, Daniel MSS, 2751, D. Ll. George to D. R. Daniel, 5 July 1888.
[12] NWOE, 6 July 1888.
[13] YGG, 11 July 1888.
[14] NWOE, 6 July 1888.
[15] W. R. P. George, The Making of Lloyd George (Llandysul, 1976), p. 115.
[16] NLW, Daniel MSS, 2751, D. Ll. George to D. R. Daniel, 5 July 1888.
[17] YHC, 10 July 1888; CDH, 13 July 1888.
[18] YGG, 11 July 1888; NWOE, 13 July 1888.
[19] Y Celt, 20 July 1888.
[20] NLW, Daniel MSS, 2752, D. Ll. George to D. R. Daniel, 10 July 1888.
[21] Ibid., 2753, D. Ll. George to D. R. Daniel, 17 July 1888.
[22] Y Werin, 27 July 1888.
[23] NWOE, 27 July 1888.
[24] Ibid.
[25] NLW, Rendel MSS, 14 (442), A. C. Humphreys-Owen to S. Rendel, 10 August 1888.
[26] CN, 17 August 1888.
[27] Y Celt, 23 August 1888.
[28] NWOE, 31 August 1888.
[29] NLW, MSS 1633, Michael D. Jones to D. R. Daniel, 4 September 1888.
[30] CDH, 21 September 1888.
[31] Y Gwalia, 23 September 1888.
[32] NWOE, 21 December 1888.
[33] Daily Post, 19 December 1888.
[34] SWDN, 19 December 1888.
[35] WM, 19 December 1888.
[36] NWOE, 21 December 1888.
[37] NLW, Lloyd George MSS, 2044A, diary, 3 January 1889.
[38] Seren Gomer, January 1888.
[39] Y Tyst a'r Dydd, 11 January 1889.
[40] NWOE, 4 January 1889.
[41] Y Gwalia, 9 January 1889.

Chapter VI

[1] *NWOE*, 25 January 1889.

[2] *Y Gwalia*, 13 February 1889.

[3] *NWOE*, 15 February 1889.

[4] Ibid.

[5] *YGG*, 3 April 1889.

[6] Ibid.

[7] Ibid., 13 November 1889.

[8] Ibid., 29 January 1889.

[9] *NWOE*, 10 May 1889.

[10] *Y Gwalia*, 11 May 1889.

[11] *NWOE*, 13 November 1889.

[12] Ibid.

[13] *CDH*, 7 February 1890.

[14] Ibid.

[15] Ibid., 15 October 1889.

[16] Ibid.

[17] Ibid.

[18] See, especially, D. Tecwyn Lloyd, *Drych o Genedl* (Swansea, 1987), pp. 26–9.

[19] Ibid.

[20] Hywel Teifi Edwards, *Cwm Rhondda* (Llandysul, 1995), pp. 221–2.

[21] Emyr Price, 'Eisteddfodau Caernarfon a Lloyd George', *Eisteddfota* (Llandysul, 1979), pp. 137–48.

[22] K. O. Morgan, *Modern Wales: Politics, Places and People* (Cardiff, 1995), p. 404.

[23] John Grigg, *The Young Lloyd George* (London, 1974), p. 43.

[24] E.g. *YGG*, 19 June 1889; also *NWOE* and *Y Werin*, same week.

[25] Ibid.

[26] NLW, George MSS, 77, 204080, D. Ll. George to M. Ll. George, 3 September 1889.

[27] *YGG*, 18 September 1889.

[28] NWL, Rendel MSS, 14 (503) 19463C, A. C. Humphreys-Owen to S. Rendel, 29 September 1889.

[29] *SWDN*, 16 October 1889.

[30] *Y Werin*, 19 October 1889.

[31] *NWOE*, 13 October 1889.

[32] For E. Herber Evans, 1836–96, see Elfed Lewis, *Cofiant y Parch E. Herber Evans* (Wrexham, 1901).

[33] *Y Celt*, 25 October 1889.

[34] *YGG*, 25 October 1889.

[35] *Y Celt*, 25 October 1889.

[36] *BAC*, 23 October 1889.

[37] *Y Tyst a'r Dydd*, 25 October 1889.

[38] *Y Goleuad*, 24 October 1889.

[39] *WM*, 19 October 1889.

[40] *CDH*, 7 February 1890.

[41] *SWDN*, 5 February 1890.

[42] *NWOE*, 14 February 1890.

[43] *SWDN*, 6 February 1890.

[44] *CN*, 7 February 1890.

[45] *Cymru Fydd*, March 1890.

[46] *CDH*, 6 February 1890.
[47] Ibid., 7 February 1890.
[48] NLW, Daniel MSS, 37, T. E. Ellis to W. J. Parry, 25 February 1890.
[49] *WM*, 5 February 1890.
[50] *SWDN*, 5 February 1890.
[51] Ibid.
[52] W. R. P. George, *The Making of Lloyd George* (Llandysul, 1979), p. 166.
[53] *NWOE*, 29 March 1890.

Chapter VII

[1] See Emyr Price, 'Lloyd George's pre-parliamentary career', ch. ix, for the political background to the Caernarfon Boroughs electorate 1832–86.
[2] Ibid., ch. ix, for social structure of the Caernarfon Boroughs constituency in 1890.
[3] Electoral registers for the electorate of Bangor and Conwy boroughs not available.
[4] Beriah Gwynfe Evans, *The Life Romance of Lloyd George* (Cardiff, 1915), p. 55.
[5] Ibid.
[6] *SWDN*, 27 March 1890.
[7] *WM*, 25 March 1890.
[8] Ibid.
[9] K. O. Morgan, *Wales in British Politics, 1868–1922* (Cardiff, 1980), p. 111.
[10] N. Masterman, *The Forerunner* (Llandybïe, 1972), p. 102.
[11] *SWDN*, 25 March 1890.
[12] *Seren Gomer*, March 1890.
[13] Bangor MSS, 1125 (158), W. Rathbone to R. D. Williams, 21 March 1890.
[14] *Y Gwalia*, 26 March 1890.
[15] *NWC*, 5 April 1890.
[16] Ibid.
[17] *NWOE*, 11 April 1890.
[18] William George, *My Brother and I* (London, 1958), p. 132.
[19] John Grigg, *The Young Lloyd George* (London, 1974), p. 82.
[20] K. O. Morgan, *Modern Wales: Politics, Places and People* (Cardiff, 1995), p. 374.
[21] William George, *My Brother and I*, p. 132.
[22] NLW, 19464C, Rendel MSS, 14 (533), A. C. Humphreys-Owen to S. Rendel, 3 March 1890.
[23] NLW, 19449D, Rendel MSS, 9 (1), A. D. Acland to S. Rendel, 1 April 1890.
[24] *CDH*, 28 March 1890.
[25] *BAC*, 2 April 1890.
[26] *YGG*, 26 March 1890.
[27] *NWC*, 29 March 1890.
[28] Ibid.
[29] *WM*, 5 April 1890.
[30] *CDH*, 28 March 1890.
[31] *Y Llan a'r Dywysogaeth*, 3 April 1890.
[32] *Y Gwalia*, 2 April 1890.
[33] *SWDN*, 3 April 1890.
[34] *Y Goleuad*, 2 April 1890.
[35] Gwynedd Archives Service, MSS 503, Lloyd George's election agent's papers (J. T. Roberts), 1890.

[36] *NWOE*, 28 March 1890.

[37] NLW, Daniel MSS, 515, diary, 9 April.

[38] Emyr Price, *Ail Gloriannu Thomas Gee* (Denbigh, 1977).

[39] *NWOE*, 4 April 1890.

[40] *YGG*, 9 April 1890.

[41] *Y Werin*, 29 March 1890.

[42] For example, *YGG*, 9 April 1890.

[43] *CDH*, 4 April 1890.

[44] *YGG*, 14 April 1890.

[45] *Y Werin*, 5 April 1890.

[46] *CDH*, 28 March 1890.

[47] *Y Gwalia*, 2 April 1890.

[48] *WM*, 9 April 1890.

[49] *Y Gwalia*, 9 April 1890.

[50] *SWDN*, 10 April 1890.

[51] NLW, 204060, George MSS, 86, D. Ll. George to M. Ll. George, 8 April 1890.

[52] NLW, Ellis MSS, 863, R. A. Hudson to T. E. Ellis, 5 April 1890.

[53] Quoted in W. R. P. George, *The Making of Lloyd George* (Llandysul, 1976), p. 168.

[54] Grigg, *The Young Lloyd George*, p. 83.

[55] *NWC*, 12 April 1890.

[56] *YGG*, 12 April 1890.

[57] Ibid.

[58] *NWOE*, 18 April 1890.

[59] Ibid.

[60] *YGG*, 16 April 1890.

[61] *BAC*, 18 April 1890.

[62] *Y Goleuad*, 17 April 1890; *Seren Gomer*, May 1890; *Y Greal*, May 1890; *Y Gwyliedydd*, 16 April 1890.

[63] *CN*, 25 April 1890.

[64] *CDH*, 11 April 1890.

[65] *Y Dydd*, 25 April 1890.

[66] *SWDN*, 12 April 1890.

[67] *Y Celt*, 18 April 1890; and *Cymru Fydd*, May 1890.

[68] *WM*, 14 April 1890.

[69] *Y Llan*, 18 April 1890.

[70] *NWC*, 19 April 1890.

[71] *NWOE*, 18 April 1890.

[72] *Liverpool Mercury*, 19 April 1890.

[73] Bangor, Coetmor MSS, 113, T. E. Ellis to W. J. Parry, 28 May 1890.

[74] K. O. Morgan, *David Lloyd George: Welsh Radical as World Statesman* (Cardiff, 1963), p. 21.

Chapter VIII

[1] See chapter VII.

[2] B. B. Gilbert, *David Lloyd George: A Political Life, 1863–1912* (London, 1987).

[3] E. Morgan Humphreys, 'Profiadau Golygydd', *Transactions of the Caernarfonshire Historical Society*, 1950.

[4] John Grigg, *The Young Lloyd George* (London, 1974), p. 141.

[5] Letter from D. Lloyd George to Richard Lloyd, quoted in W. R. P. George, *Lloyd*

6   *George, Backbencher* (Llandysul, 1983), p. 26.

7   K. O. Morgan, *Lloyd George and Welsh Liberalism* (Bangor, 1991).

K. O. Morgan (ed.), *Lloyd George: Family Letters 1885–1936* (Oxford, 1973),
8   D. Ll. George to M. Ll. George, 14 June 1890.

WM, 23 April 1890.
9   Quoted in K. O. Morgan (ed.), *Family Letters*, D. Ll. George to M. Lloyd George,
10   12 June 1890.

Ibid., D. Ll. George to M. Ll. George, 13 August 1890.
11   *Seren Cymru*, 12 June 1890.
12   *Y Cymro*, 14 June 1890.
13   *SWDN*, 16 June 1890.
14   *Y Llan*, 27 June 1890; *YGG*, 18 June 1890; *Y Celt*, 20 June 1890; *BAC*, 21 June
15   1890.

K. O. Morgan (ed.), *Family Letters*, D. Ll. George to M. Ll. George, 15 July 1890.
16   *WM*, 8 July 1890.
17   K. O. Morgan (ed.), *Family Letters*, D. Ll. George to M. Ll. George, 7 August
18   1890.

NWC, 30 August 1890.
19   *BAC*, 25 June 1890.
20   *WM*, 1 July 1890.
21   Ibid., 11 August 1890.
22   K. O. Morgan (ed.), *Family Letters*, D. Ll. George to M. Ll. George, 7 August
23   1890.

YGG, 1 September 1890.
24   Ibid., 22 November 1890.
25   *WM*, 21 November 1890.
26   *SWDN*, 18 November 1890.
27   *YGG*, 26 November 1890.
28   Ibid., 2 December 1890.
29   Ibid.
30   *BAC*, 24 December 1890.
31   *WM*, 20 December 1890.
32   *YGG*, 7 January 1891.
33   Ibid., 14 January 1891.
34   *WM*, 13 February 1891.
35   Letter from T. E. Ellis to D. Ll. George, quoted in W. R. P. George, *Backbencher*,
36   p. 55.

BAC, 24 September 1890.
37   *Seren Gomer*, 20 February 1891.
38   *YGG*, 20 February 1891.
39   Ibid., 11 April 1891.
40   NLW, Gee MSS, letter from D. Ll. George to Thomas Gee, 2 February 1891.
41   *YGG*, 18 April 1891.
42   Ibid., 27 May 1891.
43   *BAC*, 12 August 1891.
44   *SWDN*, 11 September 1891.
45   Ibid., 8 October 1891.
46   *Y Llan*, December 1891.
47   *Seren Gomer*, 11 December 1891.
48   *NWOE*, in the first edition of January 1892.
49   *Y Llan*, January 1892.
50   *WM*, 15 January 1892.

[51] *YGG*, 16 March 1892.

[52] Ibid., 30 March 1892.

[53] *WM*, 4 April 1892.

[54] K. O. Morgan (ed.), *Family Letters*, 29 April 1892.

[55] *YGG*, 8 June 1892.

[56] *Y Llan*, June 1892.

[57] NLW, Rendel MSS, letter from S. Rendel to A. C. Humphreys-Owen, 22 May 1892.

[58] *YGG*, 22 June 1892.

[59] Ibid.

[60] Ibid.

[61] *NWOC*, 8 July 1892.

[62] *YGG*, 22 June 1892.

[63] *NWC*, 2 July 1892.

[64] *YGG*, 29 June 1892.

[65] *NWC*, 2 July 1892.

[66] *YGG*, 6 July 1892.

[67] Ibid.

[68] Ibid., 13 July 1892.

[69] Ibid., 6 July 1892.

[70] Ibid.

[71] K. O. Morgan (ed.). *Family Letters*, p. 56, D. Ll. George to Margaret Ll. George, 5 July 1892.

[72] Undated letter, quoted in W. R. P. George, *Backbencher*, p. 93.

[73] J. Graham Jones, 'Lloyd George and the Caernarfon Boroughs election of 1892', *Transactions of the Caernarfonshire Historical Society*, 52–3 (1991–2), 31–50.

[74] *NWOE*, 15 July 1892.

[75] *SWDN*, 23 July 1892.

[76] William George, *My Brother and I* (London, 1958), pp. 160–1.

[77] *Y Brython Gymreig*, 5 August 1892.

Chapter IX

[1] Bangor, Lloyd MSS, 314, 449, letter from J. A. Price to J. E. Lloyd, 14 October 1892.

[2] Letter from D. Ll. George to T. E. Ellis, 16 August 1892, quoted in W. R. P. George, *Lloyd George, Backbencher* (Llandysul, 1983), p. 100.

[3] Letter from T. E. Ellis to D. Ll. George, 21 August 1892, quoted in ibid., p. 101.

[4] Letter from D. Ll. George to S. T. Evans, 19 August 1892, quoted in ibid., p. 99.

[5] *NWOE*, 16 September 1892.

[6] *Liverpool Mercury*, 20 January 1893.

[7] Ibid.

[8] *NWOE*, 20 April 1893.

[9] Ibid.

[10] Ibid.

[11] *NWC*, 20 April 1893.

[12] K. O. Morgan (ed.), *Lloyd George: Family Letters 1885–1936* (London, 1973), D. Ll. George to M. Ll. George, 2 May 1893.

[13] Quoted in W. R. P. George, *Backbencher*, pp. 146–7.

[14] Ibid., p. 147.

[15] John Grigg, *The Young Lloyd George* (London, 1974), p. 145.

[16] NLW, Ellis MSS, T. E. Ellis to D. R. Daniel, 30 April 1894.

[17] *NWOE*, 18 May 1894.

[18] Ibid.

[19] Morgan (ed.), *Family Letters*, p. 71, D. Ll. George to M. Ll. George, 17 May 1894.

[20] *NWOE*, 18 May 1894.

[21] Ibid.

[22] Letter from D. Ll. George to William Lloyd, 30 May 1894, quoted in W. R. P. George, *Backbencher*, p. 151.

[23] *Liverpool Daily Post*, 24 May 1894.

[24] *NWOE*, 25 May 1894.

[25] *BAC*, 20 June 1894.

[26] *NWC*, 20 June 1894.

[27] Ibid., 25 August 1894.

[28] *NWOE*, 6 July 1894.

[29] Emyr Wyn Williams, 'Liberalism in Wales and the politics of Welsh Home Rule, 1886–1911', *Bulletin of the Board of Celtic Studies*, 37 (1990).

[30] K. O. Morgan, *Modern Wales: Politics, Places and People* (Cardiff, 1995), p. 374.

[31] Morgan (ed.) *Family Letters*, p. 96.

[32] R. Merfyn Jones, *The North Wales Quarrymen, 1874–1922* (Cardiff, 1981), pp. 162–74.

[33] *NWOE*, 18 August 1893.

[34] Ibid., 20 October 1893.

[35] Morgan, *Modern Wales*, p. 374.

[36] Grigg, *The Young Lloyd George*.

[37] J. Graham Jones, 'Lloyd George, Cymru Fydd and the Newport meeting of January 1886', *The National Library of Wales Journal*, 1996, 449.

[38] *NWOE*, 28 September 1894.

[39] *NWC*, 29 September 1894.

[40] Ibid.

[41] *NWOE*, 28 September 1894.

[42] *NWC*, 26 October 1894.

[43] *NWOE*, 12 October 1894.

[44] Ibid.

[45] Ibid.

[46] NLW, Lewis MSS, letter from D. Ll. George to J. Herbert Lewis, 31 October 1894.

[47] *NWOE*, 23 November 1894.

[48] Ibid., 21 June 1894.

[49] Ibid.

[50] *Young Wales*, January 1895.

[51] *NWOE*, 14 December 1895.

[52] *NWC*, 15 December 1895.

[53] *SWDN*, 13 April 1895.

[54] Ibid., 17 April 1895.

[55] *NWOE*, 26 April 1895.

[56] Morgan (ed.), *Family Letters*, p. 84.

[57] *SWDN*, 27 April 1895.

[58] *NWC*, 30 April 1895.

[59] *SWDN*, 31 May 1895.

[60] Ibid., 6 June 1895.

[61] Morgan (ed.), *Family Letters*, p. 83.

[62]   Letter from D. Ll. George to William George, 9 May 1895, quoted in W. R. P. George, *Backbencher*, p. 165.
[63]   *WM*, 22 May 1895.
[64]   *NWC*, 23 May 1895.
[65]   *WM*, 27 June 1895.
[66]   *NWOE*, 26 June 1895.
[67]   *NWC*, 27 June 1895.
[68]   Grigg, *The Young Lloyd George*, p. 167.
[69]   *CDH*, 18 July 1895.
[70]   Grigg, *The Young Lloyd George*, p. 167.
[71]   *CDH*, 18 July 1895.
[72]   Ibid.
[73]   Ibid.
[74]   Ibid.
[75]   B. B. Gilbert, *David Lloyd George: A Political Life, 1863–1912* (London, 1987), p. 137.
[76]   *CDH*, 5 July 1895.
[77]   *NWOE*, 12 July 1895.
[78]   NLW, George MSS, letter from D. Ll. George to M. Ll. George, 12 July 1895.
[79]   William George, diary, 21 July 1895.
[80]   *NWC*, 20 July 1895.
[81]   William George, diary, 21 July 1895.
[82]   *Manchester Guardian*, 22 July 1895.
[83]   *NWOE*, 23 July 1895.
[84]   Letter from D. Ll. George to William George, quoted in W. R. P. George, *Backbencher*, p. 182.
[85]   *NWOE*, 23 July 1895.

Chapter X

[1]   *BAC*, 30 July 1895.
[2]   *CDH*, 2 August 1895.
[3]   *NWC*, 10 August 1895.
[4]   *SWDN*, 6 September 1895.
[5]   *NWC*, 14 September 1895.
[6]   *BAC*, 2 October 1895.
[7]   *NWOE*, 23 September 1895.
[8]   *Young Wales*, October 1895.
[9]   Ibid.
[10]   Ibid.
[11]   Ibid.
[12]   NLW, Gee MSS, letter from D. Ll. George to Thomas Gee, 9 October 1895.
[13]   *NWOE*, 18 October 1895.
[14]   NLW, Ellis MSS, 690, letter from D. Ll. George to T. E. Ellis, 4 November 1895.
[15]   J. Graham Jones, 'Lloyd George and the Caernarfon Boroughs election of 1892', *Transactions of the Caernarfonshire Historical Society*, 52–3 (1991–2).
[16]   NLW, Ellis MSS, 74A, letter from E. W. Evans to H. Asquith, 23 November 1895.
[17]   Ibid., 74, letter from H. Asquith to T. Ellis, 30 November 1895.
[18]   NLW, MSS, 20, 415C, letter from D. Ll. George to M. Ll. George, 3 June 1894.
[19]   *SWDN*, 6 November 1895.

[20] NLW, MSS, 20 45C no. 594, letter from D. Ll. George to M. Ll. George, 8 November 1895.

[21] Ibid., 594, letter from D. Ll. George to M. Ll. George, 8 November 1895.

[22] Ibid.

[23] Morgan (ed.), *Family Letters*, p. 89, D. Ll. George to M. Ll. George, 8 November 1895.

[24] *SWDN*, 8 November 1895.

[25] Morgan (ed.), *Family Letters*, p. 90, D. Ll. George to M. Ll. George, 12 November 1895.

[26] *SWDN*, 13 November 1895.

[27] *BAC*, 13 November 1895.

[28] Morgan (ed.), *Family Letters*, p. 90, D. Ll. George to M. Ll. George, 13 November 1895.

[29] Ibid., p. 92, D. Ll. George to M. Ll. George, 21 November 1895.

[30] NLW, William George MSS, letter from D. Ll. George to William George, 21 November 1895.

[31] Morgan (ed.), *Family Letters*, p. 92, D. Ll. George to M. Ll. George, 21 November 1895.

[32] Ibid., p. 91, D. Ll. George to M. Ll. George, 27 November 1895.

[33] *SWDN*, 4 December 1895.

[34] NLW, George MSS, letter from D. Ll. George to M. Ll. George, 27 November 1895.

[35] NLW, William George MSS, letter from J. Herbert Lewis to D. Ll. George, 1 January 1896.

[36] NLW, Lewis MSS, letter from D. Ll. George to J. Herbert Lewis, 11 December 1895.

[37] Ibid., letter, 28 December 1895.

[38] Ibid., letter, 31 December 1895.

[39] *NWOE*, 5 January 1896.

[40] Ibid.

[41] Ibid.

[42] NLW, Lewis MSS, letter from D. Ll. George to J. Herbert Lewis, 4 January 1896.

[43] NLW, George MSS, letter from D. Ll. George to M. Ll. George, 12 January 1896.

[44] Ibid., letter from D. Ll. George to M. Ll. George, 15 January 1896.

[45] *WM*, 17 January 1896.

[46] *NWOE*, 24 January 1896.

[47] *SWDN*, 17 January 1896.

[48] Ibid.

[49] Ibid.

[50] NLW, Lewis MSS, letter from D. Ll. George to J. Herbert Lewis, 16 January 1896.

[51] *SWDN*, 17 January 1896.

[52] Ibid.

[53] *NWOE*, 24 January 1896.

[54] NLW, George MSS, letter from D. Ll. George to M. Ll. George, 16 January 1896.

[55] NLW, Lewis MSS, letter from D. Ll. George to J. Herbert Lewis, 16 January 1896.

[56] W. R. P. George, *Lloyd George, Backbencher* (Llandysul, 1983), p. 190.

[57] NLW, George MSS, letter from D. Ll. George to M. Ll. George, 18 January 1896.

[58] NLW, William George MSS, letter from D. Ll. George to William George, 3 March 1896.

[59] NLW, George MSS, letter from D. Ll. George to M. Ll. George, 2 March 1896.

[60] *The Times*, 17 December 1896.

[61] Ibid.

[62] K. O. Morgan, *Wales in Welsh Politics, 1868–1922* (Cardiff, 1980), p. 171.
[63] Ibid.
[64] NLW, Lewis MSS, letter from D. Ll. George to J. Herbert Lewis, 11 December 1895.
[65] *Young Wales*, March 1895.
[66] J. Graham Jones, *Lloyd George Papers* (Aberystwyth, 2001).
[67] B. B. Gilbert, *David Lloyd George: A Political Life, 1863–1912* (London, 1987), p. 22.
[68] NLW, Lewis MSS, letter from D. Ll. George to J. Herbert Lewis, 21 December 1895.
[69] K. O. Morgan, *Modern Wales: Politics, Places and People* (Cardiff, 1995), p. 208.
[70] Graham Jones, p. 448.
[71] Grigg, *The Young Lloyd George* (London, 1974), p. 219.
[72] Gilbert, *A Political Life*, p. 142.

Chapter XI

[1] K. O. Morgan (ed.), *Lloyd George: Family Letters 1885–1936* (London, 1973), p. 143, D. Ll. George to M. Ll. George, undated.
[2] Ibid., p. 145.
[3] K. O. Morgan, *Rebirth of a Nation: Wales 1880–1980* (Oxford, 1981), p. 189.
[4] B. B. Gilbert, *David Lloyd George: A Political Life, 1863–1912* (London, 1987), p. 179.
[5] R. Merfyn Jones, *The North Wales Quarrymen, 1874–1922* (Cardiff, 1981).
[6] Morgan (ed.), *Family Letters*, p. 149, D. Ll. George to M. Ll. George, 11 January 1904.
[7] Morgan, *Rebirth of a Nation*, p. 112.
[8] Gilbert, *A Political Life*, pp. 305–7.
[9] Morgan, *Family Letters*, p. 149, D. Ll. George to M. Ll. George, 4 December 1907.
[10] C. Cross, *Life with Lloyd George: A. J. Sylvester* (London, 1975), p. 215, and p. 91.
[11] Quoted in C. L. Mowat, *Lloyd George* (Oxford, 1964), p. 17.
[12] Morgan (ed.), *Family Letters*, p. 151, D. Ll. George to M. Ll. George, 16 November 1909.
[13] Ibid., p. 153, D. Ll. George to M. Ll. George, 8 September 1910.
[14] Ibid., p. 145.
[15] K. O. Morgan, *Lloyd George* (London, 1974).
[16] Emyr Price, 'Labour's "breakthrough" in Caernarfon county in 1922: the election of R. T. Jones to Westminster', *Transactions of the Caernarfonshire Historical Society*, 64 (2003).
[17] Quoted in John Grigg, *Lloyd George and Wales* (Aberystwyth, NLW, 1988), p. 9.
[18] J. Graham Jones, 'E. T. John and Welsh Home Rule, 1910–1914', *Welsh History Review*, 1987.
[19] Gilbert, *A Political Life*, pp. 376–7.
[20] Morgan (ed.), *Family Letters*, p. 167, D. Ll. George to M. Ll. George, 3 August 1914.
[21] W. J. Gruffudd, *Hen Atgofion* (Caerdydd, 1936).
[22] Morgan, *Rebirth of a Nation*, p. 160.
[23] Aled Eurig, 'Agweddau ar y gwrthwynebiad i'r Rhyfel Byd Cyntaf yng Nghymru', *Llafur*, 4 (1987), 558–68.

[24] John Davies, *Hanes Cymru* (Llundain, 1990), p. 493.

[25] David Pretty, *Rhyfelwr Môn: Syr Owen Thomas* (Dinbych, 1989).

[26] Mowat, *Lloyd George*, p. 24.

[27] Ibid., p. 41.

[28] Angharad Tomos, *Hiraeth am Yfory: Hanes David Thomas a Mudiad Llafur Gogledd Cymru* (Llandysul, 2002).

[29] K. O. Morgan, *Freedom or Sacrilege* (Penarth, 1966).

[30] Morgan (ed.), *Family Letters*, p. 191, D. Ll. George to M. Ll. George, 5 January 1920.

[31] E. Morgan Humphreys, 'Profiadau Golygydd', *Transactions of the Caernarfonshire Historical Society*, 1950.

[32] Morgan (ed.), *Family Letters*, p. 193, D. Lloyd George to M. Lloyd George, 11 September 1920.

[33] John Davies, 'Wales, Ireland and Lloyd George', *Planet*, 67 (February/March 1988).

[34] K. O. Morgan, 'Lloyd George and the Irish', *The British Academy*, 1989.

[35] Emyr Price, 'Lloyd George ac Eisteddfodau Caernarfon', *Eisteddfota* (Llandysul, 1979).

[36] Emyr Price, 'Lloyd George ac Eisteddfod Machynlleth', *Y Faner*, 2 Awst 1981.

[37] John Davies, *Broadcasting and the BBC in Wales* (Cardiff, 1994).

[38] Morgan (ed.), *Family Letters*, p. 213, D. Ll. George to M. Ll. George, 9 December 1936.

[39] Quoted in Gwynfor Evans, *Seiri Cenedl* (Llandysul, 1986), p. 264.

[40] *The Welsh Nationalist*, January 1932.

[41] Gwynfor Evans, *Saer Cenedl*, p. 264.

[42] W. Hughes Jones, *Wales Drops the Pilots* (London, 1937).

[43] Emyr Price, *Megan Lloyd George* (Caernarfon, 1983).

[44] David Roberts, 'The strange death of Liberal Wales', in John Osmond (ed.), *The National Question Again* (Llandysul, 1984).

[45] Personal information provided to the author by Emlyn Hooson.

[46] Emyr Price, 'Labour's victory in Caernarfonshire: Goronwy Roberts and the general election of 1945', *Transactions of the Caernarfonshire History Society*, 2002.

[47] Robert Griffiths, *S. O. Davies: A Socialist Faith* (Llandysul, 1983).

[48] Emyr Price, *Lord Cledwyn* (Bangor, 1990).

[49] Emyr Price, 'Lord Cledwyn and the national question' (Llangefni, 2004).

[50] Ibid.

[51] Ibid.

[52] *SWDN*, 5 February 1890.

BIBLIOGRAPHY

Primary Sources

i. Manuscripts

National Library of Wales (NLW): George; William George; Castle Green; Temlwyr Da, Llŷn; W. J. Parry; D. R. Daniel; T. E. Ellis; Thomas Gee; J. Herbert Lewis; Voelas; J. Bryn Roberts; Glansevern; Rendel; Picton; Ellis Jones Griffith; Olwen Carey Evans.

Caernarfon Record Office: Breese Jones and Casson; Porthmadoc Debating Society Minute Book; Minute Book of Caernarfonshire County Council 1888–90; J. T. Roberts (Lloyd George's first election agent); Election Register for the parliamentary boroughs of Caernarfon, Nefyn, Pwllheli and Cricieth, 1890.

University of Wales Bangor Library: R. D. Williams; Coetmor; Belmont; Reports of North Wales Liberal Federation 1891, 1892; William Jones; J. E. Lloyd.

ii. Newspapers and periodicals

Baner ac Amserau Cymru (BAC); Cambrian News (CN); Carnarvon and Denbigh Herald (CDH); Cymru Fydd; North Wales Chronicle (NWC); North Wales Express (NWE); Liverpool Daily Post; Liverpool Mercury; Manchester Guardian; North Wales Observer and Express (NWOE); Seren Cymru; Seren Gomer; South Wales Daily News (SWDN); The Times; Western Mail (WM); Y Brython Gymreig; Y Celt; Y Cronicl; Y Dinesydd Cymreig: The Welsh Nationalist; Y Dydd; Y Genedl Gymreig (YGG); Y Goleuad; Y Greal; Y Gwalia; Y Gwyliedydd; Y Rhedegydd; Y Tyst a'r Dydd; Y Werin; Young Wales; Yr Herald Cymraeg (YHC); Yr Udgorn Rhyddid (UR).

iii. Official papers

Census, Caernarfonshire, 1881, 1891; Enumerator's census, Llanystumdwy, 1871; Census of Merionethshire, 1881, 1891; The Religious Census, 1851; The Royal Commission on Land (Wales and Monmouthshire), 1896; A. C. Sutton, Directory of North Wales 1888.

Secondary Sources

i. Books

Cross, Colin, *Life with Lloyd George: The Diary of A. J. Sylvester, 1931–1945* (London, 1975).

Davies, John, *Hanes Cymru* (Llundain, 1990).

Davies, John, *Broadcasting and the BBC in Wales* (Cardiff, 1994).

Davies, W. Watkin, *Lloyd George, 1863–1914* (London, 1939).

Eaton, Jack, *Judge John Bryn Roberts: A Biography* (Cardiff, 1987).

Edwards, J. H., *The Life of David Lloyd George* (Llandysul, 1976).

Evans, B. Gwynfe, *The Life Romance of David Lloyd George* (Cardiff, 1915).

Evans, E. W., *William Abraham, Mabon* (Cardiff, 1959).

Evans, Gwynfor, *Seiri Cenedl* (Llandysul, 1986).

George, William, *Cymru Fydd: Hanes y Mudiad Cenedlaethol Cyntaf* (Lerpwl, 1945).

George, William, *Atgof a Myfyr* (Wrexham, 1948).

George, William, *My Brother and I* (London, 1958).

George, W. R. P., *The Making of Lloyd George* (Llandysul, 1976).

George, W. R. P., *Lloyd George, Backbencher* (Llandysul, 1983).

Gilbert, B. B., *David Lloyd George: A Political Life, 1863–1912* (London, 1987).

Griffiths, Robert, *S. O. Davies: A Socialist Faith* (Llandysul, 1983).

Grigg, John, *The Young Lloyd George* (London, 1973).

Gruffydd, W. J., *Hen Atgofion* (Caerdydd, 1936).

Hughes Jones, W., *Wales Drops the Pilots* (London, 1937).

Humphreys, E. Morgan, *Gwŷr Enwog Gynt*, cyf. 1 a 2 (Aberystwyth, 1850, 1853).

Jones, Aled, *Press, Politics and Society* (Cardiff, 1993).

Jones, E. Pan, *Oes a Gwaith Michael D. Jones, y Bala* (Y Bala, 1903).

Jones, Ieuan Wyn, *Y Llinyn Arian: Agweddau o Fywyd a Chyfnod Thomas Gee (1815–1898)* (Dinbych, 1998).

Jones, J. Graham, *Lloyd George Papers* (Aberystwyth, 2001).

Jones, J. Ll., *Plenydd, H. J. Williams, Hanes ei Fywyd* (Caernarfon, 1929).

Jones, R. Merfyn, *The North Wales Quarrymen, 1874–1922* (Cardiff, 1981).

Jones, T. Gwynn, *Cofiant Thomas Gee* (Dinbych, 1913).

Lewis, Elvet, *Cofiant y Parch E. Herber Evans* (Wrecsam, 1902).

Lloyd, D. Tecwyn, *Drych o Genedl* (Abertawe, 1987).

Lloyd Hughes, D. G., *Hanes Tref Pwllheli* (Llandysul, 1986).

Masterman, Neville, *The Forerunner: The Dilemmas of Tom Ellis, 1859–1899* (Llandybïe, 1972).

Morgan, K. O., *Freedom or Sacrilege* (Penarth, 1966).

Morgan, K. O., *David Lloyd George* (London, 1974).

Morgan, K. O., *Wales in British Politics, 1868–1922* (Cardiff, 1980).

Morgan, K. O., *Rebirth of a Nation: Wales, 1880–1980* (Oxford, 1981).

Morgan, K. O., *Modern Wales: Politics, People and Places* (Cardiff, 1995).

Morgan, K. O., 'Lloyd George and Welsh Liberalism', in Judith Loades (ed.), *The Life and Times of David Lloyd George* (Bangor, 1991).

Morgan, K. O. (ed.), *Lloyd George: Family Letters 1885–1936* (Cardiff, 1973).

Mowat, C. L., *Lloyd George* (Oxford, 1964).

du Parcq, H., *Life of David Lloyd George* (London, 1912).

Pretty, David, *Rhyfelwr Môn, Syr Owen Thomas* (Dinbych, 1989).

Price, Emyr, *Megan Lloyd George* (Caernarfon, 1983).

Price, Emyr, *Yr Arglwydd Cledwyn/Lord Cledwyn* (Bangor, 1990).

Price, Emyr, *Lloyd George, y Cenedlaetholwr Cymreig: Bradwr neu Arwr?* (Llandysul, 1999).

Viscountess Rhondda et al., *The Life of D. A. Thomas, Viscount Rhondda* (London, 1921).

Tomos, Angharad, *Hiraeth am Yfory: David Thomas a Mudiad Llafur Gogledd Cymru* (Llandysul, 2002).

ii. Articles and lectures

Davies, John, 'Wales, Ireland and Lloyd George', *Planet*, 67 (February/March 1988).

Edwards, Hywel Teifi, 'Eisteddfod Genedlaethol Treorchi, 1928', in *Cwm Rhondda* (Llandysul, 1995).

Eurig, Aled, 'Agweddau ar y gwrthwynebiad i'r Rhyfel Byd Cyntaf yng Nghymru', *Llafur*, 1987.

Humphreys, E. Morgan, 'Profiadau Golygydd', *Transactions of the Caernarfonshire Historical Society*, 1950.

Jones, Ieuan Gwynedd, 'Merioneth politics in the mid-nineteenth century', *Journal of the Merioneth Historical Society*, 5 (1973).

Jones, J. Graham, 'E. T. John and Welsh Home Rule, 1910–1914', *Welsh History Review*, 1987.

Jones, J. Graham, 'Lloyd George and the Caernarfon Boroughs election of 1892', *Transactions of the Caernarfonshire Historical Society*, 1991.

Jones, J. Graham, 'Lloyd George, Cymru Fydd and the Newport meeting of 1896', *NLW Journal*, 25 (4), Winter 1996.

Jones, J. Graham, 'Lloyd George, the Caernarfon Boroughs and Manchester East', *Transactions of the Caernarfonshire Historical Society*, 1998.

Jones, R. Merfyn and Jones, Ioan Rhys, 'Labour and the nation', in Duncan Tanner, Chris Williams and Deian Hopkin (eds), *The Labour Party in Wales, 1900–2000* (Cardiff, 2000).

Morgan, K. O., 'Lloyd George and the Irish', *The British Academy*, 1989.

Price, Emyr, 'Lloyd George and the by-election in the Caernarfon Boroughs 1890', *Transactions of the Caernarfonshire Historical Society*, 1975.

Price, Emyr, 'Newyddiadur Cyntaf Lloyd George – Yr Udgorn Rhyddid', *Journal of the Welsh Bibliographical Society*, 1976.

Price, Emyr, 'Ail Gloriannau Thomas Gee' (Dinbych, 1977).

Price, Emyr, 'Lloyd George a rhyfel y degwm, 1886–1888'. *Transactions of the Caernarfonshire Historical Society*, 1978.

Price, Emyr, 'Lloyd George ac Eisteddfodau Caernarfon', *Eisteddfota* (Llandysul, 1979).

Price, Emyr, 'Lloyd George ac Eisteddfod Machynlleth', *Y Faner*, 2 Awst 1981.

Price, Emyr, 'David Lloyd George: y bachgen henadur a'r cenedlaetholwr Cymreig', *Cof Cenedl*, 12 (1998).

Price Jones, Frank, 'Rhyfel y degwm', *Trafodion Hanes Sir Ddinbych*, 1965.

Roberts, David, 'The strange death of Liberal Wales', in J. Osmond (ed.), *The National Question Again* (Llandysul, 1984).

Williams, Emyr, 'Liberalism in Wales and the politics of Welsh Home Rule 1886–1891', *Bulletin of the Board of Celtic Studies*, 37 (1990).

iii. University dissertations

Hughes, D. R., 'Cymru Fydd a strwythur Rhyddfryddiaeth Gymreig (1886–1896)', unpublished University of Wales MA dissertation, 1987.

Price, Emyr, 'Lloyd George's pre-parliamentary career', unpublished University of Wales MA dissertation, 1974.

Thomas, R. G., 'Politics in Anglesey and Caernarfonshire, 1826–1852', unpublished University of Wales MA dissertation, 1972.

INDEX